Lecture Notes in Computer Science 6431

Commenced Publication in 1973
Founding and Former Series Editors:
Gerhard Goos, Juris Hartmanis, and Jan van Leeuwen

W0227572

Achim Ebert   Alan Dix
Nahum D. Gershon   Margit Pohl (Eds.)

Human Aspects of Visualization

Second IFIP WG 13.7 Workshop
on Human-Computer Interaction and Visualization
HCIV (INTERACT) 2009
Uppsala, Sweden, August 24, 2009
Revised Selected Papers

 Springer

Volume Editors

Achim Ebert
University of Kaiserslautern, Computer Graphics and HCI
Gottlieb-Daimler-Straße, 67663 Kaiserslautern, Germany
E-mail: ebert@cs.uni-kl.de

Alan Dix
Lancaster University, Computing Department
Lancaster, LA1 4WA, UK
E-mail: alan@hcibook.com

Nahum D. Gershon
The MITRE Corporation
7515 Colshire Drive, McLean, VA 22102-7539, USA
E-mail: gershon@mitre.org

Margit Pohl
Vienna University of Technology
Institute of Design and Assessment of Technology
Favoritenstraße 9-11/E 187, 1040 Vienna, Austria
E-mail: margit@igw.tuwien.ac.at

ISSN 0302-9743   e-ISSN 1611-3349
ISBN 978-3-642-19640-9   e-ISBN 978-3-642-19641-6
DOI 10.1007/978-3-642-19641-6
Springer Heidelberg Dordrecht London New York

Library of Congress Control Number: 2011922135

CR Subject Classification (1998): H.5, I.3-4, J.4

LNCS Sublibrary: SL 3 – Information Systems and Application, incl. Internet/Web and HCI

Typesetting: Camera-ready by author, data conversion by Scientific Publishing Services, Chennai, India

Printed on acid-free paper

Springer is part of Springer Science+Business Media (www.springer.com)

The original version of the book frontmatter was revised:
The copyright line was incorrect. The Erratum
to the book frontmatter is available at
DOI: 10.1007/978-3-642-19641-6_12

Preface

The data available to us all is increasing because of the myriad sensors that now surround us and the networks and the Web, which links previously disparate data together. At the same time displays have changed, as well as the ubiquitous desktop or laptop screen we now also have tiny mobile phone displays as vast giga-pixel display walls creating new challenges and opportunities for visualizing this data at both ends of the scale. In numerous areas including business, healthcare, security, and environmental management the effective visualization and analysis of data is essential to understand the world around and the impact of potential actions. However, these visualizations will be impaired if not useless unless they are based on a sound understanding of the way we as humans are able to comprehend and interact.

This book is intended to give an overview of important issues concerning human–computer interaction and information visualization. It is based on an IFIP workshop that took place during the Interact 2009 conference in Uppsala. This workshop, co-organized by IFIP WG TC13.7 on "HCI and Visualization" and the European VisMaster Coordinated Action, surveyed and expanded our understanding of the cognitive and perceptual issues of interactive visualization and visual analytics and brought together researchers interested in these issues. It highlighted the research required to understand what aspects of analysis match human capabilities most closely, and how interactive visual support should be designed and adapted to make optimal use of human capabilities in terms of information perception and processing.

Throughout the discussions during the Human Aspects of Visualization Workshop, various common topics emerged among the participants and these common topics are reflected in the papers in this volume. The papers indicate that there are still many open research questions even when one considers topics that have been studied for a considerable time such as fisheye interfaces. Furthermore, they remind us that visualization is no longer confined to expert users but may be used by everyone. The book can only outline some of the most prominent problems and some potential solutions to the effective application of human–computer interaction in information visualization. It does not provide a final answer to these issues, but offers a glimpse into an exciting area of growing importance to us all.

December 2010

Achim Ebert
Alan Dix
Nahum Gershon
Margit Pohl

Table of Contents

Human Aspects of Visualization

Human Aspects of Visualization

Achim Ebert[1], Alan Dix[2], Nahum Gershon[3], and Margit Pohl[4]

[1] University of Kaiserslautern, Kaiserslautern, Germany
`ebert@cs.uni-kl.de`
[2] Lancaster University, Lancaster, UK
`alan@hcibook.com`
[3] The MITRE Corp., McLean, VA, USA
`gershon@mitre.org`
[4] Vienna University of Technology, Vienna, Austria
`margit@igw.tuwien.ac.at`

1 Introduction

This book is intended to give an overview of important issues concerning Human-Computer Interaction and information visualization. It is based on an IFIP [4] workshop that took place during the Interact'09 conference in Uppsala [3]. This workshop, co-organized by IFIP WG TC13.7 on "HCI and Visualization" [2] and the European VisMaster Coordinated Action [5], surveyed and expanded our understanding of the cognitive and perceptual issues of interactive visualization and visual analytics and brought together researchers interested in these issues. It outlined the research required to understand what aspects of analysis match human capabilities most closely, and how interactive visual support should be designed and adapted to make optimal use of human capabilities in terms of information perception and processing.

This is a challenging agenda that has to take into account many factors including user roles, tasks, collaborations, interests and previous knowledge as well as understanding the capabilities of display devices and computation methods for dealing with often very large data sets. The workshop goals required the cooperation of scientists from different disciplines addressing aspects of visualization and analysis. This enabled a mapping between foundational theories in the different research areas to support collaboration among researchers in these fields. This included researchers and developers already working at the intersection of HCI, visualization, visual analytics, and related areas such as data mining, data management, perception and cognition.

2 Goals and Issues

Displays affect the visual interaction of human with computer devices more than any other hardware component. The display determines, for example, the physical size of the viewport, the range of effective field-of-view and resolution that is possible, and the types of feasible interaction modalities. All other interactions

A. Ebert et al. (Eds.): HCIV (INTERACT) 2009, LNCS 6431, pp. 1–9, 2011.
© IFIP International Federation for Information Processing 2011

must be placed in the context of the display. Thus in recent years, two trends have been emerging.

First, visualization on large displays has become an increasingly important research topic. This is manifested in many applications in the use of wall-sized display devices. For example, large public screens enable a bigger audience to view the contents. Large displays for collaborative work provide the necessary screen real estate to allow the display of different points of view of the different users. The use of large display areas enables a more thorough immersion in virtual reality applications. And finally, large high-resolution displays enable visualization of large and complex datasets by facilitating both overview and detail views at the same time.

On the other hand, the proliferation of mobile devices requires visual applications on very small screens. With these smaller-scale displays, assumptions of the normal desktop metaphor no longer apply and mice and keyboards, designed for desktop interaction, become unsatisfactory. This calls for novel interaction devices and techniques designed for small screens of mobile devices.

Regardless of the device in use, interactive visualization methods are needed to augment cognitive resources by providing an additional, external visual resource to the human memory. They may reduce the amount of searching and make it easier to recognize patterns as well as enhance the understanding of relationships especially in large amounts of data and information. In addition, interactive visualization methods provide a medium that enables the user to have a representation of information that he or she can quickly and easily modify, restructure or consider from a different perspective. This ability to manipulate the data is of extreme importance especially for analytical reasoning and sense-making.

Research in HCI and visualization has produced numerous forms of visualization and methods for interacting with visualizations of large data sets. However, systematic understanding of the interaction issues with visualization and the human cognitive and perceptual processes involved is perhaps less well developed. Therefore, the workshop at Interact 2009 tackled the human aspects of visualization and built an inspiring platform for presentations and intensive and controversial discussions. The articles in this book capture the exciting presentations and discussions about these issues.

3   The Articles in This Book

The following section is a short overview of the papers in this book. All but the paper of Bob Spence – the keynote speaker at the workshop – are listed in alphabetical order (name of the first author).

3.1   The Broker
Bob Spence (Keynote)

There is a considerable amount of existing perceptual and cognitive knowledge that is highly relevant to information visualization. Nevertheless, it is difficult to directly apply it to the design of information visualization. Much of the research is very abstract in nature. Some results might be context-dependent and could not be easily generalized to information visualization applications. In his keynote lecture, Bob Spence, therefore, advocated that "Brokers" should mediate between cognitive scientists and information visualization designers. "The task of a Broker is to interpret relevant knowledge acquired by cognitive and perceptual psychologists and bring it suitably to the notice of interaction designers, thereby avoiding the need for that designer to have knowledge of cognition and perception."

A suitable method to do this brokerage is to develop Design Actions. Design Actions are structured forms that provide design guidance at a useful level of detail. In a way, they translate knowledge from cognitive psychology into a "language" that can be understood by designers. Basically, they are guidelines, but they also contain information about the empirical evidence supporting them, and advantages and disadvantages of following the guideline.

Bob Spence's article provides a valuable foundation for the following papers, many of which try to connect psychological research with design issues of information visualization.

3.2 Comparing Different Layouts of Tag Clouds: Findings on Visual Perception
Stephanie Deutsch, Johann Schrammel, Manfred Tscheligi

Tag clouds are an example of casual information visualization as described in the article of Andreas Kerren (see below). They can support users who want to get a comprehensive overview of the annotations that are often chaotically made by communities on the web. Clustering can produce meaningful units within tag clouds, but these units have to be presented in a way that can be easily perceived and understood.

The authors argue that, while tag clouds are intuitively comprehensible and attractive for users, they have certain limitations, e.g. the amount of redundant annotations or the problem that concepts are understood differently by various users. In addition, more possibilities for interaction would be advantageous. They also emphasize the importance of developing a solid foundation in perceptual psychology, especially with regard to visual perception and eye movement. Their empirical study indicates that semantic clustering (in contrast to traditional methods of tag-cloud-generation) might be useful for classifying annotations. However, they point out that there are still open questions regarding the design of such visualizations.

3.3 The Personal Equation of Complex Individual Cognition During Visual Interface Interaction
Tera Marie Green, Brian Fisher

Green and Fisher discuss approaches from cognitive psychology that might guide the design of interactive visual interfaces. They point out that the interaction with visual interfaces consists of complex cognitive behavior. So far, evaluation studies have focused on low-level cognitive processes (e.g. pre-attentive processing). This turns out to be interesting but not sufficient. In this context, they discuss theories of reasoning, especially the so-called sense-making loop. They point out that human reasoning processes can vary widely and therefore it is not easy to develop comprehensive theories of human reasoning. Models like the sense-making loop may form a general framework, but cannot guide concrete design decisions.

The authors also argue that human cognition is fundamentally influenced by individual differences (e.g. how humans categorize information, how they perceive visually or which problem-solving behaviors they adopt). Based on this assumption, they developed the Human Cognition Model, an operational framework to guide the design of collaborative interactive systems.

3.4   Faceted Visual Exploration of Semantic Data
Philipp Heim, Jürgen Ziegler

Heim and Ziegler address the problem of searching and exploring semantic data, in particular whether faceted search might be a possible way to support such search processes in Semantic Web data. In faceted search, the search space is divided based on independent search dimensions that serve as filters. To support users in their exploration of semantic data they developed a graphical tool representing facets and search results as nodes in a visualization that exploits the graph-based structure of linked semantic data. This graphical representation can help users to develop a coherent cognitive model of the target domain.

Heim and Ziegler argue that searching semantic data differs from using relational databases and conventional information retrieval. The tool they developed is specifically targeted at searching and exploring semantic data and especially supports exploration and hypotheses refinement processes.

3.5   Fisheye Interfaces – Research Problems and Practical Challenges
Mikkel Rønne Jakobsen, Kasper Hornbæk

One of the major problems in information visualization is the representation of large amounts of data and information. Cognitive overload resulting from the display of large amounts of data has to be avoided by an appropriate and effective design. There are several possibilities to reach this goal, one of which is focus+context interfaces (e.g. fisheye interfaces). Although using fisheye interfaces is a well-known technique dating back many years, Jakobsen and Hornbæk argue in their article that many problems concerning this technique are still not solved. They point out that, for example, the notion of focus is not very well defined in the literature. Consequently, different systems are developed with a large variety of interaction strategies. This makes it difficult to give an overall assessment of such systems. In addition, fisheye interfaces are seldom integrated into practical applications where they could probably be most useful.

Jakobsen and Hornbæk address some of the open questions they describe in their empirical research. Their work indicates that even for well-known techniques, many usability issues are still not solved. Apart from that, their discussion also deals with more general questions of the representation of large datasets on the screen and raises issues relevant for the information visualization community as a whole.

3.6 Visualization of Workaday Data Clarified by Means of Wine Fingerprints
Andreas Kerren

In his contribution, Kerren discusses the topic of information visualization for the masses, also called casual information visualization. Originally, information visualization was predominantly developed for expert users who needed sophisticated applications for complex problems. Nowadays, an increasing number of non-specialist users are interested in such tools, but may only occasionally need them or encounter them. Such systems have to be more intuitive and easier to learn than the ones geared for professional users. Potential visualizations for such systems are simple node-link diagrams, tag clouds or treemaps.

Kerren points out that intuitive and easy to learn interfaces are not always obvious. In his research, he initially assumed that treemaps would be easier to understand for casual users than bubble diagrams; however, this assumption was found to be incorrect. It is anticipated that simple visualizations will become even more important because of the increasing utilization of social software to support, for example, the perception of relationships between members of communities in Facebook.

3.7 Staying Focused: Highlighting-on-Demand as Situational Awareness Support for Groups in Multi-display Environments
Olga Kulyk, Tijs de Kler, Wim de Leeuw, Gerrit van der Veer, Betsy van Dijk

In recent years, there has been an increase in research on cooperative problem solving using information visualization techniques. It is hoped that multi-display environments may support group decision-making capabilities, as the displays can act both as communication tools and information devices. The authors point out that group decision processes are often flawed, for example, because of the dominance of single group members or because group members ignore alternative solutions.

Cooperative information visualization tools might overcome such problems by giving a comprehensive overview of existing possibilities and enabling group members to draw attention to various solutions by highlighting them. Technologies like tabletop computers or large tablets might be especially valuable in this context if they are appropriately designed and well integrated into the decision process.

3.8   Using Gaze Data in Evaluating Interactive Visualizations
Harri Siirtola, Kari-Jouko Räihä

Siirtola and Räihä discuss the difficulties in carrying out effective evaluations of interactive visualizations. Because of these difficulties, evaluations of such systems have often been missing. Thus, it is difficult to assess whether interactive visualizations are really useful. One of the reasons for this lack of evaluation studies might be that carrying out effective evaluations is both time-consuming and costly. They propose a simpler methodology for evaluation by using eye tracking.

In recent years, eye tracking has become more attractive for evaluation studies because the systems have become cheaper and easier to use. Nevertheless, the authors point out that the volume of data and the lack of methodologies to generalize these data is still a problem. This is especially difficult for animations when it is difficult to measure fixations on moving objects. In addition, there are still many open questions as far as interpretation of the data is concerned.

3.9   Giga-Scale Multi-resolution Volume Rendering on Distributed Display Clusters
Sebastian Thelen, Jörg Meyer, Achim Ebert, Hans Hagen

Large high-resolution displays have proven to be beneficial in various kinds of collaborative scenarios. They allow users to physically navigate the space in front of the screen and interact with applications in a highly dynamic way. Due to their extended screen space, large high-resolution displays are often employed by user groups to explore data sets that, because of their size, could not be perceived entirely on a regular small desktop display. However, visualizing such data sets is challenging since their size can exceed the computational resources of render nodes by several orders of magnitude, thus making data exploration more complicated.

Thelen et al. describe a technique to visualize and explore gigabyte-sized volumetric data sets on distributed display clusters, such as tiled monitor walls or tiled projector walls. Their method uses a wavelet-based multi-resolution approach in combination with octree-based space subdivision to significantly increase the level-of-detail that each render node in the cluster is able to display. The paper describes the underlying visualization approach and analyzes the results obtained with various data sets. The implementation was successfully tested on a tiled display comprised of 25 compute nodes driving 50 LCD panels. The system was able to produce renderings of volumetric data sets larger than the texture buffer size of a single graphics card at significantly higher levels of detail than on a single desktop display.

3.10   Teaching Visual Design as a Holistic Enterprise
Gerrit C. van der Veer, Corné Verbruggen

Van der Veer and Verbruggen argue that approaches in Visual Design education are often limited because of a focus on the design of the computer screen. Such an approach does not take into consideration that the interpretation of visual representations is often influenced by a specific context and by the experiences and attitudes of the observers. Designers of the visualization tools usually cannot anticipate users' reactions and therefore develop tools that are not adaptable to users' needs. This gap between designers' and users' mental models has often been described in Human-Computer Interaction textbooks and it is the main reason for recommending user studies. But, the argumentation of the authors goes beyond this; they point out, for example, that visualization tools do not merely produce representations on the screen but also introduce physical artifacts that are part of the display device – each device has specific characteristics like portability, opportunity for dialogue, visibility in daylight or in a building.

Design education has to take all of these aspects into consideration. In this sense, it should be holistic and address more than screen design. Consequently, usability is just one aspect of the story. Other factors to be considered are, for example, that the audience is often heterogeneous and comes from different backgrounds and that one needs to take into account the rules of human perception that could be analyzed by Cognitive Psychology.

4   Summary

Throughout the discussions during the "Human Aspects of Visualization" workshop, several common topics among the participants emerged and these common topics are reflected in the papers.

A common theme that is probably essential for this area is the relationship between research from cognitive psychology and design of interactive visualization systems. This problem was mentioned by Bob Spence in his keynote address, but can also be found in other articles in this book. Green and Fisher, for example, describe theories of reasoning and problem-solving and point out that there is no single theory in this area that might effectively explain the design of information visualizations, and therefore, one needs to make use of a number of different theories. This makes it difficult to formulate guidelines for explaining effective designs of information visualizations. Deutsch et al. also discuss psychological theories as foundation for research in information visualization. Kulyk at al. extensively discuss research from social psychology and sociology to substantiate their results. Related issues are also elaborated in van der Veer and Verbruggen's discussion of a holistic approach in design education; they point out that many different disciplines are necessary to develop successful visual designs, not only psychology but also, for example, media theory or sociology because the functioning of visual design depends on the social context and on the characteristics of the media being used.

Another common topic was information visualization for non-experts. As information visualization systems are increasingly adopted by non-expert users, their design will have to be adapted to this population. Kerren explicitly discusses this problem and tries to give an outline of possible solutions. This is also mentioned in the paper by Deutsch et al.

Methodological issues also played an important role in the workshop discussions. One open question is whether traditional methods of cognitive psychology or HCI are appropriate for the investigation of perceptual and cognitive aspects of information visualization. Methodologies such as eye-tracking (discussed by Siirtola and Räihä as well as by Deutsch et al.) offer the potential for radically different ways of approaching evaluation. However, these are themselves areas of substantial complexity. One problem is the appropriate interpretation of the data gained from eye-tracking studies and the definition of the variables that could be measured by this technology.

Another important issue that should play an important role in the future of visualization and HCI is the design of visualization systems supporting cooperative activities (see the contribution of Kulyk et al.). Technologies like tabletop computers might be the medium of choice in group situations. The papers indicate that there are still many open research questions even when one considers topics that have been studied for a considerable time like fisheye interfaces. The book can only outline some of the most prominent problems and some potential solutions to the effective application of human-computer interaction in information visualization.

As already mentioned above, the workshop at the Interact conference was co-organized by IFIP WG TC13.7 on "HCI and Visualization" (HCIV) and the European VisMaster Coordinated Action.

HCIV is a major program in Human Computer Interaction and Visualization that started in 2006. The aim of this initiative is to establish a study and research program that will combine the knowledge of both the science and the practice in the fields of HCI and Visualization. One of the main steps in organizing this program is a workshop series with world-renowned experts in the fields of Human Computer Interaction and Visualization. Since 2009, HCIV is an official working group of IFIP Technical Committee on Human-Computer Interaction (TC.13). In addition, all HCIV workshops since 2009 have been approved as an official IFIP event (including the Interact 2009 workshop on human aspects of visualization).

VisMaster is a European Coordination Action Project focused on the research discipline of Visual Analytics. The main strategic goal of this action is the shaping of a new research community for the field of Visual Analytics. It explicitly addresses issues of human cognition, perception and decision-making. To support the human visual and reasoning abilities efficiently, tools for visual analysis tasks have to be designed appropriately. The workshop helped in shaping the Visual Analytics community and hereby provided valuable input to the VisMaster project; in particular creating a foundation for the discussion of perceptual and cognitive issues in the European Visual Analytics roadmap "Mastering the Information Age" [1].

References

1. Keim, D., Kohlhammer, J., Ellis, G., Mansmann, F. (eds.): Mastering The Information Age: Solving Problems with Visual Analytics. Eurographics (2010) ISBN 978-3-905673-77-7
2. Human Computer Interaction and Visualization (HCIV), http://www.hciv.de
3. Gross, T., Gulliksen, J., Kotzé, P., Oestreicher, L., Palanque, P., Prates, R.O., Winckler, M. (eds.): INTERACT 2009. LNCS, vol. 5726, 5727. Springer, Heidelberg (2009)
4. International Federation for Information Processing (IFIP), http://www.ifip.org
5. VisMaster: Visual Analytics - Mastering The Information Age, http://www.vismaster.eu

The Broker

Bob Spence

Department of Electrical and Electronic Engineering,
Imperial College London,
SW7 2AZ, United Kingdom
r.spence@imperial.ac.uk

Abstract. The task of a Broker is to interpret relevant knowledge acquired by cognitive and perceptual psychologists and bring it suitably to the notice of interaction designers, thereby avoiding the need for that designer to have knowledge of cognition and perception. The task is first illustrated by an example based on the concept of Design Actions and demonstrates the implication, for two different design challenges, of certain properties of the human visual processing system. It is then argued that the task of the Broker can be eased by the definition and classification of relevant concepts, in the illustrative example those of browsing, interaction and visualization. Finally, a current need for a Broker's expertise is illustrated in the context of the interactive and dynamic exploration of the relationships associated with a multivariable system.

To explain the title of this contribution I must point out that I'm an engineer who first became an interaction designer, with a concern for visualization, in 1968 when I started to design (Figure 1) an interactive-graphic CAD system for electronic circuit design [1] that eventually (Figure 2) became a commercial product in 1985. During that time I was very much aware that the perceptual and cognitive abilities of the human being – the circuit designer in my case – would be ignored at one's peril. Few others in the industry appeared to share my view but, as an engineer and not, definitely not, a psychologist, I had to get things done – in my case the creation, with colleagues, of the first commercial interactive-graphic CAD system for electronic circuit designers (MINNIE). I therefore had some sympathy with Isambard Kingdom Brunel because I did not have, at my disposal, all – or even a little – of the knowledge about human factors that would better inform my design. So a great deal of intuition had to be applied, and we know how dangerous a substance that can be. I did involve psychologists in my research to a limited extent, but their activities could only provide a very small fraction of the knowledge I was seeking.

So for a very long time I've been aware of the need for some means of interpreting relevant knowledge acquired by cognitive and perceptual psychologists and bringing it *suitably* to the notice of interaction designers. I shall call the person responsible for doing that The Broker.

To illustrate the task of a broker and how it might be supported I first present an example; to the same end I then advocate more attention to definitions and

A. Ebert et al. (Eds.): HCIV (INTERACT) 2009, LNCS 6431, pp. 10–22, 2011.

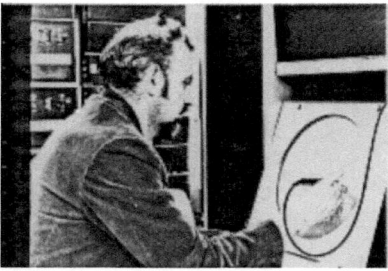

Fig. 1. The MINNIE interactive-graphic CAD system, 1968

Fig. 2. The commercially available MINNIE system for CAD, 1985

classification; and, finally, I illustrate a current need for action by a broker. Because a keynote is often based on personal experience I make no apology for the fact that many of the references are to the work of myself and my colleagues.

1 An Example

My psychologist colleague Dr. de Bruijn and I had an idea that required the services of a broker. The idea was based on the fact that an interaction designer has to design an interface to support some type of human behaviour. The designer knows that such behaviour is controlled by cognitive and perceptual processes associated with the human user, *but may have little or no understanding of that subject*. Let's take an example of behaviour – that of search browsing. That behaviour will certainly be affected by the human visual processing system. However, as I have emphasised, the interaction designer almost certainly has no knowledge of such processes. So our view was that he or she would benefit from suitably presented guidance that is based on knowledge about the human behaviour that has to be supported by the designed interface. We suggested that it is possible – and this is where the Broker comes in – to identify the human processes relevant to the behaviour to be supported – one of which is human visual processing – and generate what we called Design Actions [2] (Figure 3).

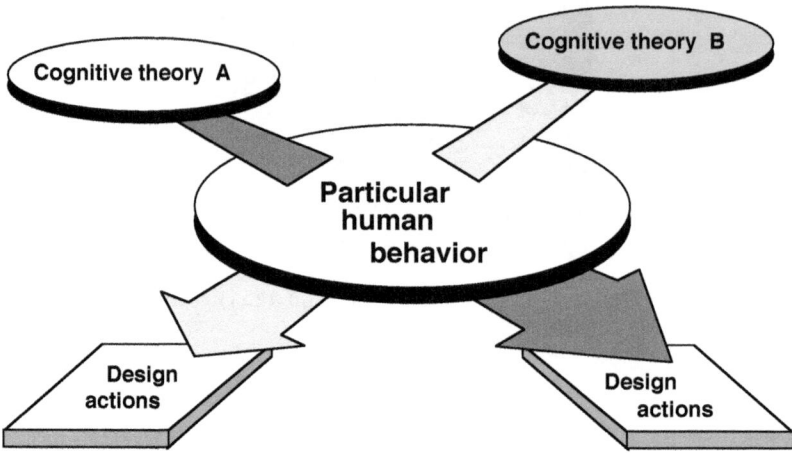

Fig. 3. The conceptual basis of Design Actions

They tell the interaction designer how to create a good design and they relieve that designer of the need to understand human cognitive and perceptual processes.

Very briefly, Design Actions are tables that provide design guidance, and at a useful level of detail. Figure 4a shows the structure of a Design Action. First there is a brief title, followed by a clarification of that title. The next line says that if you, the interaction designer, take a particular design decision, a particular outcome can be achieved. Next, because any design decision has its pros and cons, it is helpful for the designer to know what they are. Then there are related issues that the designer might beneficially consider. Finally there is a reference to the HCI principles involved in case the designer is curious. Figure 4b shows one example of a Design Action relevant to a situation in which you want a user to respond very rapidly to the appearance of a target image. Design Actions do not, of course, constitute the only methodology available to the interaction designer: a comparison with Alexander Patterns [3] is provided in [2].

The concept of Design Actions is extremely general – that's one of its potential attractions. To illustrate that potential we focused [2] on a particular behaviour, that of browsing, with two applications in mind. One concerned the rapid search, on a mobile, for an interesting news item among a collection of such items, using the technique of Rapid Serial Visual Presentation (RSVP) [4]. The other concerned involuntary browsing (defined later) where, for example, small icons moving very slowly around the periphery of a coffee table (Figure 5a) [5] might catch the *latent* interest of a person sitting at that table. This table was originally designed to be located within an area such as a pub or library: the little icons refer to activities going on in the local community: sight of one of them might trigger some latent interest. Pushing the little icon (Figure 5b) into the centre provides more information, in this case about a chess tournament.

Title	Design objective
Description	Clarification of title
Effect	"If you do this, that will happen"
Upside	The advantages of doing it
Downside	The disadvantages of doing it
Issues	Considerations
Theory	Reference to theoretical basis of Design Action

(a) The format of a Design Action

ID	DA2
Title	Presentation for immediate action
Description	If selectable information sources are each represented by an image (with or without brief text), ensure that each item can be fixated for at least 100ms, and that an immediate response can be initiated as soon as a relevant item is encountered.
Effect	This action gives reasonable certainty that the meaning of each fixated item can be established and that items that match a relevance threshold can trigger an appropriate action
Upside	Many information items can be presented in a relatively short period of time either sequentially or concurrently
Downside	The lower limit of 100ms will, for a given application, establish an upper limit to the number of images that can be presented concurrently with the expectation that, during the normal - and often random and involuntary - eye gaze activity, a relevant one will be identified.
Issues	(1) undirected/random eye-gaze activity is such that only a very short (e.g., 50 to 300ms) fixation on an information item may take place, further supporting the need for pictures of familiar objects and scenes. Conscious attention should not be necessary to recognise words and images within the information items. (2) The actions that are triggered in response to the interpretation of items need to be simple so that they can be executed without delay and consideration.
Theory	The ability to automatically and rapidly match an information need with a viewed image.

(b) An example of a Design Action

Fig. 4. The format of a Design Action and an example

The question we had to address was "what knowledge about human visual processing exists that will help us with these two quite different design challenges?" Answering that question is the task of a broker.

Human visual processing was obviously fundamental to both these applications. For that reason we found the book *Fleeting Memories* [6] to be most helpful, and especially the chapter [7] by Mollie Potter of MIT who was responsible for proposing the concept of Conceptual Short Term Memory (CSTM). Basically Potter proposed the CSTM model – our own illustration of which is shown in Figure 6 – to describe the processing of a visual stimulus in the first few hundred milliseconds after its initiation. Almost immediately following the arrival of that stimulus in sensory storage it is categorized by reference to previously stored knowledge in long-term memory (LTM): it may be categorized as 'a cat in front of a house' or 'a briefcase' or 'coloured wiggly lines'. That categorization

(a)   (b)

Fig. 5. A coffee table designed to trigger the latent interests of the coffee drinker

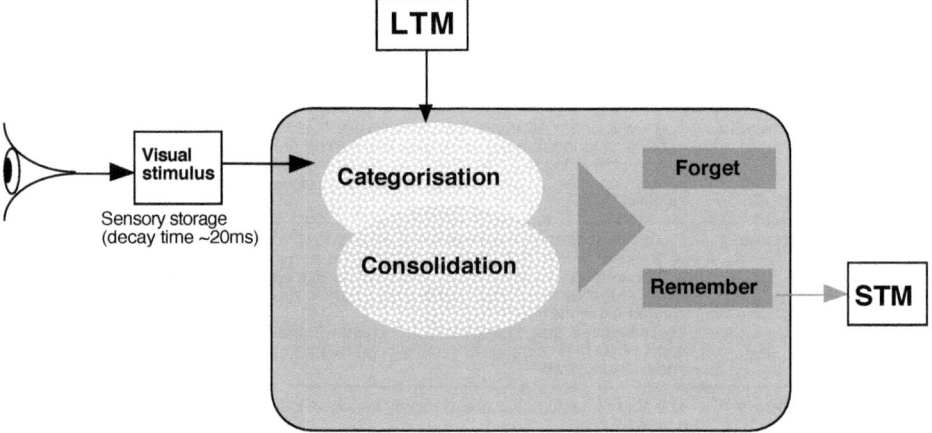

Fig. 6. A representation of Conceptual Short-term Memory

may well be 'primed' [8] by the task being performed: it is thought to occur in about 100ms and is performed essentially unconsciously.

The meaning or relevance of the stimulus is then interpreted, again unconsciously, in a process called consolidation. If there is relevance it is passed to short-term memory (STM); if there is not, then forgetting occurs. Potter points out that the whole cycle – identification of stimulus, memory recruitment, structuring, consolidation and the forgetting of irrelevant data – may occur in less than a second and, essentially, is achieved unconsciously.

We then examined various experiments that had been carried out by cognitive psychologists over a number of decades to see how they could be associated with CSTM. I'll identify three (Figure 7), although we made use of seven. One is the discovery [9] that if images are presented at a rate as fast as 10 per second, the search for a known target image will be essentially successful. Another is that if two targets are being sought during such a presentation, one will not be

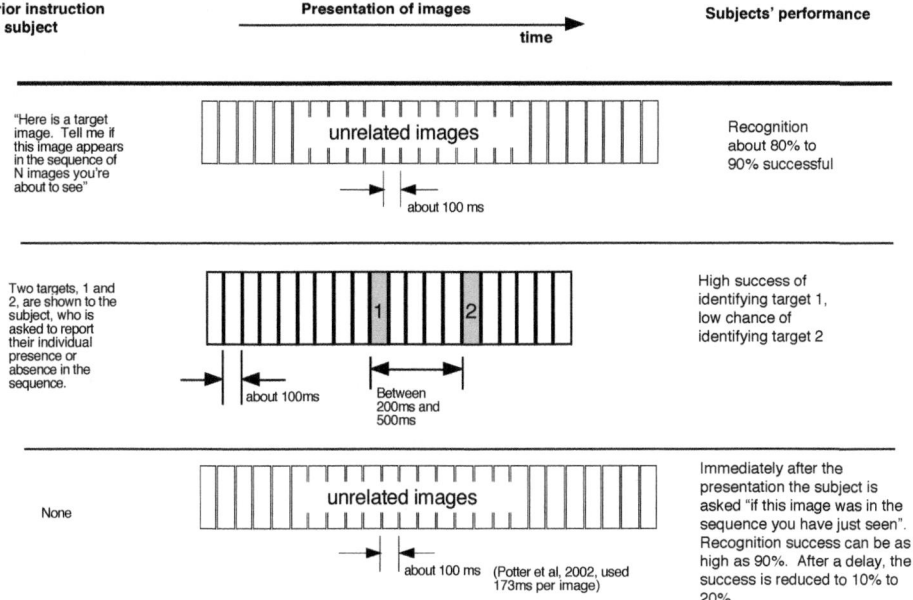

Fig. 7. Three experiments concerned with human visual processing

detected if it occurs shortly after the first to be detected, a phenomenon known as Attentional Blink [10]. A third concerns one's memory of what has been seen that had not been seen before – in general it is pretty poor [11].

To cut a very long story short, reference to these experiments enabled us to associate, with the original CSTM model, a scale indicating the earliest permissible onset of a following image if a certain task had to be successfully performed with the current image. I'll give three examples. If a 'satisficing' task is involved, a following image should not appear until 100ms after the appearance of the preceding image. If the task is to select the most appropriate image from a collection – we called that an 'optimising task' – then the separation must not be less than 500ms. If the task is of the 'preview-consider-select' type, the separation must be at least 1500 ms.

Using this model, we were able to derive, for the activity of browsing, various Design Actions [2] that should be brought to the attention of an interaction designer when designing, in one case, the RSVP presentation of news items and, in the other, a coffee table presentation of icons representing activities within a local community. The outcome was encouraging in the sense that what the extended CSTM model suggested turned out experimentally to be reasonable, though the framework we proposed requires much more use and evaluation.

Obviously there are hidden dangers in what we did as brokers, because psychologists are still trying to unravel the mysteries of human visual processing. Also, there are many other factors relevant to interaction design that we have not yet taken into account. Indeed, for any particular behaviour such as finding a news channel of interest on a mobile, there will be more than one relevant cognitive theory and therefore more than one set of Design Actions. However, I'm talking here about engineering design: and as a designer I need answers *right away*. So I feel that HCI professionals have a duty to provide models – however approximate – that will inform design. Having something reasonably well understood to go by is better than having nothing. Brunel did not, to my knowledge, have access to a finite element analysis package, but he produced some remarkable results.

2   Definitions

In this second of three sections I want to talk about definitions. I have a view – a philosophy, if you like – as to how they can facilitate the transfer of knowledge from cognitive psychology to the interaction designer.

My opinion is that although we are all of a scientific persuasion we seem to shy away from precise definitions. Take the term *browsing*, for example. Ask an HCI specialist what is meant by this frequently used term and you often get a very fuzzy reply (usually containing the term 'casual') and a lot of arm waving. I think that is not good enough: and goodness knows what students trying to adopt a scholarly approach to HCI will think. It turns out that in the work I've just described, reasonably precise definitions and taxonomies were of considerable help to the brokers. For example, based on Norman's Action Cycle [12] we defined three types of browsing using, as their defining parameters, Goal, Intention and Action Plan. The three types of browsing we defined are Search Browsing, characterised by a goal, a conscious intention and an action plan; Opportunistic Browsing with no immediate goal, but with an intention and an action plan; and Involuntary Browsing which is characterised by a latent goal [13] (of which we each have many) and therefore no conscious intention or action plan.

With these reasonably precise definitions and classification – though acknowledging that the topic of browsing is still under discussion – we were able to be quite specific about the Design Actions we derived.

I have two more examples where I feel that definition is important. The first concerns the definition of 'visualization'. I'm frankly surprised that many experts seize upon the 'visual' in that term and, for example, totally ignore the encoding of data in sound, a tendency that is not helped either by the new term 'Visual Analytics' [14] or by the legacy of our past computer-graphics-based approach to visualization. As I've said on many previous occasions, visualization has nothing to do with computers and is simply defined in some very respected dictionaries as

Visualise: to form a mental image of something.

As a consequence we have (at least) four classes of visualization (vision, sound, touch and smell) depending upon the human sense by which encoded data is perceived.

Interaction is another term we frequently use, so we had better find some classification scheme. We will certainly have to if we're to achieve the goal, described by Thomas & Cook [14] of creating a Science of Interaction. My own suggestion for a classification of interaction [15], which I have found to be helpful for interaction design, is again based on dictionary definitions and leads to three types:

Stepped interaction (such as a mouse click) which causes a discrete movement in information space,

Continuous interaction, as occurs during scrolling, for example, and

Sensory interaction: here something happens between user and computer that is experienced by one of the senses (e.g., reading a book, inspecting an image).

We can use classifications of visualization and interaction to form a two dimensional space (Figure 8) which, for emphasis, has been simplified by the omission of incidental interaction [16] and the mention of the status-event concept [17]. We can then perhaps introduce our browsing classification to create a 3-dimensional space. I think such a space can be very helpful when seeking frameworks to support interaction design. What I think is unfortunate is that the scope of this space is not fully explored by researchers seeking a framework to inform interaction design, first because the very term Visual Analytics restricts the sense involved in the perception of encoded data; second because sensory interaction does not seem to be accepted as a class of interaction; and third because involuntary browsing receives little attention. By ignoring such a large part of this space there may be a danger that any Science of Interaction that might be discovered will be rather impoverished.

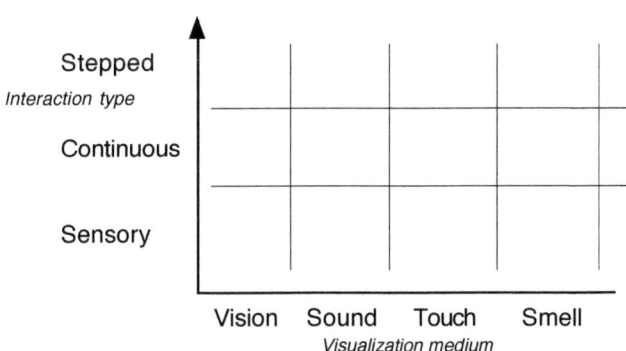

Fig. 8. The interaction-visualization space

So my plea, to all HCI practitioners, initially concerns science rather than engineering: "please can we have more precise definitions of familiar terms, because we can then more readily derive some frameworks that can inform interaction and visualization design". In any case there is no excuse for saying "everyone knows what we mean by..." – if everyone *does* know, then let's write it down.

3   Need

In this third section I want to identify – by an illustrative example – a specific need for the services of a broker. Again I base my example on work I have done with colleagues.

In 1970 we had devised an efficient algorithm [18] that allowed us to implement a scheme [19] whereby the designer of an electronic circuit could first point to a component whose effect on the performance of a circuit must be explored: then, following execution of the algorithm, the component's value could be varied manually and its effect *immediately* seen. The aim of that interface was to support exploration and the improvement of the designer's mental model.

Later, in 1996, my group went on to invent the Influence Explorer [20] – another interface designed to support the interactive exploration of data – though again without the benefit of knowledge of any relevant psychological literature. Let me first, and again necessarily briefly, illustrate the idea.

An electric lamp is to be designed [21]. It contains, internally (Figure 9), a structure supporting a filament. The structure is described by four dimensions (X_1 to X_4) that the lamp designer can choose. Interest lay in the effect of these dimensions on four stresses within the lamp (S_1 to S_4). The mathematical model (Figure 10) expressing all Ss in terms of all Xs provided no insight whatsoever for the lamp designer. So we (easily) simulated 400 random *but possible* designs and displayed the results (Figure 11) in the form of histograms. Alone they don't

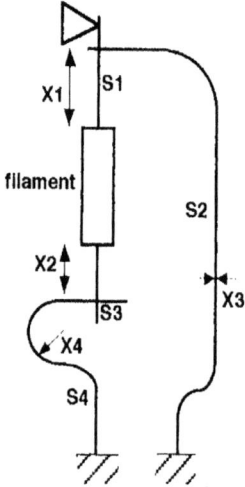

Fig. 9. A structure supporting the filament of an electric lamp

$$S_4 = 60.4 + 23X_1 - 3.8X_2 + 631.2X_3 - 26.4X_4 - 79.7X_1X_3 + 4.8X_2X_3 + 2.6X_1X_4 - 2.6X_1^2 - 278.2X_3^2 + 5.7X_1^2X_3$$

Fig. 10. An expression relating a structural stress to four designable dimensions

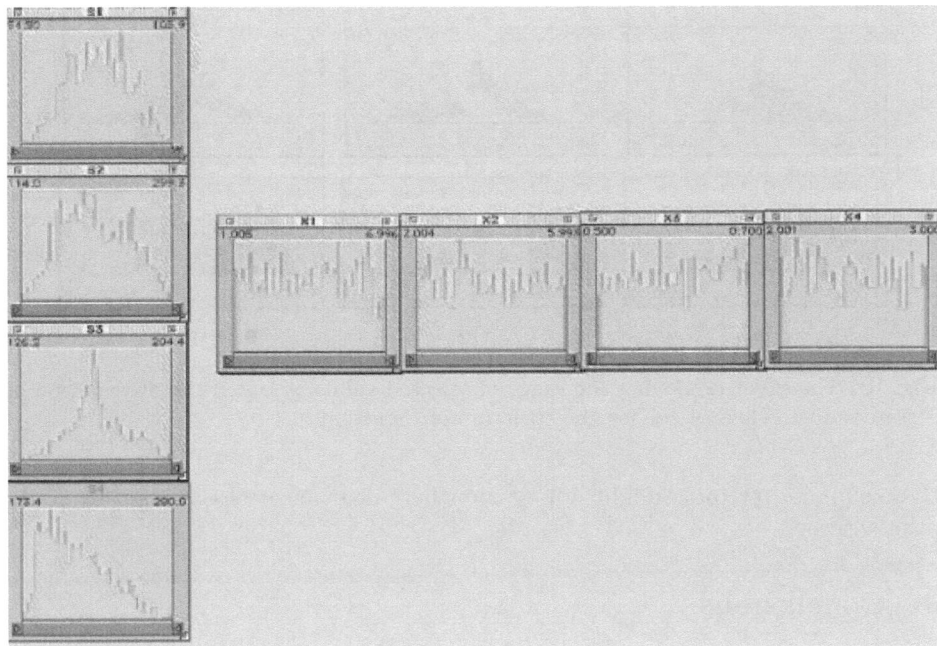

Fig. 11. Interactive histograms showing the result, for four stresses in the structure of Figure 9, of a random selection of designs (i.e., choices of X_1 to X_4)

tell you very much, but they certainly can if interaction is made possible. For example, if the designer interactively selects those designs that have low values of S_4, and especially move the range of selected values of S_4, they immediately notice a trade-of with S_3 (Figure 12) as well as a correlation with S_2 and with the designable parameter X_1. The mental model thereby gained by the designer of that lamp was immensely valuable and rapid. The same principle can be applied to many other disciplines including, for example, financial design.

What I have described is a very powerful technique allowing an investigator to gain insight into the complex relationships between variables and functions of those variables in a wide variety of multi-variable systems. Not surprisingly, some people are developing this idea [22] because the potential it offers is considerable. But I don't know – except from intuition based on experience – how best to design such an exploration tool. So I want the answers to many questions having to do with navigation, representation, 'near miss' information, the influence of task, how exploration can be automated [23] (in which case what is a good representation?), the awareness of desirable and undesirable regions of multidimensional space [24], design to provide useful overviews, useful computations – the list is long. These questions are not restricted to the Influence Explorer: recent exciting developments in interactive exploration [25] pose similar questions.

It may well be that some answers are already available in the psychological literature, in which case I want to know about them. If not, our design of

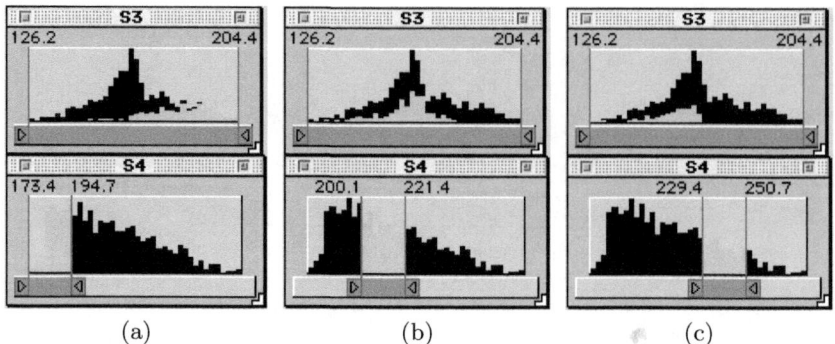

Fig. 12. The effect of moving the range of selected values of S_4 on the distribution of corresponding values of S_3, for the structure of Figure 9)

these exploratory tools might not be anywhere near as successful as they could otherwise be.

4   Conclusions

My conclusion is simply stated: that there's a need to package knowledge gained by psychologists in a form that will inform an interaction designer, and that to do so effectively we must pay more attention to definition and classification.

Acknowledgments. Much of the work I have referred to has been carried out in collaboration with Dr. Oscar de Bruijn of the Manchester Business School, and for that association I am most grateful. Earlier work on the development of MINNIE, the Influence Explorer and other examples involving interaction and visualization stretches back 40 years: the list of collaborators is very long, but they know who they are!

References

1. Spence, R., Apperley, M.: The interactive-graphic man-computer dialogue in computer-aided circuit design. IEEE Transactions on Circuits and Systems 24, 49–61 (1977)
2. De Bruijn, O., Spence, R.: A new framework for theory-based interaction design applied to serendipitous information retrieval. ACM Transactions on Computer-Human Interaction 15, 1–38 (2008)
3. Borchers, J.O.: A pattern approach to interaction design. In: Gill, S. (ed.) Cognition, Communication and Interaction, pp. 114–131. Springer, London (2008)
4. Spence, R.: Rapid, serial and visual: a presentation technique with potential. Information Visualization 1, 13–19 (2002)
5. Stathis, K., de Bruijn, O., Macedo, S.: Living memory: agent-based information management for connected local communities. Interacting with Computers 14, 663–688 (2002)

6. Coltheart, V. (ed.): Fleeting memories: cognition of brief visual stimuli. MIT Press, Cambridge (1999)
7. Potter, M.C.: Understanding sentences and scenes: The role of conceptual short-term memory. In: [6], ch. 2, pp. 13–46
8. Neely, J.H.: Semantic priming effects in visual word recognition: A selective review of current findings and theories. In: Besner, D., Humphreys, G.W. (eds.) Basic Processes in Reading: Visual Word Recognition, pp. 264–336. Lawrence Erlbaum Associates Inc., Hillsdale (1991)
9. Potter, M.C., Levy, E.I.: Recognition memory for a rapid sequence of pictures. Journal of Experimental Psychology 81, 10–15 (1969)
10. Raymond, J.E., Shapiro, K.L., Arnell, K.M.: Temporary suppression of visual processing in an rsvp task: An attentional blink? Journal of Experimental Psychology: Human Perception and Performance 18, 849–860 (1992)
11. Potter, M.C., Staub, A., Rado, J., O'Connor, D.H.: Recognition memory for briefly presented pictures: the time course of rapid forgetting. Journal of Experimental Psychology: Human Perception and Performance 28, 1163–1175 (2002)
12. Norman, D.A.: The Design of Everyday Things. Basic Books, New York (2002)
13. Zeigarnik, B.: On finished and unfinished tasks. In: Ellis, W.D. (ed.) A source book of Gestalt psychology, pp. 300–314. Trubner & Co., Ltd, Kegan Paul (1938)
14. Thomas, J.J., Cook, K.A.: Illuminating the Path: The Research and Development Agenda for Visual Analytics, National Visualization and Analytics Center (2005)
15. Spence, R.: Information Visualization: Design for Interaction, 2nd edn. Pearson Education, London (2006)
16. Dix, A.: Incidental interaction (2002),
    http://www.comp.lancs.ac.uk/~dixa/topics/incidental/
17. Dix, A.: Status-event analysis (2010),
    http://www.comp.lancs.ac.uk/~dixa/topics/status/
18. Leung, K., Spence, R.: Multiparameter large-change sensitivity analysis and systematic exploration. IEEE Transactions on Circuits and Systems 22, 796–804 (1975)
19. Spence, R., Apperley, M.: On the use of interactive graphics in circuit design. In: Proceedings of the International Symposium on Circuits and Systems, pp. 558–563. IEEE, Los Alamitos (1974)
20. Tweedie, L., Spence, R., Dawkes, H., Su, H.: Externalising abstract mathematical models. In: CHI 1996: Proceedings of the SIGCHI Conference on Human factors in Computing Systems, pp. 406–412. ACM, New York (1996)
21. Su, H., Nelder, J.A., Wolbert, P., Spence, R.: Application of generalized linear models to the design improvement of an engineering artefact. Quality and Reliability Engineering International 12, 101–112 (1996)
22. Neufeld, E.M., Kristtorn, S.K., Guan, Q., Sanscartier, M., Ware, C.: Exploring causal influences. In: Erbacher, R.F., Roberts, J.C., Grohn, M.T., Borner, K. (eds.) Visualization and Data Analysis. SPIE, vol. 5669, pp. 52–62 (2005)
23. Colgan, L., Spence, R., Rankin, P.: The cockpit metaphor. Behaviour & Information Technology 14, 251–263 (1995)
24. Tweedie, L., Spence, R.: The prosection matrix: A tool to support the interactive exploration of statistical models and data. Computational Statistics 13, 65–76 (1998)
25. Elmqvist, N., Dragicevic, P., Fekete, J.D.: Rolling the dice: Multidimensional visual exploration using scatterplot matrix navigation. IEEE Transactions on Visualization and Computer Graphics 14, 1148–1539 (2008)

Videos

It is difficult to convey the considerable potential of interactive exploration via the written word and static image. Some of the effects mentioned in this paper can be better appreciated by viewing short videos. The references to which they relate, and their source, are listed below

[19]: Video V2 on the DVD associated with reference [15]
[20,21]: Video V31 on the DVD associated with reference [15]
[22]: Video V33 on the DVD associated with reference [15]

Comparing Different Layouts of Tag Clouds: Findings on Visual Perception

Stephanie Deutsch[1], Johann Schrammel[1], and Manfred Tscheligi[1,2]

[1] CURE - Center for Usability Research & Engineering, Modecenterstr.17/ Objekt 2
A-1110 Vienna, Austria
[2] ICT&S Center, University of Salzburg, Sigmund-Haffner-Gasse 18
A-5020 Salzburg, Austria

Abstract. With the emergence of social tagging systems and the possibility for users to extensively annotate web resources and any content enormous amounts of unordered information and user generated metadata circulate the Web. Accordingly a viable visualisation form needs to integrate this unclassified content into meaningful visual representations. We argue that tag clouds can make the grade. We assume that the application of clustering techniques for arranging tags can be a useful method to generate meaningful units within a tag cloud. We think that clustered tag clouds can potentially help to enhance user performance. In this paper we present a description of tag clouds including a theoretical discourse on the strengths and weaknesses of using them in common Web-based contexts. Further recent methods of semantic clustering for visualizing tag clouds are reviewed. Findings from user studies that investigated the visual perception of differently arranged depictions of tags follow. The main objective consists in the exploration of characteristical aspects in perceptual phenomenons and cognitive processes during the interaction with a tag cloud. This clears the way for useful implications on the constitution and design factors of that visualisation form. Finally a new approach is proposed in order to further develop on this concept.

1 Introduction

Ever since social tagging systems began to gain popularity as a tool for annotating web resources, extensive amounts of unordered information have found their way into every day life in Web 2.0 surroundings. In order to differentiate between personally relevant information and irrelevant content, tagging and bookmarking have become a powerful routine among internet users. Essentially, once a selected item of information has been extracted from the enormous set of cumulated web content it has to be captured by the user for later use. An information source which has been tagged once should allow the user to re-find the content easily and at any time, while the meaning of that information in given contexts must remain comprehensible through the meaning of the adequately chosen tag. As people obviously differ in their personal conceptions and derive

A. Ebert et al. (Eds.): HCIV (INTERACT) 2009, LNCS 6431, pp. 23–37, 2011.

inter-individually different associations from one and the same information content many tags are dedicated to stand for fewer resources, filling the "tagging space" with more and more personalized keywords.

The need for managing this plenitude of cumulated tagging data, i.e. "folksonomies", provided reason for the emergence of a simple visualization form named the "tag cloud", a visual depiction of user-generated tags, in which words that act like links and connect to subsequent information content. In contrast to their great popularity, however, efforts to understand the underlying cognitive and perceptual processes related to the interaction with tag clouds have so far been moderate. Hence in our work we set the focus on tag clouds as a useful search tool that provides access to large amounts of user-collected data. As contents and resources in folksonomies are subjectively denominated by users without any limitations on vocabulary, a viable visualization form needs to integrate unclassified and difficult to define content into meaningful representations. A few variants have been proposed to enhance the interaction within a search process, e.g. mediating the relevance of the tags by varying visual features such as font size, color and position; or alternating the tags structural arrangement within a tag cloud. Additional innovative approaches have dealt with improvement of data management i.e. consolidation (for example [Viegas2004]). Accordingly, clustering methods have previously been used either to integrate tags into a coherent whole according to their semantic interrelations or to create new visual variants of tag clouds [Hayes2007],[Hassan-Montero2006],[Bielenberg2005]. In our opinion, semantic clustering for arranging tags can be a viable method to generate meaningful units within a tag cloud in order to enhance user performance and augment users' personal gain from the interaction. Facing the potentially great value within information visualization issues, our objective for improving tag cloud representations can be justified by their perpetual popularity as well as by the fact that their typical organisation and appearances have not yet seen much innovative activity.

In a first step, this work provides a detailed description of tag clouds, including an elaboration of the basic concept, common shapes and application methods; this introduction serves to hilghlight some cogent arguments regarding tag clouds practical limitations. Further, we excerpt some essentials from research into visual perception and eye movement, in order to touch on considerations in the discourse on perceptual aspects of the interaction with the tag cloud visualization. Additional attention is then given to the different uses of semantic clustering methods for the meaningful implementation of tag cloud applications, including some of the stringent findings attained with eye tracking methodology. We emphasize the analysis of the cognitive background of the observed behavior related to the interaction with tag clouds. A section is dedicated to illustrating the attempt of a stepwise dissociation of the different attentional and conscious and cognitive stages occurring during a typical interaction. Once the underlying processes have been illustrated we finally discuss some design- and concept-related considerations for the future use of tag clouds as a simple and viable tool for visualizing user-generated annotation content in the Web.

2   Tag Clouds

2.1   The Concept

The concept of a tag cloud is as popular as it is simple to comprehend. A tag cloud consists in an agglomeration of lexical items including words, parts of words, expressions, symbols, and combinations of the latter. All items are usually placed nearby to one another on a dedicated part of the display. Taken together they build a certain form due to their proximity one to each other, such as an angular or rounded shape. An example of a common tag cloud layout as can be found in the Web is presented in Figure 1. Each item, called a "'tag"', represents a hyperlink to a specific informational resource on a Website. Thus users are able to re-find their bookmarked resources through the use of keywords. Furthermore the tags can be used to organize several resources within specific topics.

Tags are usually weighted according to their occurrence and popularity within a representation, whereby the bigger the tag the more it has been frequented by users or the more often it occurs on a website (see Fig.1). In this way tag clouds allow for the easy highlighting of important information among the remaining content, set apart from the typical text-based website appearance. An additional property that can be varied in tag cloud visualizations concerns the order of the tags. Although a few solutions exist for the spatial organization of tags, their arrangement within a tag cloud typically follows an alphabetic order, as is the case for the tag cloud in Figure 1.

2.2   Application

Several web tools exist today (e.g. Tag Cloud Generator, TagCrowd [1]) that let users built their own tag cloud. Thus they can organize personal web space and provide a quick overview or a first orientation for insight-seeking visitors. Due to their great popularity tag clouds remain a widely used tool among internet and social media users for the visualization of metadata. More concretely, tag clouds can be used in several contexts: firstly, when a website owner wants to visualize the main topics on his site, he can use a tool to process the most frequented terms as weighted tags in order to form a cloud. In this case visitors are supposed to get an idea of "aboutness" of the website content. Secondly, many web services exist which allow users to individually bookmark information content using self-created keywords. These keywords support them in their ability to accurately organize relevant data. These user-generated tags can then be embedded into a graphical frame, i.e. a tag cloud within the users personal profile. A tag cloud can also serve as a categorization method for special content items where the font size of each tag reflects the quantity of subsequent content items in a given category. Keeping in mind these different tasks where tag clouds can be involved, user-related factors such as individual skills and familiarity with this kind of tool will always have an impact on the resulting performance during an interaction. It is

---

[1] http://www.tag-cloud-generator.com, http://tagcrowd.com

therefore important to consider that different search scenarios exist, originating from personal search intentions in various search contexts. Different browsing contexts depend on the goals and intentions of the users, which lead to different browsing behaviors. We will discuss the significance of these scenarios later in this work.

Fig. 1. Example from a TagCrowd[1] tag cloud

2.3   Practical Limitations

The initial idea behind this tool was to provide uncoded and intuitively comprehensible keywords that help to better organize and to refind miscellaneous web content (see Fig. 1). Beside their ease of use, tag clouds are perceived to loosen the appearance on a website as usually dominated by primarily text-based contents. In practice, however, the operability of tag clouds suffers from obvious limitations. First of all, tag clouds have to deal with weaknesses concerning the quality and syntax of folksonomies [Mathes2004]. An important issue concerns the lack of vocabulary control within social tagging data, where identical words leading to similar resources are written differently and so the variety and plenitude of redundant annotations continuously grows every day. Often contents are tagged by symbols or codes that cannot be comprehended by uninvolved people, but allow others to remember and re-find certain information via the use of these mnemonic tricks. As already mentioned, people have varying abstract concept understanding for everything they perceive. Each individual derives different associations from one and the same informational content. Hence efforts to generate meaningful ontological organizations from user-generated social tagging data often run up their limits. Users obviously like to make efficient use of this tool. Hence when reflecting on ways to optimize tag clouds, restrictions related to vocabulary control can not be up for discussion.

Another observation concerns the interaction with a tag cloud which is often limited. Former studies have shown that usually tags with larger font size are frequented over a longer time than are smaller tags [Halvey2007],[Shepitsen2008]. As the most frequented tags are displayed with larger font size, tags with smaller size become redundant. The result is that the perception of a tag cloud is dominated by a few number of very large tags, where the smaller tags earn much less attention from the users. For the insight-seeking user the interaction with a tag cloud visualization often ends here without having exploited the full informational content. Now, one can raise the question if the systematic variation of the visual features runs the risk of becoming counterproductive for a sensible interaction, when the larger tags systematically distract from the remaining content. In this context the advantages of just weighting tags following their popularity remain to be discussed [Hayes2007].

The variation of the font size provokes further inconsistency. In many tag cloud visualizations the appearance is affected by the occurrence of some areas of white space between the lines (see also Fig.1). As the bigger tags need more space than do the smaller, much space is utilized when a line contains only one big tag but many tags with small font size [Kaser2007]. The waste of empty space on a website not only disturbs the appearance of the tag cloud itself but also leads to issues dealing with page layout and design aspects. Influence of white space on perceptual factors will be discussed in a subsequent section.

We can assert at this point that the manipulation of the visual features has a major impact on the appearance of a tag cloud. Although the variation of the tag font size is predominantly used other ways should be elaborated. To do so the principles of human visual perception in relation to tag cloud "reading" and similar tasks must first to be outlined.

3   Basics on Visual Perception

A classic approach to how visual information is processed by the human has been delivered by Ann Treisman [Treisman1980]. In the feature integration theory she claims for the existence of a pre-attentive subsystem, which at the earliest stage of visual processing decomposes a visual stimulus into its elementary features [Treisman1980],[Duchowski2002]. At a more focused attentive level, then, these independent basic features are recomposed in order to obtain an integrated perception of an object and the world. Pre-attentive vision is supposed to happen around 200 ms after stimulus onset and can be manipulated by pre-attentive cues such as color, size, or proportion difference of objects [Bruce2006].

As tag clouds provide quick access to information without the demand of great mental efforts, special interest is dedicated to those moments of early processing before complex cognitive activities of reasoning are engaged. In order to quantify visual perceptual processes physiological parameters can be derived from the recording of eye movements during a given task.

3.1   The Eye Tracking Approach

Usually when interacting with visual interfaces what we perceive from the outer world is principally determined by what our eyes capture for us. The systematic observation of eye movements potentially offers a viable approach for the derivation of physiological correlates of visual perception and processing in a non invasive manner. Relevant metrics for measuring gaze behavior are frequency, duration and spatial distribution of fixations and saccades.

The recording of eye gaze is considered as an empirically approved method to derive important aspects for the understanding of visual perception. In relation with our current research interests the main intention is to compare the visual perception of tag clouds with processes running during other visual tasks. Also different patterns of visual inspection behavior that exist for different visual stimulation variants can be identified. In respect to findings on the basic characteristics of eye movements in information processing selected patterns shall be briefly described in the following section.

3.2   Perceptual Aspects in Similar Tasks

Tag clouds have to be processed by capturing the lexical characters and similarly integrating the formal aspects of their graphical frame. This is why the perceptual aspects of related tasks such as reading text and anticipating the meaning of graphically presented information will be outlined.

A major part of the eye movement research has been extended from initial examinations of reading behavior, and many studies have dealt with the visual perception of textual information. Apart from the individual factors of intention, motivation and strategy, eye movements are affected by textual and typographical variables such as the manipulation of various visual features. When *reading text*, indicators for visual processing are the so-called fixations, saccades, or scan-paths [Rayner1998]. Saccades are the rapid eye movements that the eyes perform during a visual task lasting between 20 and 35 milliseconds (ms). More exactly, during the activity of reading, a saccade of 2° has an average duration of approx. 30 ms [Rayner1998]. Eye fixations occur between the saccades when the eyes remain relatively still during a time window of 200 to 300 ms. Depending on the context, fixations are meant to represent the critical moments for the synchronization of perceptual and attentive processes, from physical input at the sensory receptors of the eye to the encoding and integration of information.

The *perceptual span* is the region from which useful information can be captured during an eye fixation [Rayner1998]. During reading this region is known to reach not more than 3 to 4 letters from the beginning of the actual fixation point to the left and about 13-14 letters to the right (parafoveal vision)(see Figure 2). For a mean saccade size the *perceptual span* is said to correspond up to 7 to 9 letter spaces. More concretely, the maximum acuity of the eye can be attained in the central 2° of vision (foveal), whereas acuity shrinks in parafoveal vision and even more in its periphery, as is illustrated in Fig. 2.

Worth noting is that during saccades no encoding activity is supposed to happen. The so-called regressive saccades (back-tracking eye movements) can

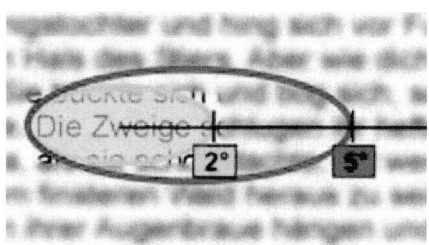

Fig. 2. Visual field during a reading activity; foveal vision (turquoise), parafoveal (red)

serve as an indicator for task complexity and encoding difficulties. Whereas some studies have demonstrated that lexical processing is not suppressed during saccades, others argue that cognitive processes are suppressed (for example see [Irwin1998]). For the current analyses of tag clouds, however, the examination of eye fixations remains our principal indicator for visual processing.

These facts can aid us in finding out about the acuity of tag perceptions within a tag cloud. We are interested in how strong fixations on bigger tags or on semantically charged tags favor or disrupt the perception of neighbored tags (parafoveal field). Of further interest is if tags in the parafoveal field are perceived depending on their semantic content, i.e. if the latter has an influence on the integration of pre-attentive captured information.

For a better understanding of the visual perception of tag clouds, the consideration of the perceptual and cognitive aspects of *graph comprehension* can also be useful. Carpenter and Shah recorded peoples eye movements while they were examining graphs showing complex interactions. They argue for an iterative character of graphical feature identification processing [Carpenter1998]. Due to the increase of online information platforms and newspapers, new paradigms have been generated where people deal with more complex scenes in form of multimodal representations, i.e. when a web page contains text and graphical content. Interestingly, studies showed that when observing selected advertisements (ads) on the Web viewers do not alternate fixations between the text and picture part of the ads. They rather tend to read the large print, then the smaller print, and then they look at the picture [Rayner2001]. Accordingly, a question of particular interest is how people process a tag cloud, comprised of both textual and graphical information. Overall active tasks such as visual search or reading text seem to generate shorter fixation duration and larger saccades than do passive viewing of natural scenes or simple patterns.

As tag clouds mostly serve for browsing website content or annotated resources, parallels to the behavioral processes during *web search* generally have to be considered. The examination of eye movements in order to understand how users search for information on the Web showed that most people perform a linear strategy during the inspection of search results, in which every result is evaluated in turn before a person proceeds with the list [Kloeckner2004]. The question is now if people adopt similar strategies for browsing tag clouds, or if the graphical context stimulates different patterns.

Finally, we have no doubt that these perceptual, attentional, and cognitive processes for the integration of visually distributed material are influenced by motivational factors during the interaction (e.g. for aborting an unsuccessful search). Of course the context in which a search task is performed has a strong influence on the outcome. Every activity requires energy and demands a certain amount of an individuals cognitive capacities and motivation. According to this, behavioral data should be analyzed in order to extract peoples level of motivation to use the tool (i.e. trying out and continuing to use), and to observe corresponding typical *behavioral tendencies* respectively.

Taken together these findings and in order to better understand the mechanisams of human information processing when handling with tag clouds, open questions exist such as:

- How font size affects the perception of a tag cloud?
- Do semantically relevant tags earn attention within parafoveal vision?
- How both graphical and lexical information is processed within a tag cloud?

Before trying to answer those questions, however, we need to examine the various visualization approaches that use different clustering techniques in order to learn more about perceptions of tag clouds.

4   Layouts of Tag Cloud Visualizations

4.1   State of the Art

Current innovations in the field of information visualization enable the implementation of highly sophisticated techniques based on graph theory, topological algorithms, physical models, geometrical and geographical representations [2]. Existing solutions for visualizing conglomerates of unordered and semantically interrelated data must not only fulfill principal functional requirements but also meet aesthetic demands. Similarly, in addition to the variation of the visual features, solutions with different tag arrangements have been realized.

Work on tag clouds has been done with the motivation to embed the semantic relations between tags into a graphical frame. For example [Fujimura2008] generated an algorithm displaying tag clouds within a topographic image context, where the cosine similarity of tag feature vectors (terms and their weight generated from a set of tagged documents) was used to measure tag similarity. A tag cloud layout was then calculated where the semantic relatedness was displayed as the distance between tags. Others tried to generate map-based visualizations of large collections of geo-referenced pictorial data [Jaffe2006]. Using a summarization algorithm pictures were ranked and organized into a hierarchically clustered structure. Additionally, [Begelman2006] provided a technique to measure similarity among tags in order to use a selected clustering algorithm for adequately displaying semantically-related tags. As contents vary significantly

---

[2] VC: http://www.visualcomplexity.com/vc

within different contexts, Begelmann and colleagues further advocate the implementation of separate clusters for different communities. They also recommend re-running the algorithm periodically in order to keep the data updated. This observation refers to a phenomenon that has been named "user drift" i.e. the inconsistency of social tagging data over time [Hayes2007]. A circular cloud layout as opposed to the common rectangular layout of tag clouds has also been proposed [Bielenberg2005].

Furthermore [Kaser2007] discuss the waste of white space in classic tag clouds, in particular as it is found to become problematic in small-display (e.g. mobile) devices. They seek to optimize the tag cloud layout with electronic design automation (EDA) tools. Having inconsistent white spaces between the lines is not as trivial as it seems as - following the proximity law of Gestalt - the white spaces can give impression of grouped lines as entities, which biases the perception in an unintended direction (see Fig.1). Here a robust algorithm could prevent from such side effects.

Some investigations also encountered the phenomenon of a majority of infrequently used tags in a cloud as mentioned before. They partitioned data using content clustering [Hayes2007].

Overall, depending on the nature of the task in question we assume that semantic mapping techniques to visualize tags and their interrelations can be useful, as reading and handling maps is part of most human procedural knowledge and memory abilities.

4.2   Empirical Evidence

Effects of tag position on user perception have not been confirmed yet. However evidence exists that larger displayed tags earn more attention than smaller tags. Fig. 3 shows an example of how the gaze can get stuck on larger tags. Results from eye gaze analysis with tag clouds showed that generally the upper left quadrant of the display is the most frequented [Schrammel2009b]. This trend may be understood by the fact that people in western cultural areas usually read texts from top left to bottom right. Knowing that the bigger tags earn more attention than the smaller ones, tags with small font size positioned in the bottom right quadrant risk being neglected by the users attention. This observation should be a principal motivator for conceptual adaptations in future design considerations.

Tag clouds with semantically clustered tag arrangements have been implemented by a series of research groups. Semantic relatedness is most often defined by the means of relative co-occurrence between tags (see section 4.1). Whereas some could determine a better search performance of their participants for the interaction with a semantically clustered tag cloud [Hassan-Montero2006], the results in our experiments did not show such an improving effect [Schrammel2009b]. Nevertheless the study showed that semantically clustered tag clouds can provide improvements over random layouts in specific search tasks. Also, semantically structured tag clouds were preferred by about half of the users for general search tasks, whereas tag cloud layout did not seem to influence the ability to remember tags.

Fig. 3. Gaze plots showing fixations on tags with large font size

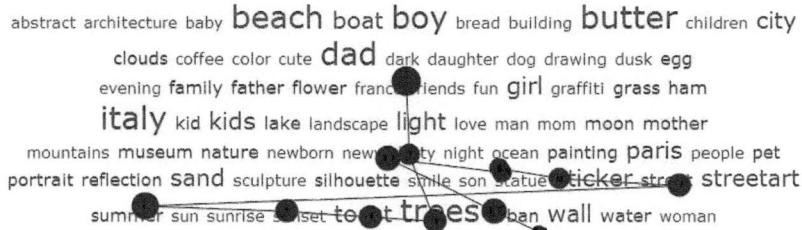

Fig. 4. Targeted search behavior for the target tag "'water"' (alphabetic layout)

Here the quality of the applied algorithm may have an essential role, noting that social tagging data are known to be not clearly definable in their semantic concept. In one case, related tags were situated in the same line of text, whereas our algorithm grouped the semantic clusters over several lines. According to the quadrant effect and reading direction in western cultural areas the use of line-by-line clusters by [Hassan-Montero2006] (i.e. each line contains only items of one cluster) may be more appropriate for the linear-scanning users.

Although our findings did not show any significant differences, we have to underline that search strategies can differ within various search contexts. An opportunistic search where no explicit target tag is searched may engage different patterns than a specific tag search. When looking for a specific tag the alphabetic arrangement may be useful. When searching for any term belonging to a certain topic a semantic layout is thought to be more practicable. Given that the user identifies the semantic arrangement of the tags he can choose from a pool of tags. For the semantic layout, however, specific patterns could not yet be observed or dissociated from patterns in other layout conditions.

Another aim in previous studies was to examine whether users perform characteristic search patterns within a search task. Eye gaze analysis showed that depending on the task users can adopt certain patterns but no traceable strategy within a search process could be determined: some use a *chaotic search* patterns, others perform a *serial scanning* in a "zigzag" pattern (see Fig. 6). Again others alter their gaze behavior during the search process between chaotic searching and serial scanning (i.e. beginning to search chaotically and after a moment of unsuccessful performance proceeding with serial search and so on). Generally search behavior may be influenced by individual factors such as personal levels of impulsivity and accurateness in search tasks. Those users, however, who often alternated their search strategy within one search often took more time to solve it.

Interestingly, serial search is not always performed until the last line of a tag cloud. Some users abandon the serial search for conducting chaotic search again. In this case the same tags are fixated several times. This could be due to reciprocal blocking of memory traces. The trace of tags scanned during one search strategy probably does not include the short memory trace from the other strategy and vice-versa.

According to the scanning phenomenon some authors think that people scan tag clouds rather than read them [Halvey2007]. These perceptual aspects related to processing depth have to be considered in further information visualization discources. Independently from the layout (alphabetic, randomized, semantic) people performed similar gaze combinations for several stimuli right after onset. Considering the existence of *scanpaths*, some users performed for example a "circle loop", or an "S"- scan (see Fig. 5). It is still open if there are characteristic orders of alternating those patterns within one search process, i.e. if inter- and intra-individual regularities in task strategies can be identified. Again, systematic differences due to the various search contexts could not yet be examined.

Fig. 5. Example of a "S - scan" (left) and a "right loop" (right) pattern

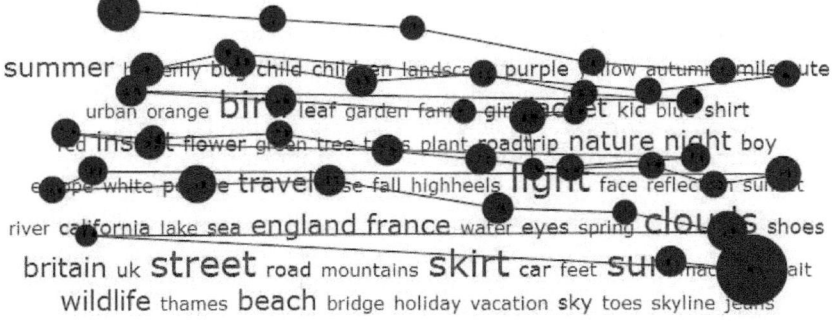

Fig. 6. Gaze plot for serial search using zigzag pattern (semantic layout); note the upward dislocation of the gaze plot due to unsystematic head motor activity of the participant

Focusing on performance in different layouts, research on the perception of alphabetically ordered tag clouds showed that search processing becomes much more targeted once the user recognizes this principle of organization (see Fig. 4) [Kaser2007], [Schrammel2009b]. An example is shown in Figure 5 where the gaze heads first to a very large tag at the bottom of the cloud. Scanning inverse to reading direction is then initiated until the alphabetic order is recognized. Eye movements turn to the region where the target tag is estimated, following the perceived principle of organisation.

This means that as soon as a structural feature has been identified the search behavior is efficiently adjusted. This observation may lead to the assumption that a better task performance can be achieved if the user is aware of the semantic organisation in a tag cloud. In this case all the more appropriate visual features of tag clouds are required to be well developed for ensuring an enhanced interaction within the latent information, i.e. tagging space.

5   From Perceptual to Cognitive Integration

Essentially a tag cloud consists in a visual representation of data mined content, i.e. information resources reduced to a certain quantity of selected tags. This concept may invite users to search for single items rather than for entities, keeping the perceptual processing more pre-attentive, i.e. lowering cognitive load. This is in line with approaches from cognitive psychology which underline the fact that attention focus is limited, e.g. naming the spotlight-metaphor within visual attention discourses [Posner1980].

Within neuropsychological research, the postulation of a limited capacity control system (LCCS) of attention has been widely discussed [Eysenck1995]. It is assumed that the information integration begins with pre-attentive appraisal of the visual features, in this case, the font size of the tags. In case of a mismatch, when the larger tags do not meet the search intention of the user, an orientation reaction (OR) occurs. With the OR the user abandons the irrelevant cues to adjust the attention to other targets. In line with the findings on tag clouds, we can assume that a chaotic pattern is initialized by the upcoming OR in succession of the mismatch. Via the LCCS, an effort mechanism is then triggered for a more conscious coordination and comparison of contents in short-term versus long-term memory stores. If the new search strategy also fails (influenced by motivational factors) a new OR is engaged. We further suppose that the motivation to find the target tag by chance (e.g. chaotic browsing) is sometimes higher than the patience to accomplish a certain strategic pattern (e.g. serial scanning).

In general, however, such effort mechanisms are accompanied by higher energy costs in the central nervous system and finally take more time. These considerations taken together could explain why people in previous experiments took more time to detect the underlying hierarchical structure within the tag cloud than they needed to recognize the alphabetical order [Schrammel2009b]. Accordingly people perceived the semantically clustered tag cloud as less helpful than the alphabetic condition.

Hence we suggest that once a cluster has been identified as being semantically related, cognitive load should be relatively low to proceed with search. We can distinguish between first, the cognitive effort needed to comprehend an underlying semantic structure within a visualization form, and second, the search process within a coherent context. In order to attain the latter i.e., to favor the conjunction of semantically related tags into an integrated percept, users simply could be alerted by a note when a tag cloud contains semantic clusters.

Further we claim for the elimination of the artificially generated separations between tags (see section 4.1). White space should only separate tags of different clusters, such as in the form of several "mini clouds". However, the initial conception of tag clouds would then need to be redefined. To encourage the awareness of arrangement structure, future design implications could profit from the physiological phenomenon of context dependency [Eysenck1995]. This refers to the phenomenon that objects with similar attributes are seen as related, i.e. embedded in a common context. In line with the arguments of the Gestalt theories [Eysenck1995], semantic clusters of tags could be visualized with manipulated visual features, such as differently colored tags for each cluster within a tag cloud. An item thus integrated in a certain context - even if not familiar - could initiate contextual cueing processes and provide much more informational content to the user than a cumulated representation of items. By modulating light and color conditions of related tags, entities could be better recognized following the law of similarity. For the technical implementation of these propositions, however, issues of keeping system load to a minimum have to be taken into account.

6   Conclusion

Based on our experience, we think that semantic clustering methods are useful for classifying annotations in social tagging systems, i.e. tag clouds, as their strength lies in the procurement of meaning on a meta-level, and clustering here meets the needed standards. As the core interest in research lies in the effort to enhance interaction with tag clouds, future efforts should focus on the synchronization of the perceptual user capacities and the conceptual conditions of that visualization form. Summarizing the approaches above, we see potential for improvement of clustering techniques for use in tag clouds. We expect that the cognitive processes of chunking could be engaged through visual stimulation, e.g. becoming clusters signalized as entities. As evidence now exists that performance can be enhanced when the user is aware of the tag arrangement (as for alphabetic layout), design implications could involve the visual accentuation of the clusters. We conclude that this can be solved by triggering the perceptual system on a pre-attentive level.

Although they are not appropriate for all contexts [Sinclair2008], tag clouds still remain useful in their simplicity of visualization, and in their ease of use and manipulation. The interaction with a visualization based on a semantic structure demands semantic processing by the user, i.e. the processing of meaning, which occurs at a higher processing level that of scanning a display for single lexical expressions. In our opinion we cannot expect from users to autonomously search for semantic relations within such a simple visualization form; there must be an indication of the underlying structural attributes. In order to enhance the dynamic character of the interaction, the user could be allowed to vary the number of displayed clusters within a tag cloud, where he/ she could easily switch between the different views. An option to display the evolution of tagging data over time could also provide some additional insight into information content for the interested user. Altogether we hold the position that semantically clustered tag clouds represent a viable visualization form for displaying social tagging data. They potentially enhance users ability to represent knowledge and improve retentiveness of given knowledge. Along with the findings on perceptual aspects, new approaches have been formulated that integrate important factors of visual processing and attention capturing. In this regard, elaboration on the graphical appearance of tag clouds cannot yet be seen as completed, and provides material to further research.

References

[Bielenberg2005] Bielenberg, K., Zacher, M.: Groups in Social Software: Utilzing Tagging to Integrate Individual Contexts for Social Navigation. Masters Thesis, Universitt Bremen (2005)

[Begelman2006] Begelman, G., Keller, P., Smadja, F. Automated Tag Clustering: Improving search and exploration in the tag space. In Proc. WWW 2006

[Bruce2006] Bruce, V., Green, P.R., Georgeson, M.A.: Visual Perception: Physiology, Psychology and ecology, 4th edn. Psychological Press, San Diego (2003)

[Carpenter1998] Carpenter, P.A., Shah, P.: A model of perceptual and conceptual processes in graph comprehension. Journal of Experimental Psychology: Applied 4, 75–100 (1998)

[Chung1998] Chung, M.M., Jiang, Y.: Contextual Cueing: Implicit Learning and Memory of Visual Context Guides Spacial Attention. Cognitive Psychology 36, 28–71 (1998)

[Duchowski2002] Duchowski, A.T.: A Breadth-First Survey of Eye Tracking Applications. Behavior Research Methods, Instruments, and Computers 34(4), 455–470 (2002)

[Eysenck1995] Eysenck, M.W., Keane, M.T.: Cognitive psychology: a student's handbook, 3rd edn. Lawrence Erlbaum Associates, Mahwah (1995)

[Fujimura2008] Fujimura, K., Fujimura, S., Matsubayashi, T., Yamada, T., Okuda, H.: Topigraphy: visualization for largescale tag clouds. In: Proc. WWW 2008, pp. 1087–1088. ACM Press, New York (2008)

[Halvey2007] Halvey, M.J., Keane, M.T.: An assessment of tag presentation techniques. In: Proc. WWW 2007, pp. 1313–1314. ACM Press, New York (2007)

[Hassan-Montero2006] Hassan-Montero, Y., Herrero-Solana, V.: Improving tagclouds as visual information retrieval interfaces. In: Proc. InfoSciT 2006, Mrida, Spain (October 2006)

[Hayes2007] Hayes, O., Avesani, P.: Using Tags and Clustering to identify topic-relevant Blogs. In: International Conference on Weblogs and Social Media, ICWSM (2007)

[Henderson1990] Henderson, J.M., Ferreira, F.: Effects of Foveal Processing Difficulty on the Perceptual Span in Reading: Implications for Attention and Eye Movement Control. Journal of Experimental Psychology 16(3), 417–429 (1990)

[Irwin1998] Irwin, D.E.: Lexical Processing during Saccadic Eye Movements. Cognitive Psychology 36(1), 1–27 (1998)

[Jaffe2006] Jaffe, A., Tassa, T., Davis, M.: Generating Summaries and Visualization for Large Collections of Geo- Referenced Photographs. In: Proc. MIR 2006, pp. 89–98. ACM Press, New York (2006)

[Kaser2007] Kaser, O., Lemire, D.: Tag-Cloud Drawing: Algorithms for Cloud Visualization. In: WWW Workshop on Tagging and Metadata for Social Information Organization, pp. 1087–1088 (2007)

[Kloeckner2004] Kloeckner, K., Wirschum, N., Jameson, A.: Depth and breadth-first processing of search result lists. In: Ext. Abstracts CHI 2004, pp. 1539–1539. ACM Press, New York (2004)

[Posner1980] Posner, M.I., Snyder, C.R.R., Davidson, B.J.: Attention and the Detection of Signals. Journal of Experimental Psychology 109(2), 160–174 (1980)

[Rayner1998] Rayner, K.: Eye movements in reading and information processing: 20 years of research. Psychological Bulletin 124, 372–422 (1998)

[Rayner2001] Rayner, K., Rottello, C.M., Stewart, A.J., Keir, J., Duffy, S.A.: Integrating Text and Pictorial Information: Eye Movements when Looking at Print Advertisements. Journal of Experimental Psychology: Applied 7, 219–226 (2001)

[Schrammel2009a] Schrammel, J., Leitner, M., Tscheligi, M.: Semantically Structured Tag Clouds: An Empirical Evaluation of Clustered Presentation Approaches. In: CHI 2009, Boston, MA, USA (April 3-9, 2009)

[Schrammel2009b] Schrammel, J., Deutsch, S., Tscheligi, M.: The Visual Perception of Tag Clouds Results from an Eye Tracking Study. In: Gross, T., Gulliksen, J., Kotzé, P., Oestreicher, L., Palanque, P., Prates, R.O., Winckler, M. (eds.) INTERACT 2009. LNCS, vol. 5727, pp. 819–831. Springer, Heidelberg (2009)

[Mathes2004] Mathes, A.: Folksonomies - Cooperative Classification and Communication Through Shared Metadata. UIC Technical Report (2004)

[Rivadeneira2007] Rivadeneira, A.W., Gruen, D.M., Muller, M.J., Millen, D.R.: Getting our head in the clouds: toward evaluation studies of tagclouds. In: Proc. CHI 2007, pp. 995–998. ACM Press, New York (2007)

[Shepitsen2008] Shepitsen, A., Gemmell, J., Mobasher, B., Burke, R.: Personalized Recommendation in Social Tagging Systems Using Hierarchical Clustering. In: Proc. RecSys 2008, pp. 259–266. ACM Press, New York (2008)

[Sinclair2008] Sinclair, J., Cardew-Hall, M.: The Folksonomy Tag Cloud: When is it Useful? Journal of Information Sience 34(1), 15–29 (2008)

[Treisman1980] Treisman, A.: A feature-integration theory of attention 12, 97–136 (1980)

[Viegas2004] Viégas, F.B., Wattenberg, M., Dave, K.: Studying cooperation and conflict between authors with history flow visualizations. In: CHI 2004: Proceedings of the SIGCHI Conference on Human Factors in Computing Systems, pp. 575–582. ACM, New York (2004)

The Personal Equation of Complex Individual Cognition during Visual Interface Interaction

Tera Marie Green and Brian Fisher

School of Interactive Arts + Technology
Simon Fraser University
terag@sfu.ca

Abstract. This chapter considers the need for a better understanding of complex human cognition in the design of interactive visual interfaces by surveying the availability of pertinent cognitive models and applicable research in the behavioral sciences, and finds that there are no operational models or useful precedent to effectively guide the design of visually enabled interfaces. Further, this chapter explores the impact of individual differences, and in particular, inherent differences such as personality factors, on complex cognition. Lastly, it outlines how knowledge of human individuality, coupled with what is known about complex cognition, is being used to develop predictive measures for interface interaction design and evaluation, a research program known as the Personal Equation of Interaction. . . .

1 Introduction

Generally speaking, interactive visualizations are considered to have a number of advantages over more conventional visual interfaces for learning, analysis, and knowledge creation. Much of the support for these claims comes from a variety of sources, such as user evaluations, comparative studies of error rates, time to completion, etc., as well as and designer/developer intuition. One common claim concerns the development of insight. From early on, visualization has been proposed as a preferable interface approach for generating insight (e.g. [3], [39].[43]). As a concept, however, insight is a construct that is often either loosely defined as some variety of meaningful knowledge or is left undefined (e.g. [40],[44]). More recently there have been efforts to define insight, although not in ways that might enable it to be quantified. For example, North described insight as a broad construct, which is complex, deep, qualitative, unexpected, and/or relevant [27], without characterizing the cognitive processes that give rise to it, or the outcomes that are generated by it. Chang et al. defined insight as comprising two categories: knowledge-building insight, which is a form of learning and/or knowledge generation, and spontaneous insight, which is method of problem-solving for previously intractable problems, commonly described as an a-ha! moment. This dual definition has advantages over a unitary definition in that it supports focused analysis of the component aspects of the overall construct. Spontaneous insight, however, has been an elusive notion for researchers in several disciplines;

A. Ebert et al. (Eds.): HCIV (INTERACT) 2009, LNCS 6431, pp. 38–57, 2011.
© IFIP International Federation for Information Processing 2011

neuroscientists and psychologists have studied the phenomenon, but as yet do not know how insight is triggered [4].

By any definition, there is little empirical evidence that supports claims of visualization superiority in insight generation, though user evaluations are often conducted to demonstrate visualization efficacy over other types of interface. Plaisant et al. [30] identified four current themes in the evaluative literature: controlled experiments comparing design elements, usability evaluation, controlled experiments comparing two or more tools, and in situ case studies. In all four groups, evaluations and comparative studies have largely focused on perception, motor learning, focal attention, target recognition and/or target acquisition. For example, musing behaviors were used as a predictor of user focus in a geospatial visualization [1]. Jeong et al. compared two visualization tools to determine in which interface users were more efficient in finding outliers and identifying highly correlated items in a matrix [22]. Nodes were the subject of an evaluation of target identification in large tree tools [29]. And Wang et al. evaluated whether users could focus on the count of visualized objects (in this case, paper proposals) over a period of time [52]. In these evaluations as well as in cognition as a whole, perceptual, cognitive, and motor processes are important to the overall interaction. However, each of these identified cognitive systems are feeder processes. That is to say, they support and inform the more complex processes, such as reasoning, problem-solving, and knowledge generation, which form the backbone of systematic analysis or task solution. These complex processes are impacted demonstrably, as we will see, by the individuality of the interface environment, the knowledge domain, and the inherent differences within the user, over which visualization design has no control. To date, visualization evaluation has insufficiently considered the complexity of human cognition. This, in turn, has hampered the design of intuitive interfaces capable of mixed-initiative collaboration.

In this chapter, we will explore a variety of challenges to the consideration of cognitive complexity in visual analytics design, from the current lack of operational models and applicable research to a consideration of individual differences. We will then explore how an consideration of how these complex processes impact the understanding of common visual analytics tasks, and discuss a continuing exploration of how human individuality can be measured and charted, leading to a differentiating set of predictive measures that can not only predict interface performance, but guide visualization design. We call this the Personal Equation of Interaction.

2   The Challenge of Complex Cognition

Very little research examines the use of what is commonly known as higher cognition during interaction, which includes processes such as reasoning, problem-solving, and decision-making. Frequently, when a visualization design or evaluation argues that a specific technique or tool improves insight (which is learning and/or problem-solving) or analysis (which involves every major cognitive process), the evidence is actually task completion times for single-step tasks, improved target identification, or other simple outcomes. One reason for this, perhaps, is the practice of inferring the success of complex behaviors from measurements of simpler ones. A common example is the generalization of findings from simple, semantically-unrelated target acquisition tasks to human problem-solving as a whole, without a discussion of which of the many problem-solving theories or heuristics the finding might speak to (e.g.[8] , [35]). This practice over-simplifies the complexity of cognition, but is understandable, given that our best complex cognitive models are black box or descriptive. We will now consider the best known of these descriptive models, the sensemaking model.

2.1   The Sensemaking Loop

The most familiar approach to descriptively outline task-oriented processes is Pirolli and Cards sensemaking loop ([31], [38]). See Figure 1. Russell et al. defined sensemaking as *the process of searching for a representation and encoding data in that representation to answer task-specific questions* [38]. In the rest of this section, we will summarily explore the complexity of analytical cognition through a brief discussion of the sensemaking loop in the broader context of human reasoning. This seems necessary, for, as valuable as the sensemaking loop is to describing certain analytical tasks, its use tends to be overgeneralized in the visualization literature. Indeed, *sensemaking* is often the term given to most or all of the cognitive processes analysts employ during visual analytics tasks (e.g. [47], [31], [20]).

Sensemaking, as defined in the previous paragraph, creates a mental or physical representation (i.e. a "mental model" or "story"). This singular representation may well be necessary for problem solving, but may not be in itself sufficient for generating valid implications. Analyses may create multiple alternative mental representations of a situation in order to compare them in a variety of ways, using a variety of evaluative heuristics in order to draw their conclusions. At this larger scale of problem solving strategy, analytical cognition exhibits a great deal of variability, and is informed by both human and task individuality. For example, the sensemaking loop makes an effort to delineate top-down and bottom-up task descriptions. However, as some of Pirolli and Cards participants indicated, the cognition involved in the early tasks of the loop can rarely be so cleanly categorized. Further, though seemingly simplistic, even the first steps of the sensemaking loop (the "lower-effort" tasks of searching and filter) require complex cognition in the form of various reasoning heuristics to categorize, evaluate, and assemble pertinent information. These heuristics could be elimination heuristics like elimination by aspects [51], or satisificing [24] or they could be more complicated, such as the comparing possible shoebox members (concepts the analyst has gathered during sensemaking and think may be related to each other) to an ideal before addition. According to the Loop, pertinent shoebox members become part of and Evidence File which is used as part of the formal structure of the Schema, which is a sturctured narrative of how the evidence collected thus far fits together [31]. Thus, while sensemaking effectively describes

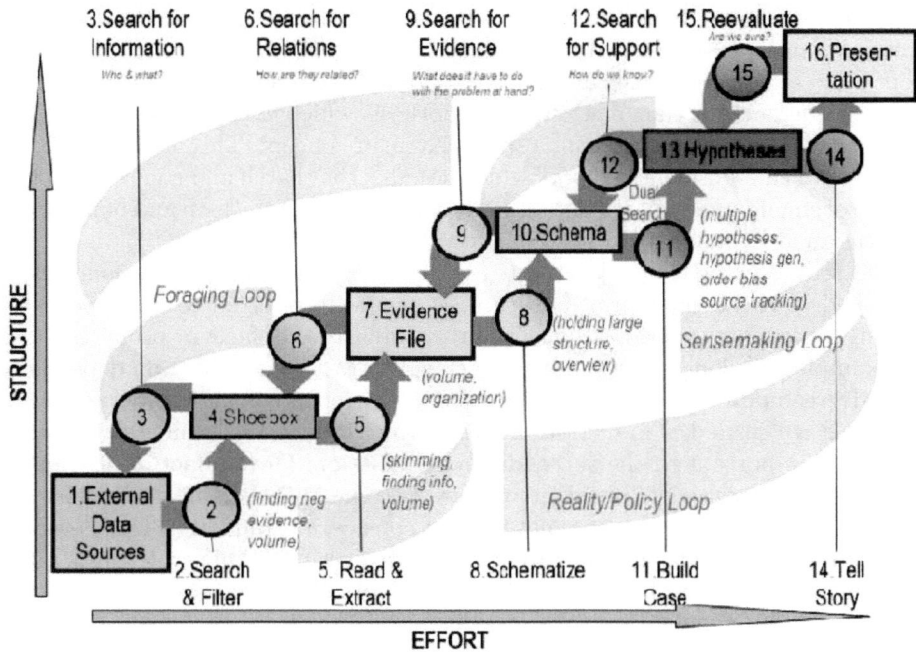

Fig. 1. The Sensemaking Loop. From [38].

one key component of the complex cognitive processes involved in the generation of insight, it does not claim to capture higher levels of abstraction, i.e. generation of problem-solving strategy, nor does it attempt to capture lower-level pattern recognition processes that support its operation. The latter set of processes are arguably the most critical for visualization to support, since they are precisely those aspects that are most closely tied to the visual systems own information processing capabilities (i.e. Irving Rocks logic of perception [36]).

Similarly, Cherubinis "models to rules mechanization" [6] suggests that the formation of schemata and hypothesis generation are not necessarily higher effort tasks. According to Cherubini, after human reasoning uses the generated model (which does require some cognitive effort to create in novel instantiations), the human infers a rule from the knowledge structure in the mental model. Or in his own words: *After grasping the common structure of the problems, most people should be able to devise a simple rule to solve all problems with the same structure (i.e., a domain-specific rule), disregarding the number of possibilities underlying them.*[6] This rule may be created after only one or two uses of a newly created model. Thus, depending on the information under consideration, hypothesis generation could actually require less cognitive bandwidth than the initial information search.

At a higher level, the sensemaking loop articulately describes one subset of reasoning, that of reasoning types which generate inferred hypotheses or generalized rules, or abduction and induction. Abduction (or abductive reasoning) is process of approaching seemingly unrelated information with the assumption that the data points or concepts are indeed interconnected; abduction creates and infers relations between two previously unrelated data points; the end product of abductions series of inferences is the creation of a hypothesis which explains these relational inferences [41], and usually about a specific item or concept. This fits well with the structure of the sensemaking loop, which situates the search and compartmentalization of small, unassociated details in the early stages of the loop and builds from there to an identifiable hypothesis or story.

The sensemaking loop also illustrates induction. Inductive reasoning, as is described in the behavioural literature, is generally referred to the process of making acceptable generalizations from the similarities of facts or properties (see for example [34], [50]). The validity or strength of the generalization depends in large degree upon the strength of these similarities. One of the characteristics of induction which makes induction different from abduction is that relationships are not as important to the successful generalization. Once a fact(s) or similarity has been accepted as valid, it or they become the basis of generalization; additional information may or may not be considered. Induction is a powerful form of reasoning that allows us to quickly categorize and infer rules; it is often referred to as a form of bottom-up reasoning, but can utilize top-down cognition as is needed. To some degree, the sensemaking loop describes induction, as this type of reasoning tends to build from smaller facts to a broader concept. However, unlike with hypothesis generation and analysis, induced generalizations do not necessarily require vetting, e.g. careful consideration of available evidence for the generalization. Induced hypotheses can jump past multiple steps, such as the shoebox or schema creation, straight to a generality.

While abduction or induction may accurately describe behavior during discovery or during exploration of novel problems for which the analyst does not already have a script or mental model to guide her as to what to do next, most problem-solving or decision-making tasks are driven by an articulated goal, theory or hypothesis from the start. These reasoning heuristics are neither abductive, which ends with a hypothesis, nor inductive, ending in an inferred rule, but rather deductive.

One of the more actively studied reasoning types, deductive reasoning falls outside of the sensemaking loop. By deduction (or, for that matter, induction), we are referring to reasoning as the subject of decades of empirically conducted research, which is usually evaluated through use of normative tasks like those that we will briefly itemize in the next section. A discussion of the philosophy of deduction, such as the traditional deduction of Aristotle, propositional (or first order) deduction, or natural deduction ([21], [10]), and the similarities or differences between these definitions, is neither intended nor implied.

There are several theories of deduction in the behavioral literature, but we will focus on two of the broader categories of deduction, which assume that human deductive reasoning is either rule based or model based. This dichotomy of rules vs. models raises interesting issues for visual analytics interfaces. Rule-based theories assume that humans use a script or a formal sequential logic while working through a deductive task (e.g. [53]). From this perspective, the content or information manipulated during the task doesnt demonstrably influence the reasoning, because the inferences drawn during induction are part of this formal process[54]. From the rules perspective, for the development of more intuitive deductive visual analytics tools, it would only be important to uncover the pertinent rules the analyst would use; theoretically, these deductive rules would generalize to all similar visual analytics tasks.

Model-based theories, however, are quite different. Models can be either concrete or abstract, complete or incomplete, pictorial or conceptual (e.g. [53],[54]). Models are also flexible; they can change as pertinent information changes, and can quantify degree (such as few or often), as well as causal conditions. Models depend heavily on semantic relationships, and so can be heavily influenced by the content of the information at hand. This, too, influences visualization design, for what data is presented when, and in what context, can influence the development of the model, as well as its completeness and validity. From the model-based perspective, discovering quickly inferred rules is not nearly as helpful as assuring that the human has all pertinent information readily at hand. With pertinent information, the human can generate a mental model, which can be manipulated as needed to reasoning through the task to a valid conclusion. Shneidermans Mantra [42]: Overview first, zoom and filter, details-on-demand assumes deductive reasoning. The big picture, or hypothesis, drives the interactive behavior. It is not surprising, then, as powerful as models would seem to be in the successful use of visual analytics interfaces, that they have a place in the visual analytics literature, even if the theory and implications of models are rarely discussed.

This has been only a brief, general discussion of the sensemaking loop and how it fits into the broader context of common reasoning types. Human reasoning is about reaching a usable or verifiable conclusion, but the ways in which we reach these conclusions, as we have seen, can vary widely. For this reason, it is easy to see why analytical reasoning processes have yet to be operationalized in a manner that meaningfully informs research and design. For while descriptive models like the sensemaking loop do much to frame the big picture, intuitive interfaces will require a more detailed working-order understanding of what lies inside the frame.

2.2   The Absence of Precedent

As we saw in the last section, there is, as yet, no unifying theory of reasoning (if such a thing is even possible). What does exist is a complication of decades of research into specific laboratory tasks, usually characterized by small-scale problems, which are intended to uncover reasoning heuristics and biases. These are of limited use for real-world applications, and in particular map poorly onto visually enabled human reasoning (e.g. interactive visualization for cognitive tasks). Further, the theories that motivate these studies are often bound to a particular task and environment. Thus the field of behavioural research as a whole is characterized by contradictory, often esoteric theories that fail to explain the narrative of reasoning from beginning of task to end.

For example, deductive reasoning is almost entirely studied in a laboratory trials. Both rule based and model-based deduction has traditionally studied by presenting participants with syllogisms and evaluating the conclusions that are drawn. Phillip Johnson-Laird often uses syllogisms to study aspects of reasoning, which can take forms such as this inference about object properties:

> Only one of the following statements is true:
> At least some of the plastic beads are not red, or
> None of the plastic beads is red.
> Is it possible that none of the red beads is plastic? ([23], pg. 150).

Other common uses of syllogisms involve mental reasoning and inferences about spatial relationships, such as:

> The cup is on the right of the plate.
> The spoon is on the left of the plate.
> The knife is in front of the spoon.
> The saucer is in front of the cup.
> What is the relation between the knife and the saucer? ([23], pg. 130)

Cherubini and Johnson-Laird [5] studied qualified inferences in iterative reasoning through word problems like the following:

> Everybody loves anyone who loves someone.
> Anne loves Beth.
> Does it follow that everyone loves Anne?
> .. ..
> Does it follow that Carol loves Diane?

Cherubini and Mazzocco also evaluated the mental models to rules mechanization through use of a computer program loaded with a series of virtual card problems [6] as illustrated in Figure 2. The participant was asked whether, based on the presented cards, a proposed sentence was *certainly true*.

Gigerenzer, in his evaluation of "fast and frugal" reasoning heuristics, used what he considered to be common knowledge about cities in questions about which he asked participants to make quick reasoning decisions. The questions were simple, such as *Is this [city name] the capital of the country?* [11]. Gigerenzer postulated that humans could make quick decisions based on very simple elimination heuristics which depended on accumulated general knowledge. These decisions were found to be more accurate than more sophisticated human and computer reasoning simulations.

The behavioral literature contains decades of research similar to the research we have discussed, with each study having its own novel, usually non-real world, problem formulation. Study problems are often designed to study some small subcategory of reasoning (iterative inferred, probabilistic, etc.) and very few or no studies are published which are designed to explain how humans solve a complex problem from start to finish.

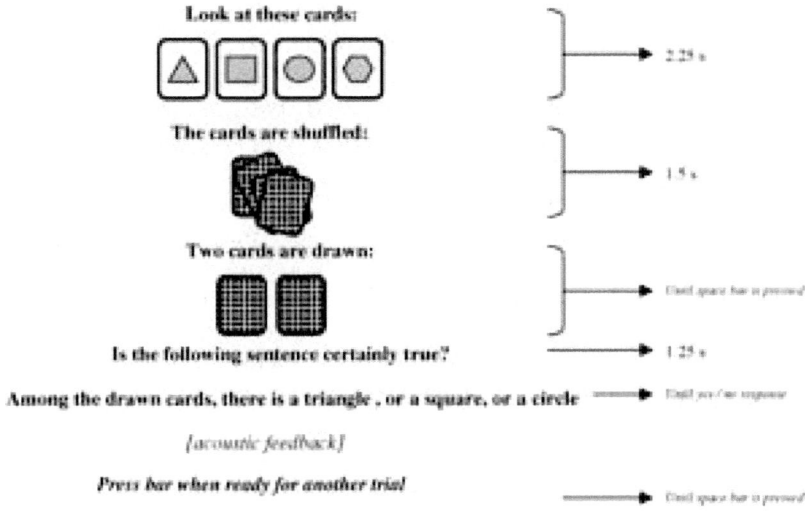

Fig. 2. The reasoning task from Cherubini [6]

Perhaps it is not surprising then that, with all of this research, there is still a lack of precedent on how to conduct research into visually enabled reasoning. It is not at all clear how one might evaluate interfaces with respect to their ability to scaffold higher-order cognitive tasks. Further, unlike many of the simpler cognitive tasks, higher cognition is almost never binary, sequential, or singly threaded. It is, in practice, dynamic, combinatorial, and capable (at least to some degree) of parallel processing. Which heuristics are used during complex cognition and when will depend on the task, the environmental framing, and, as we will now discuss, differences in how an individual assimilates and manipulates new information.

3   Individual Differences

Complex cognition, for all of its variety, is also influenced by human individuality. There is no standardized unit of human cognition. It is influenced, sometimes profoundly, by the users distinctive abilities and bottlenecks, beliefs about the world, preferred methods of categorizing and prioritizing information, and other individual differences. This is one reason that the modeling of reasoning has traditionally been difficult. Human behavioral research has demonstrated the impact of individual differences on learning and analysis in traditional environments.

There is also a plethora of examples in the behavioral literature of how individual differences impact cognition; for the sake of brevity, we will focus on the impact of personality factors, which also have a broad literature of their own. For example, personality factors predicted preferences and visual perception of landscapes [26]. Visual impairment in children is heavily influenced by individual personality differences [7]. Individual differences also affect how humans categorize, including the categorizing of stereotyping and prejudice [19]. Palmer found that interactive behaviors in information search can be categorized by personality factors [28]. Another study found that problem-solving behaviors could be predicted by responses to the Thematic Apperception Test [37]. In reasoning behaviors, individual differences impact rationality and reasoning as well ([45],[46]). These are just a handful of studies in a deep literature of individuality and the impact of these differences on every major cognitive process, as well as behavioural outcomes, such as academic or organizational performance. The question is not whether individual differences impact cognition, but how we can use individual differences to improve our understanding of visually enabled analysis. In addition, users in a particular domain can share personality characteristics and learning preferences, both inherent and institutional, which implies that some common traits can be aggregated into specific user profiles which can inform superior design requirements and aid in evaluation protocols. These differences will be discussed as part of the Personal Equation of Interaction in a following self-titled section.

4   The Human Cognition Model

In earlier work ([12], [13],[14]) we outlined an operational framework, the Human Cognition Model (HCM), whose objective was to inform customization of human-computer cognitive collaboration in mixed-initiative interactive systems. Todays information visualization applications tend to be passive; primary interface processes sit and wait for user initiation. This is not a problem if the user knows exactly where to go and what to do. But for the large semantically-rich datasets which visualizations are increasingly called upon to capture, and the complex analytical reasoning the visualization must scaffold and support, a truly intuitive interface must be capable of initiating a variety of processes on its own. The HCM identifies many of these tasks and the varieties of cognition the tasks.

The central process identified by the HCM is Knowledge Discovery. (See Figure 3.) This was envisioned as a human and computer paired process: the interface presents information and the human user indicates interest in a specific area or point, which the computer in turn presents in a related context. If Knowledge Discovery is goal oriented, the human will, among other processes, use temporally moderated perception, semantic categorization, and elimination reasoning heuristics to search and filter through the information space. If the discovery is not goal-oriented, the user may browse, stopping the explore data items that stand out or that are associated to items of interest.

Other processes in the HCM include information search by pattern and example. Search is an interesting cognitive task, as it is deceptively simple. Some types of search are simply target identification, utilizing perceptual logic, manipulating the interface and information space through a procedural script, and using the simplest of elimination heuristics (a binary filter that asks a question: Is this the specific item Im looking for?). Other types of search can be much more

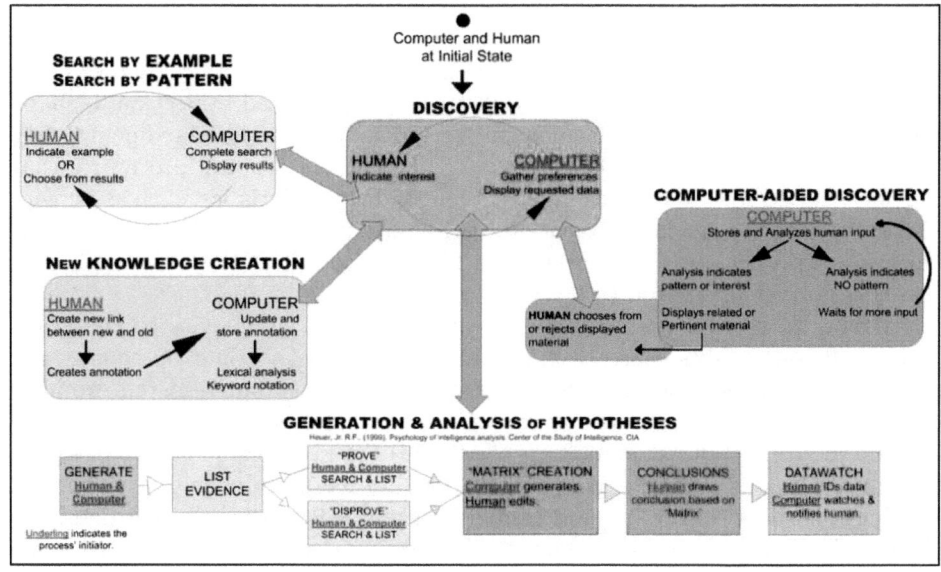

Fig. 3. The Human Cognition Model[13]

complex. When the task is to find items similar to an exemplar, for example, all the cognitive processes from the simpler search tasks serve to feed more complex processes, such as inferential and deductive reasoning, which utilize more complicated models or rules for comparison and contrast. Thus, even in the more routine of interface tasks, complex cognition cannot be ignored.

The HCM also outlines the creation and analysis of hypotheses. As discussed in previous sections, hypotheses can be created in a variety of ways, from the loose associations in abduction to the use of more demanding heuristics. Sometimes hypothesis are brought to the task by the user, and drive the interaction from the start. Wherever hypotheses are generated, they serve an important function. They drive discovery and search behaviors, they determine how information is viewed and filtered, and they promote some data-derived conclusions over others. For these reasons, interfaces which promote the generation of valid hypotheses, either through framing, adaptive search, or more intuitive interaction, might be considered more valuable than others.

Other pertinent processes discussed in the HCM literature (e.g. [13]) include an interface being aware of and predicting user intent in order to keep pertinent information visible, supporting human working memory, caching data subsets of interest to introduce them in a sequence and timing that will support the flow of reasoning and ongoing discovery, and conducting analyses and providing their findings in a contextual framework, which supports a variety of hypotheses generation. In short, the HCM sketches out an interface that collaborates on cognitive processes per se, informed by a growing understanding of human preferences, abilities and limitations.

5   The Personal Equation of Interaction (PEI)

Humans are cognitive individuals. As we have seen, humans individuality influences cognitive performance. These differences, as discussed in Section 3, shape the way we approach and perform cognitive tasks. We have discussed personality and self-beliefs in this chapter for sake of brevity, but we are also aware that humans also exhibit differences in psychophysical characteristics, such as perceptual categorization, focused attention, and haptic preferences. These individual variations interact with each other and the task to which they are applied in manners not yet understood.

Further, as we have seen, there is great variety and complexity to analytical tasks, and so it makes sense that not all cognitive tasks would be equally impacted by the same inherent differences. For example, in our research, we have found that persons who tend to believe in that good things that happen to them are due to "luck" (an external locus of control) are predictably slower in target identification. [15]. But the same cannot be said for more cognitively complex problems, such as comparing and contrasting multi-dimensional glyphs [16]; for these tasks, believing in luck seems to give users a decided advantage. (See the section on Research in Personal Equation of Interaction.) It makes sense, then, that not all cognitive tasks would be equally impacted by the same inherent differences; some reasoning tasks may be better predicted by one collection of inherent traits over others.

5.1   The Personal Equation of Interaction Defined

Our goal of parameterizing a general model in order to predict performance of a particular individual builds upon foundational work in human perception conducted in the early 19th century by Friedrich Bessel [2]. Bessel recognized that the variability of reports of astronomical observations could be separated into the differences between the average ratings of observations made by each individual observer (in statistical terms, the between-subject variance around the global mean) and variation within observations made by a given observer (the within-subject variance around that individual's mean for a given task and situation). While within-subject variability could not be easily factored, the deviation from the overall mean judgment for a given individual was relatively consistent over a range of similar situations. The error for a given individual could be measured to generate a "personal equation" for that individual. This could be used to factor out their characteristic error to bring their data into agreement, more or less, with the global mean. This meant that data from fewer observers were needed in order to achieve the same level of precision. In addition, one could predict any given observer's raw measurement to a reasonable degree of accuracy given the global mean and their personal equation.

Much of the research [32], [9], [16] in our laboratory has been devoted to defining a modern version of the personal equation, the "personal equation of interaction". The PEI uses quantifiable interaction of human perceptual, motor, and cognitive limitations during tasks and perceptual stimuli that are generated by modern visual information systems. In Po et. al., we demonstrated that system variables such as cursor visibility and display lag interact with individual differences to produce characteristic patterns of behavior for subpopulations of individuals [32]. These effects are unlikely to be observed by perceptual testing that does not focus on the particular characteristics of active visual information displays and how they differ from those we experience in the physical world that have informed both human evolution and visual experience of individuals.

There are three goals in current efforts in the PEI: first, to to predict how a given individual will perform on a given task and information display; second, to build a framework for interface design that to support customization of a visual information system along dimensions that are psychologically valid (i.e. that would track aspects of individual differences in such a way that their accurate fit to an individual's capabilities would measurably improve their performance with the system); and lastly, to build increasingly accurate and comprehensive estimates of personal equations and methods for assessing them. This includes both persistent differences between individuals (e.g. color blindness) and short-term shifts in capabilities (e.g. their performance under stress). The latter could potentially be generated "on the fly" by an attentive system and applied as conditions changed to maintain optimal performance over changes in the capabilities of the human operator.

Our approach builds on existing psychometrics methods and materials. However the goal of this particular line of inquiry is to build towards a natural science of human-information interaction. By focusing on the specific kinds of changes in perceptual and interactive experience that are generated by modern visual information systems, we can address how changes in the properties and statistical regularities of information displays interact with the human visual system in general, and that of an individual observer in particular. For example, many studies in perception (e.g. [25]) show how our ability to parse complex visual scenes given limited perceptual information (the so-called "poverty of the stimulus") is supported by our internal expectations, which in turn are built through a lifetime of sampling the statistical regularities of our physical environment. Phenomena such as change blindness [18], [33] demonstrate the adaptation of human vision to an environment where abrupt changes are rare. Our visual system is not optimized to detect those changes, but pays a small price for this in the physical world. Active updating of visual displays increase the frequency of abrupt display events, and the probability increases that one will coincide with the observer's saccadic eye movement and so escape detection. Thus we find that the study of human performance with information systems cannot simply rely on applying perceptual and cognitive science research taken from the literature. It is necessary to actively seek answers to questions that arise from the use of information systems in cognitive task performance, and to do so using methods from the natural sciences.

It is an open question to what extent aspects of the PEI are inherent and what aspects are acquired through experience with complex visualizations. Some factors such as low vision, color and stereo blindness etc. clearly fall into the former category. Estimation of these factors might require psychophysical testing of a given individual, but may also be estimated by covariates of the given conditions, whether or not we can establish a causal link between them. To the extent that these covariates are predictive, they can be used to support the design and customization of information systems now, as well as contributing to ongoing research about human differences.

The first clustering factor for individual differences is through cognitive experience, e.g. in a given institution or profession. Members of a professional or skilled cohort tend to share jargon and conceptual understanding. Additionally, they are often practiced in methodologies and task heuristics that are specific to the group. These methodologies become a part of the way in which the user searches for and uses information, and can impact the conclusions drawn. They can also introduce group-specific biases that might not be found in the general user population. For these reasons among others, understanding an institutional user profile is important to the design of an expert system interface. A second factor might be perceptual and perceptuomotor experience through interaction with some specific environment.

We define the Personal Equation of Interaction as a compilation of predictive measures based upon inherent individual differences, including but not limited to personality; each measure will be validated to predict performance for one type of cognitive task integral to analysis. The PEI has three current and future end goals: the prediction of analytical performance based on inherent differences [15], [16], the ability to inform real-time interface individuation, and the creation of fuller-bodied user profiles, broken down by the reasoning tasks performed [17].

The first goal – that of performance prediction – is being undertaken through a series of human research studies. Participants are asked to complete a series tasks similar to common interface tasks, such as interface learnability, target identification, categorization, etc. The measured outcomes vary by task, and include completion times, errors, self-reported insights and free response feedback. In addition to the performance and qualitative feedback, participants are asked to complete hundreds of items from a battery of psychometric measures we have chosen for their inter-relatedness and their relationships to learning outcomes in the behavioral literature. Post-study analysis includes evaluating the trending of the psychometric items with measured outcomes. In addition, followup testing such as factor analysis is done to isolate highly predictive psychometric items or groups of items, such as in [15] for a particular type of reasoning task. This allows us to delineate our findings by cognitive process and compare multiple interfaces or problem-solving environments in hopefully a more even fashion. Currently, we can predict performance on simple outcomes like completion times in a variety or common interface tasks; these findings are being replicated and expanded. Not surprisingly, this research is currently quite fluid, and continues to inform the second goal of what matrices will be needed to support real-time interface adaptation. In addition, having hundred of participants complete these studies has allowed us to sketch out initial user profiles, or describe inherent characteristics of a user based how the user performs on an analytical task [17].

The goal of the PEI is not, at least in the short term, to tell designers and developers specifically which visualization techniques to use and which to avoid generically, but rather to give interface creators a robust understanding of what the individual analyst needs in order to optimally support the analytical tasks that must be performed. The Personal Equation of Interaction does not replace interface design; it augments design by making designers aware of user strengths and weaknesses. It cannot replace user studies for a particular interface, but it provides new metrics with which to evaluate study outcomes. And as a research program, it amplifies visual analytics as the study of analytical reasoning supported by interactive visual interfaces by adding to the body of understanding on analytical reasoning and analytical reasoners.

These are aggregated to build an ever more comprehensive and accurate personal equation of interaction that could be used by an application to parametrically modify its display of information in such a way as to optimize the cognitive performance of an individual decision-maker. As research progresses we hope to find a way to integrate system models with models of human interaction to better predict the course of fluent human-information interaction.

5.2   Research in the Personal Equation of Interaction

Our research has demonstrated that inherent differences can and do influence learning and analytical performance during interface interaction. In combination with the environmental and institutional variations, there is evidence that the impact of inherent differences could theoretically be used to derive a personal equation of interaction.

Our recent research has demonstrated that personality factors can predict efficiency during varying task types [15]. We designed a series of tasks we asked participants to complete in two visual interfaces using the same dataset: menu-driven web application, and an information visualization using direct interaction on hierarchical graphs. These tasks were designed to test two very different types of learning: procedural and inferential. Procedural learning, as defined for this study, was the ability to use the interface to find target information. This type of learning tends to be inductive: a rule is inferred which generalizes to other similar target identification tasks in the interface. Other the other hand, the inferential learning tasks were highly deductive. Participants were asked to evaluate a multi-dimensional exemplar and find another conceptual object in the hierarchy that was similar to (or different from) the exemplar for the specified dimensions. This type of reasoning involves the creation of a mental model, which is then used to evaluate complex concepts to reach a valid conclusion. For each task, we tracked errors, completions, as well as qualitative feedback.

In addition, we administered several longstanding and well-documented psychometric measures to participants [15]. These measures were created to measure personality traits such as neuroticism (a tendency toward emotional instability), extraversion (a tendency toward sociability or seeking the company of others), and trait anxiety, which is a tendency to be more anxious generally, regardless of

the environment. Trait anxiety differs from state anxiety, which is the tendency
to be anxious when in a situation that triggers anxiety.

Item (Originating Meaure)	How scored	PCA Component
Unable to Relax (Beck's Anxiety Inventory)	0(never) to 3(severely)	
Fear the Worst (Beck's Anxiety Inventory)	0(never) to 3(severely)	1
Heart Pounding (Beck's Anxiety Inventory)	0(never) to 3(severely)	
What we are used to is always preferable to what is unfamiliar. (Tolerance of Ambiguity)	1(strongly disagree to 7(strongly agree)	2
Talk to a lot of people. (Extraversion)	1(low) to 5(high)	
Hands Trembling (Beck's Anxiety Scale)	0(never) to 3(severely)	3
Numbness (Beck's Anxiety Inventory)	0(never) to 3(severely)	
Don't talk a lot. (Extraversion)	1(low) to 5(high)	
Am easily disturbed. (Neuroticism)	1(low) to 5(high)	

Fig. 4. Items in the 9 item short measure. Adapted from [15].

Another personality trait that proved to have a demonstrable impact was locus of control, which is a measure of how in control a person feels he or she is
over the events in life. Persons with an external locus tend to believe strongly
that they are not in control, and attribute events to factors outside themselves,
such as luck, other people, or circumstances outside of their control. On the other
hand, persons with an internal locus tend to believe that they are responsible for
both positive and negative events in their lives. They are more likely to attribute
events to some behavior or attitude of their own than to outside influences, and
tend to give very little credence to luck.

Other measures designed to test other personality factors, such as a discom-
fort with problem-solving situations where important factors are unknown (an
intolerance of ambiguity) or self-regulation, which is the ability to hold it together emotionally when the problem or situation becomes difficult, were also
evaluated but were not found to be particularly predictive in performance of the
tasks under study.

Results of Study 1. Results demonstrated [15] that whole score locus of control predicted inferential task efficiency in the data visualization; participants with a more external locus were able to complete the deductive inferential tasks more quickly.

For the inductive procedural tasks, no singular full measure could predict behavior, which was not unexpected, given that none of these psychometrics were designed to evaluate these traits in this interface environments. But factor analysis uncovered 9 items, largely from the trait anxiety measure, that predicted target identification efficiency across both interfaces. Participants who were more trait anxious found target items more quickly, even when the target was buried several layers down in the hierarchy.

Results indicated that no single personality factor measure could predict errors in either interface.

Results of Study 2. Results of a similar study using procedural tasks [16], currently under submission) expanded these findings somewhat. This study used the same interfaces and similar procedural tasks. The scores and outcomes of participants in both studies were combined for greater statistical power (N = 105). Results demonstrated that both neuroticism and extraversion predicted efficiency; the more neurotic/extraverted participants found items more quickly. Additionally, analysis of the combined set found that locus of control predicted procedural performance, in directly the opposite way to that of the inferential tasks. Participants with an internal locus (a belief that they were in control of life events) found targets more quickly than those with an external locus. This evidence alone demonstrates that not only that personality factors affect interface interaction performance, but that different tasks are impacted differently by inherent individual differences. See Figure 5.

	Completion times	Errors	Insights
Interface	faster times in MapViewer	fewer errors in MapViewer	more insights in Gvis
Locus of Control	internal locus faster times	none	external locus more insights
Extraversion	more extraverted faster times	none	less extraverted more insights
Neuroticism	more neurotic faster times	none	less neurotic more insights

Fig. 5. Summary of findings from Study 2. From [16].

<u>Discussion of Results.</u> The existence of significant trending between personality factors and interface interaction outcomes is interesting for a variety of reasons. First, it demonstrates that even complex cognition can, at least to some degree, be predicted. Secondly, it demonstrates that inherent individual differences, over which we as designers have no control, could inform design if we knew the psychometric makeup of our target user group. This holds potential for experts systems, which are designed for users whose differences are likely to trend in similar ways. Thirdly, these studies open a promising doorway; if these few personality factors can predict performance, what else about complex cognition might we be able to predict if we knew more about our users, as well as about the expert cohorts for whom we design visually enabled interfaces?

6 Conclusion

The reasoning used during task analysis is complex. In this chapter, we have discussed this complexity by highlighting a handful of reasoning heuristics. We have underscored this complexity with a discussion of Pirolli and Cards sensemaking loop. And we have explored how this complexity complicates the current state of design and evaluation thanks to the absence of applicable reasoning research and pertinent precedent in the behavioural literature.

We have also broadly discussed the impact of human individuality on every primary cognitive process, and surveyed our current research in pursuit the generation of new system development models that optimize the cognitive performance of human decision-makers. Optimization in this context must include complex criteria such as insight, innovation, creativity and awareness in uncommon, unique and novel problems and situations. Research has shown that inherent individual differences between users impacts the task and learning performance in visually embedded interfaces. Our previous work in the development of the Human Cognition Model continues to inform our research direction. Our ongoing research in the Personal Equation has highlighted the need to study not only inherent differences in personality factors, but also other user differences, including those in which affect other inherent individualities as well as differences in institutional cohort and environment. These individual differences in human capabilities are great enough that any unitary system will be at best a compromise between the needs of the various sub-populations of users. Our ongoing research seeks to take advantage of human individuality, rather than to ignore it. While still in the early stages of this research, we have already highlighted several inherent differences which predict performance, depending on reasoning task. We intend to explore further, with the expectation of isolating and understanding influential individual differences and how they impact interface interaction, which could benefit visual analytics interface designers by informing design requirements and opening up new areas for innovation.

References

1. Aoidh, E.M., Bertolotto, M., Wilson, D.C.: Understanding geospatial interests by visualizing map interaction behavior. Information Visualization 7, 275–286 (2008)
2. Brooks, G., Brooks, R.: The Improbable Progenitor. Journal of the Royal Astronomical Society of Canada 73(1), 9–23 (1979)
3. Card, S., Mackinlay, J.D., Shneiderman, B.: Readings in Information Visualization Using Visualization to Think. Morgan Kaufmann, San Francisco (1999)
4. Chang, R., Ziemkiewicz, C., Green, T.M., Ribarsky, W.: Defining insight for visual analytics. Computer Graphics and Applications 29(2), 14–17 (2009)
5. Cherubini, P., Johnson-Laird, P.N.: Does everyone love everyone? The psychology of iterative reasoning. Thinking and reasoning 10(1), 31–53 (2004)
6. Cherubini, P., Mazzocco, A.: From models to rules: Mechanization of reasoning as a way to cope with cognitive overloading in combinatorial problems. Acta Psychologica 243, 223–243 (2004)
7. Corn, A.L.: Visual function: A theoretical model for individuals with Low Vision. Journal of Visual Impairment and Blindness 77(8), 373 (1983)
8. Dou, W., Jeong, D.H., Stukes, F., Ribarsky, W., Lipford, H.R., Chang, R.: Recovering reasoning processes from user interactions. IEEE Computer Graphics and Applications 29(3), 52–61 (2009)
9. Fisher, B.: Science and Smart Graphics. Information Technology 3, 142–148 (2009)
10. Gentzen, G.: Investigations into Logical Deduction, pp. 68–131. North-Holland, Amsterdam (1969); Translation printed in M. Szabo The Collected Papers of Gerhard Gentzen (1934/5)
11. Gigerenzer, G., Goldstein, D.G.: Reasoning the fast and frugal way: Models of bounded rationality. Psychological Review 103(4) (1996)
12. Green, T.M., Ribarsky, W., Fisher, B.: Visual analytics for complex concepts using a human cognition model. In: Proceedings of IEEE Visual Analytics Science and Technology, Columbus, OH, USA (October 2008)
13. Green, T.M., Ribarsky, W.: Using a human cognition model in the creation of collaborative knowledge visualizations. In: Proceedings of Hot Topics in Visual Analytics, SPIE Defense + Security, Orlando, Florida, USA (2008)
14. Green, T.M., Ribarsky, W., Fisher, B.: Building and applying a human cognition model for visual analytics. Information Visualization 8(1), 1–13 (2009)
15. Green, T.M., Jeong, D.H., Fisher, B.: Using personality factors to predict interface learning performance. In: Proceedings of Hawaii International Conference on System Sciences, Koloa, Hawaii, USA, January 2010, vol. 43 (2010)
16. Green, T.M., Fisher, B., Jeong, D.H.: Towards the personal equation of interaction: The impact of personality factors on visual analytics interface interaction. In: Proceedings of IEEE Visual Analytics Science and Technology, Salt Lake City, UT, USA (2010)
17. Green, T.M., Fisher, B., Jeong, D.H.: The impact of personality factors on interface interaction and more robust user profiles: Next steps in the Personal Equation of Interaction. Journal of Management Information Systems, Special issue on Hawaii International Conference on System Sciences 43 (2010) (invited, under review)
18. Grimes, J.: On the failure to detect changes in scenes across saccades. In: Akins, K. (ed.) Perception (Vancouver Studies in Cognitive Science), vol. 2, pp. 89–110. Oxford University Press, New York (1996)
19. Heaven, P.C.L., Quintin, D.S.: Personality factors predict racial prejudice. Personality and Individual Differences 34, 625–634 (2002)

20. Heer, J., Agrawala, M.: Design considerations for collaborative visual analytics. In: IEEE Symposium on Visual Analytics Science and Technology. IEEE Computer Society Press, Sacramento (2007)
21. Jaskowski, S.: On the Rules of Suppositions in Formal Logic. In: Studia Logica v.1, Polish Logic 1920-1939, pp. 232–258. Oxford Univ. Press, Oxford (1934); Reprinted in S. McCall (1967)
22. Jeong, D.H., Green, T.M., Ribarsky, W., Chang, R.: Comparative Evaluation on Two Interface Tools in Performing Visual Analytics Tasks. In: Proceedings of BELIV Workshop, CHI 2010, Atlanta, GA, USA (2010)
23. Johnson-Laird, P.: How We Reason. Oxford University Press, Oxford (2008)
24. Kozielecki, J.: Elements of a psychological decision theory. Studia Psychologica 13(1), 53–60 (1971)
25. Marr, D.: Vision. MIT Press, Cambridge (1982)
26. Macia, A.: Visual perception of landscapes: Sex and personality differences. Our national landscape: A conference on applied techniques for analysis and management of the visual resource, General Technical Report PSW-35: 279-285 (1979)
27. North, C.: Toward measuring visualization insight. IEEE Computer Graphics and Applications 26(3), 6–9 (2006)
28. Palmer, J.: Scientists and information: II. Personal factors in information behaviour. Journal of Documentation 3, 254–275 (1991)
29. Plaisant, C., Grosjean, J., Bederson, B.B.: SpaceTree: Supporting exploration in large node-link tree: design evolution and empirical evaluation. In: Proceedings of IEEE Symposium on Information Visualization, pp. 57–64 (2002)
30. Plaisant, C.: The challenge of information visualization evaluation. In: Proceedings of the Working Conference on Advanced Visual Interfaces, Gallipoli, Italy (2004)
31. Pirolli, P., Card, C.: The sensemaking process and leverage points for analyst technology as identified through cognitive task analysis. In: Proceedings of International Conference on Intelligence Analysis, McLean, VA, USA (2005)
32. Po, B., Fisher, B., Booth, K.S.: Pointing and Visual Feedback for Spatial Interaction in Large-Screen Display Environments. In: Butz, A., Krüger, A., Olivier, P. (eds.) SG 2003. LNCS, vol. 2733. Springer, Heidelberg (2003)
33. Rensink, R.A., O'Regan, J.K., Clark, J.J.: To see or not to see: The need for attention to perceive changes in scenes. Psychological Science 8, 368–373 (1997)
34. Rips, L.J.: Inductive judgments about natural categories. Journal of Verbal Learning and Verbal Behavior 14, 665–681 (1975)
35. Robinson, A.: Collaborative synthesis of visual analytic results. In: IEEE Visual Analytics Science and Technology, Columbus, OH USA, October 2008, pp. 67–74 (2008)
36. Rock, I.: The logic of perception. MIT Press/Bradford Books, Cambridge, MA (1985)
37. Ronan, G.F., Senn, J., Date, A., Maurer, L., House, K., Carroll, J., Vanhorn, R.: Personal problem solving scoring of TAT responses: Known groups validation. Journal of Personality Assessment 67 (1996)
38. Russel, D., Card, S.: The Cost of Sensemaking. In: Proceedings of Interact 1993 (1993)
39. Saraiya, P., North, C., Duca, K.: Evaluation of microarray visualization tools for biological insight. In: IEEE Symposium on Information Visualization, Austin, TX, USA, pp. 1–8 (2004)
40. Saraiya, P., North, C., Duca, K.: An Insight-Based Methodology for Evaluating Bioinformatics Visualizations. IEEE Transactions on Visualization and Computer Graphics 11, 443–456 (2005)

41. Sebeok, T.: You Know My Method. In: Sebeok, T. (ed.) The Play of Musement. Indiana, Bloomington (1981)
42. Shneiderman, B.: The Eyes Have It: A Task by Data Type Taxonomy for Information Visualizations. In: Proceedings of the IEEE Symposium on Visual Languages, Washington, DC, pp. 336–343. IEEE Computer Society Press, Los Alamitos (1996)
43. Spence, R.: InformationVisualization. Addison-Wesley, Reading (2001)
44. Springmeyer, R.R., Blattner, M.M., Marx, N.L.: A Characterization of the Scientific Data Analysis Process. Proceedings of IEEE Visualization, 1235–1242 (1992)
45. Stanovich, K.E., West, R.F.: Individual differences in reasoning: Implications for the rationality debate? Behavioral and Brain Sciences 23, 645–726 (2000)
46. Stanovich, K.E.: Who is rational? Studies of individual differences in reasoning. Erlbaum, Mahwah (1999)
47. Stasko, J., Gorg, C., Liu, Z., Singhal, K.: Jigsaw: Supporting Investigative Analysis through Interactive Visualization. In: Dill, J., Ribarsky, W. (eds.) Proceedings of 2007 IEEE Symposium on Visual Analytics Science and Technology, pp. 131–138. IEEE CS Press, Sacramento (2007)
48. Sternberg, R.J.: Intelligence, Information Processing and Analogical Reasoning. Erlbaum, Hillsdale (1977)
49. Sternberg, R.J., Gardner, M.K.: Unities in inductive reasoning. Journal of Experimental Psychology: General 112(1), 80–116 (1983)
50. Tversky, A.: Elimination by aspects: A theory of choice. Psychological Review 79, 281–299 (1972)
51. Wang, T.D., Plaisant, C., Quinn, A.J., Stanchak, R., Murphy, S., Shneiderman, B.: Aligning temporal data by sentinel events: discovering patterns in electronic health records. In: Proceeding of the twenty-sixth annual SIGCHI conference on Human factors in computing systems, Florence, Italy, April 05-10 (2008)
52. Beth, E.W., Piaget, J.: Mathematical Epistemology and Psychology. D. Reidel, Dordrecht (1966)
53. Johnson-Laird, P.N.: Deductive Reasoning. Annual Review of Psychology 50, 109–135 (1999)
54. Johnson-Laird, P., Byrne, R.M.J.: Deduction. Psychology Press, San Diego (1991)

Faceted Visual Exploration of Semantic Data

Philipp Heim[1] and Jürgen Ziegler[2]

[1] Visualization and Interactive Systems Group, University of Stuttgart, Germany
`philipp.heim@vis.uni-stuttgart.de`
[2] Interactive Systems and Interaction Design, University of Duisburg-Essen, Germany
`juergen.ziegler@uni-due.de`

Abstract. Tools for searching and interactively exploring the rapidly growing amount of semantically annotated data on the Web are still scarce and limited in their support of the users' manifold goals and activities. In this paper we describe a method and a tool that allows humans to access and explore Semantic Web data more effectively, leveraging the specific characteristics of semantic data. The approach utilizes the concept of faceted search and combines it with a visualization that exploits the graph-based structure of linked semantic data. The facets are represented as nodes in a graph visualization and can be interactively added and removed by the users in order to produce individual search interfaces. This provides the possibility to generate interfaces with different levels of complexity that can search arbitrary domains accessible through the SPARQL query language. Even multiple and distantly connected facets can be integrated in the graph facilitating the access of information from different user-defined perspectives. This approach facilitates searching massive amounts of data with complex semantic relations, building highly complex search queries and supporting users who are not familiar with the Semantic Web.

Keywords: Graph visualization, faceted search, query building, SPARQL, hierarchical facets, pivot operation.

1 Introduction

The amount of semantically described data available on the Web has been growing considerably in recent years, turning the vision of a Semantic Web as proposed more than a decade ago by Tim Berners-Lee [1] more and more into reality. The growing volume of information in the Semantic Web can be seen in large information pools such as *DBpedia* [2] or in the *LOD initiative* (Linked Open Data [3]) which aims at semantically linking a large number of different open, publicly available data sets. In these datasets information is represented by semantic structures expressed in formal languages such as *RDF* (Resource Description Framework) or *OWL* (Web Ontology Language). The structures consist of statements about real world (e.g. 'Berlin') or virtual objects referenced by a *URI* (Uniform Resource Identifier), an assigned ontological class, such as 'city' or 'country', and an arbitrary number of properties that define links to other

A. Ebert et al. (Eds.): HCIV (INTERACT) 2009, LNCS 6431, pp. 58–75, 2011.

objects, such as 'is capital of'. These techniques allow to search for information based on their semantic descriptions and to make data interoperable between different datasets by linking objects that have the same meaning.

The predominant view on the purposes of a Semantic Web was, and still is to enable machines to process distributed data on the Web more effectively. In recent years, however, there has been an increasing focus on the interactive use of semantic data. The Semantic Web can also help users directly to answer focused questions and to retrieve unknown factual information. In contrast to the conventional Web, however, there are a number of properties of semantic data that may impede human use unless appropriate support for searching and exploring the data is provided.

Conventional Web pages are predominantly structured and designed as coherent documents, intended and suitable for human consumption and perusal. Information units are embedded in other textual or multimedia content, providing context for clarification and a better understanding. Semantic data, on the other hand, are represented in the form of single subject-predicate-object statements and thus constitute more elementary pieces of information than standard Web pages. While the information contained in a single statement may indeed be the target of a focused search, for exploring and understanding the data, more context is usually required. The semantic relations between individual resources can be exploited to create such context. Since a pool of semantic data forms a large RDF graph, a context of interest can essentially by of arbitrary size. Users should therefore be able to define and visualize the context of some focal concept in a flexible and user-controlled fashion.

For this purpose, suitable tools are needed that support users throughout the information seeking process starting from an initial query formulation over the flexible selection of relevant context through to the identification and use of the information needed. One of the objectives of this paper is to propose a conceptual search model that is appropriate for describing the different user activities involved in searching and exploring semantic data. Since the information space to be searched can be very large, such a process typically requires the use of search and exploration activities in combination. Even if the target of the search is not well-defined at the outset, users will have to define a starting point for follow-up explorations based on some textual query. For experts, artificial query languages such as $SPARQL$[1] are available that allow to formulate precise queries on the basis of a well defined information need. For non-experts, free text search is more appropriate for initiating the search process. In contrast to Web search, however, the result is not comprised of Web pages but can be concepts that match the query terms. In the following stages, user activities are typically more of an exploratory nature, iteratively refining or modifying the search until the desired information is found.

A promising approach for supporting exploratory search processes is faceted search [4]. In faceted search, the search space is partitioned using orthogonal conceptual dimensions based on the properties of some set of objects and their

---

[1] http://www.w3.org/TR/rdf-sparql-query/

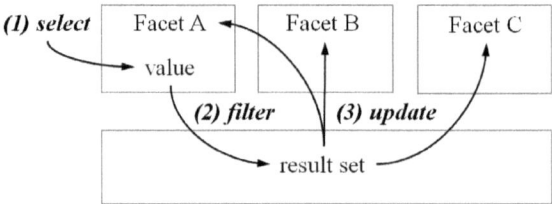

Fig. 1. In faceted search, selecting a value in a facet (1) filters the result set (2), with subsequent updating of the other facets (3)

corresponding values which serve as independent filters for narrowing down a result set. Selecting a value of a facet adds this value to the query and filters the result set accordingly. Whenever the result set changes, all facets are updated to show only those attributes that can be used for further filtering (Fig. 1). Therefore, users always see only those values that can further constrain the result, but which do not result in an empty set. While faceted search was originally developed for searching relational databases, the concept can be extended to semantic data, exploiting the well-defined classes and properties of semantic data for creating facets.

In a domain such as 'football', for example, a faceted search would allow football players to be filtered by their clubs, their birthplaces, or their ages. Even so the concept of faceted search has been successfully applied in popular applications such as *Apple's iTunes*[2], using it to seek information in the Semantic Web entails several new problems that are not yet sufficiently solved. Most of the problems result from the vast number of objects, classes and properties. According to [5], the LOD cloud alone contained approximately two billion statements in 2008 already.

In this paper we introduce *Facet Graphs*, a new approach based on the concept of faceted search which allows the intuitive formulation of search queries for semantic data. Facet graphs are composed of set-valued nodes and labeled semantic relations between these nodes. Users can choose a node as the desired result type as well as related nodes that serve as facets for filtering the results, thereby producing a personalized search interface. The graph provides a coherent representation of multiple, even distantly connected facets on a single page, avoiding browsing and preventing users from losing track of the relationships. Each node in a facet graph contains a list of items that provides sorting, paging and scrolling functionalities and thereby enables an easy handling of even large amounts of objects. Users can build queries to filter the result list by just clicking on items in the facet nodes. Filtering is indicated by colored highlighting around the nodes affected, helping users to understand and keep track of the filtering constraints applied. Users can also at any time change their search perspective by turning results nodes into facets of related nodes.

---

[2] http://www.apple.com/de/itunes/

The combination of a graph visualization with faceted search allows for an easy formulation of even complex, semantically unique search queries and thus for seeking semantically annotated information without expert knowledge.

The rest of this paper is organized as follows. First we review related work and motivate our work based on shortcomings of the existing approaches. In section 3, we propose a general information seeking model for searching and exploring semantic data. We then describe the approach of Facet Graphs and the tool gFacet in detail, and evaluate its usability in a comparative user study. In the discussion, we relate our findings to the proposed search model and analyze Facet Graphs in terms of general requirements for information search. Finally, we present a conclusion and an outlook on future work.

2   Related Work

Several approaches using faceted search have been reported in the literature, both for relational and semantic data. Most approaches display the facets as well as the result set as lists at different positions on the screen. Examples are tools like *mSpace* [6], *Flamenco* [4], *Longwell* [7] and *Haystack* [8]. In most cases, only facets directly connected to the result set are used. For example, football players could be filtered by facets containing the clubs they are playing for, the city they are living in or the number on their shirts. By selecting, for example, the football club 'FC Chelsea' in a 'club' facet, football players would be filtered to only those players employed by this club. Hierarchical filtering, however, that allows also indirectly connected facets to be used for query building (e.g. get only players playing for clubs in the Premier League) is not supported by these tools.

Tools like *Parallax* [9] (Fig. 2a), *Humboldt* [10], *Tabulator* [11] (Fig. 2b) and the *Nested Faceted Browser* [12], by comparison, allow for hierarchical filtering. Therefore, football players could be filtered by the cities where clubs they are playing for are located. Thus the possible options for building a query are not restricted to the direct periphery around a result set but can include dimensions that are distantly connected by other facets. Depending on the directness of their

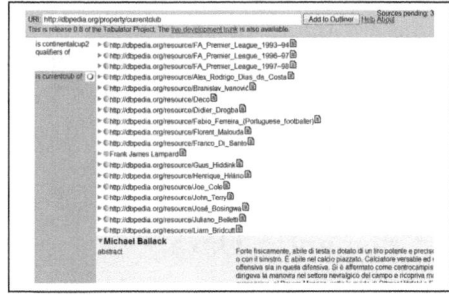

(a)   (b)

Fig. 2. a) Screenshots of Parallax and b) Tabulator

connections to the current result set, they can be integrated in a hierarchy and are therefore called *hierarchical facets*.

In Parallax, Flamenco and Humboldt, the hierarchy of facets is never completely visible to the user. By providing ways to browse through the facet hierarchy, users are able to include attributes of also distantly connected facets in their search query. For complex queries, it is getting more difficult for users to keep an overview of all included attributes since the corresponding facets are often scattered over several different pages.

Tools like Tabulator and the Nested Faceted Browser, on the other hand, allow the whole hierarchy to be displayed on one page. By using a tree structure to display all available hierarchical facets, users can open and close distantly connected facets in one coherent view and thus keep an overview of all attributes that are included in their queries. Since tree structures are used to depict all kinds of taxonomies in a wide range of well known applications, users need no extensive period of training to gain an understanding of how to use them.

In Tabulator and the Nested Faceted Browser, every attribute defines its own subtree that can be expanded by the user in order to see distantly connected facets and their attributes, which again can be expanded and so on (cp. Fig. 2b). So for the football players, one of the clubs they are playing for (e.g. 'FC Chelsea'), could be expanded by the user to see, for example, the city of its location (here: 'London'). Selecting 'London' would cause the list of players to be filtered to only those that are playing for 'FC Chelsea' or any other club located in this city. A combined list of all the cities that could be selected in order to filter the clubs and also the players, however, is not provided by the tree structure. The cities are partitioned in different subtrees, each for every club, that all need to be expanded in order to see all available cities. Having many subtrees opened, however, places attributes that actually belong to one facet at many different positions in the tree, leading to an increased tree structure that can possibly not be displayed on one screen. If an attribute is shared by more than one object (e.g. many clubs are located in London), it also occurs repeatedly in different subtrees.

Tree structures are well suited for visualizing and interacting with hierarchical data; however, when used for hierarchical facets, they tend to produce large and highly subdivided structures that cannot easily be overviewed by users. In this paper we therefore propose an alternative, graph-based approach to visualize and interact with hierarchical facets that aims at preventing large and confusing tree structures and hence facilitates an easy generation of semantically unique queries by the user.

3   A Three-Stage Model for Searching and Exploring Semantic Data

Searching and exploring linked semantic data differs in a number of aspects from conventional search paradigms as proposed, for example, in the area of information retrieval. Conventional information search is usually either completely based on free-form textual search or uses a limited well-defined set of metadata. Free text search is the main paradigm in Web search while metadata-based search is a predominant model in more structured domains such as digital library search. Semantic data, on the other hand, are more structured than free text documents but may contain an arbitrary number of semantic relations which makes it hard or, in the case of large or open corpora, even impossible to build up a complete and coherent cognitive model of the underlying structure. This latter aspects also distinguishes semantic data search from querying conventional relational databases. A further important distinction refers to the granularity of the search results. While conventional search aims at retrieving a set of relevant information ressources at the document level, the size of a single chunk of semantic data is typically much smaller, containing individual factual statements describing relations between elementary units of information.

A variety of models have been proposed for describing user behavior when searching and exploring collections of information. Classical models from information retrieval focus either on the sequential process from the formation of the search goal to the use of the results or analyse the different levels of abstraction in the search process [17,18]. Kuhlthau, for example, describes the information seeking process from a user perspective in six stages: task initiation, selection, exploration, focus formulation, collection and presentation [16].

While these models have demonstrated their usefulness in general information retrieval, they do not take into account the specific properties of semantic data which can be assumed to have a significant influence on the cognitive tasks and search strategies of the user. When searching semantic data, users can make use of the explicit semantic relations which link information instances among each other as well as with the conceptual structure of the dataset expressed in terms of ontologies describing the domain(s) at hand. The search process can therefore be separated in actions selecting the concept of interest and actions that explore information at the instance level. Once a conceptual starting point for the search has been determined, the semantic relations can be used as 'guiding rails' for a systematic exploration of the environment of the initial concept. Based on these observations, we can identify a model consisting of three stages of searching and exploring semantic data which forms the conceptual basis for the gFacet tool described in the next section.

1. **Goal formation and concept search:** In the initial phase, users form the search goal which can be specified at very different levels of concreteness. For explorative tasks, this goal will typically be at the concept level, specifying one or more concepts that determine the initial search space the user is interested in. Since the number of concepts in a datapool or linked data is far too high to start the search with a visual exploration, this goal (for instance 'find out more about German footballers' in our running example) is translated into textual search terms (e.g. 'football' that are used for identifying a relevant start concept 'e.g. German football clubs'. This concept (or class)

along with its instances, i.e. information elements of this type, constitute a point of departure for the explorative activities in the second stage.

2. **Construction of the exploration space:** At this stage, the user incrementally builds up a space for exploring the relevant semantic neighborhood of the starting concept. For this purpose, she can exploit the different semantic relations (object properties) linked to the starting concept. By incrementally adding relations and the instance sets (ranges) linked through these relations, users can flexibly construct subspaces of the entire dataset that are relevant to their information goal . Since these relations are independent of each other, they can be used for constructing independent facets and chains of facets. These facets can be used for providing visual tools that facilitate constructing and exploring the space.

3. **Multi-perspective exploration and sensemaking:** Once a relevant exploration space has been constructed by the user it can be used in various ways to explore it and to make sense of the information and relations contained in it. The semantic relations are a valuable asset to support the sensemaking process. First of all, they can help to filter the information by using related concepts as facets to narrow down the number of items of a target concept. Since semantic relations can be viewed in both directions by exchanging the roles of facet and target concepts, they support changes of perspective that are important for getting a better and more comprehensive understanding of the data and their relationships. At any time in this process, the user may choose to further expand or prune the exploration space when new information of interest is found. Stages 2 and 3 of this model are therefore closely intertwined and may be executed in an iterative fashion.

This model of searching and exploring semantic data forms the conceptual basis of the method and tool described in the next section. While other search and exploration strategies are possible and may be supported by other types of tools, the model focuses on the linking aspect of semantic data and provides a systematic method for exploring datasets the structure and content of which are largely unknown to the user. We therefore postulate that the model is particularly suited to searching open linked data due to their enormous volume and complex link structure for which users will only be able to build up partial mental models.

4   Visualizing Semantic Data with gFacet

In Facet Graphs, facets and result set are represented as nodes in a graph visualization (see also [19]). The semantic relations that exist between facets and result set as well as facets and other facets are represented by labeled directed edges between the nodes. Fig. 3 shows *gFacet*[3], a prototypical implementation of our approach of Facet Graphs.

---

[3] A description of an early version of this prototype with limited functionalities and access to dummy data only can be found in [13].

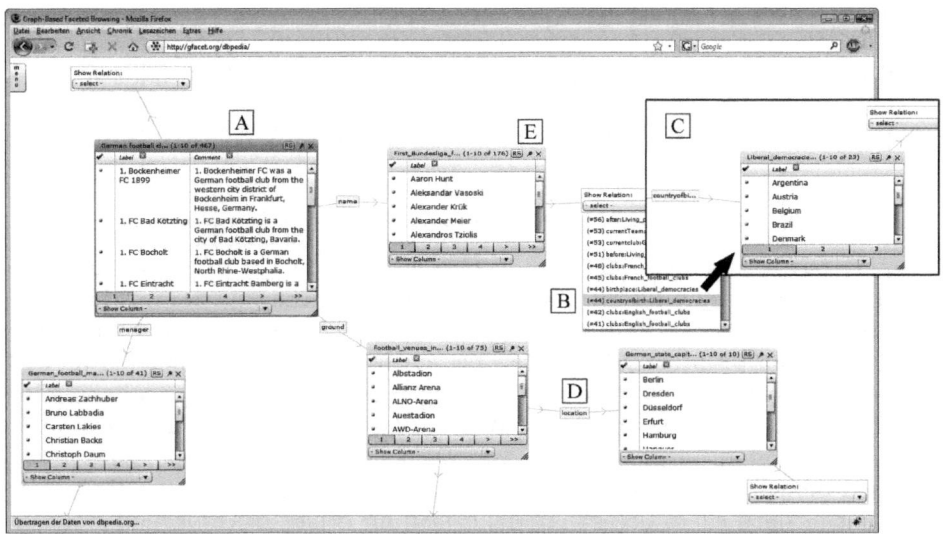

Fig. 3. In gFacet, the result set (A) and the facets are represented by nodes and connected by labeled edges (D). By selecting properties out of drop-down-lists (B), further facets can be added as new nodes to the graph (C).

In gFacet, the node representing the result set is marked by a darker background color (cp. Fig. 3, A) to better distinguish it from the nodes representing facets. The attributes of each facet are listed within one single node, which can be scrolled, paged and sorted to handle large sets of facet values. The graph can be interactively expanded by adding nodes that serve as additional facets. Facets can be added via a drop-down list from which related concepts can be selected (e.g. 'First Bundesliga Footballers' in Fig. 3, B). Facets in the drop-down lists are ordered by the number of values. Selecting a facet (e.g. the one containing the countries where footballers are born), adds it to the graph and connects it to the existing node by a labeled edge (cp. Fig. 3, C). In this way, the user can iteratively construct a graph of facets that serves as an exploration space and fosters the user's understanding of the relationships among items.

The nodes in the graph are positioned in an aesthetically pleasing way with a force-directed layout algorithm [14]. To prevent nodes from changing their position in the visualization too frequently, we apply a pinning mechanism that forces nodes to hold their position. When a new node is added, pinning is executed after a short time delay. This delay allows the force-directed algorithm to position new nodes in an appropriate way and at the same time prevents already existing information to change their location. Pinned nodes are indicated by a pin symbol in the upper right corner (cp. Fig. 3, E) which can also be used to control pinning manually.

The general benefits of representing hierarchical facets as nodes in a graph are:

1. The attributes for each facet are grouped into one node.
2. All nodes are shown in a coherent presentation on one page.
3. Semantic relations between the nodes are represented by labeled edges (Fig. 3, D).
4. Facets can be flexibly added and removed by the user (Fig. 3, C).

4.1 Extracting Facets and Searching for a Start Concept

To make facets selectable by the user, they first have to be extracted from the underlying data structure. In gFacet, we build SPARQL queries on the client side, send them to SPARQL endpoints using HTTP requests and extract the facets from the resulting XML data. The client-server communication as well as the graphical user interface are implemented in *Adobe Flex*[4] and compiled to a Flash movie, which runs in all Web browsers with Flash Player installed. An implementation of gFacet that uses DBpedia's SPARQL endpoint can be accessed online[5]. Since gFacet does not need any modification on the server side, it can be used to access information from other SPARQL endpoints as well.

Extracting facets from semantic structures is performed on the basis of semantic links. The links are defined by properties like 'plays for' and connect objects such as 'Franck Ribry' with, for example, 'FC Bayern Munich'. So given a list of football players, a possible facet to filter this list would be the football clubs at least one of the players in the list are playing for. Links from facet concepts to other concepts allow to construct facets hierarchically.

Since the number of concepts or classes as well as relations in a semantic data set is typically very large and cannot be shown simultaneously, users first have to identify a start concept or ontological class which is shown as the first node in the visualization. This step is done by entering textual search terms (e.g. 'german football' in Fig. 4). While entering terms, matching classes are immediately shown in a selection list.

The corresponding SPARQL query, which returns all the classes with labels containing the words entered by the users (here: "german football"), is given in the following:

```
SELECT DISTINCT ?class ?label COUNT(?o) AS ?numOfObj
WHERE { ?class rdf:type skos:Concept .
?o skos:subject ?class .
?class rdfs:label ?label .
?label bif:contains "german and football" .
FILTER (lang(?label) = "en") }
ORDER BY DESC(?numOfObj) LIMIT 30
```

The found classes are initially ordered according to the numbers of objects contained in each class. The class selected by the user becomes the first node in

---

[4] http://www.adobe.com/products/flex
[5] http://gfacet.semanticweb.org.

Fig. 4. List of suggested classes to define the initial search space based on user input

the graph and also the current result set (e.g. 'German football clubs'), listing all the objects of the selected class (cp. Fig. 3, A).

Based on the properties of the objects in the result set, available facets are extracted automatically and displayed in a drop-down next to the result set. Each facet in this list consists of a property (e.g. 'ground') and a class of objects this property leads to (e.g. 'Football venues in Germany'). It is thus possible to have several facets with the same property but different target classes, or with different properties but the same target class. The corresponding query looks as follows:

```
SELECT DISTINCT ?prop ?newClass
COUNT(DISTINCT ?objNewClass) AS ?numOfObj
WHERE { ?objCurrClass skos:subject <URIofGermanFootbalClubs> .
?objCurrClass ?prop ?objNewClass .
?objNewClass skos:subject ?newClass .
?newClass rdf:type skos:Concept .}
ORDER BY DESC(?objNewClass) ?prop ?newClass LIMIT 40
```

Similarly to adding first order facets to the result set, also facets of second or higher order can be added to the graph and used for filtering. In higher order facets, only those objects are shown that are connected to objects in other visible facets that are in turn directly or indirectly connected to objects in the result set. Fig. 5 shows a result set on the left, a first order facet in the middle and a second order facet on the right together with a schematic representation of the visible (black) and invisible (gray) objects. The gray dots in the second order facet represent objects of that class which are not connected to any object in the result set and therefore not visible. In this way, all the facets in the graph only contain objects that can be used for filtering but will never result in an empty result set.

4.2   Exploring the Search Space

After selecting at least one facet node in addition to the result node, it can be used to build semantically unique search queries. By selecting one of the objects

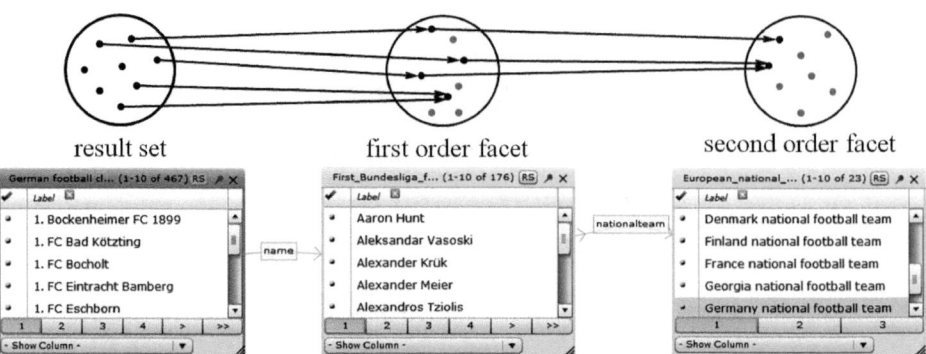

Fig. 5. Only objects that are connected to the result set are visible in the hierarchical facets: Here the national teams for which players of German clubs are playing

in a facet, the result set is filtered to only objects that are directly or indirectly connected to the selected one. For example, the selection of 'Germany national football team' in the second order facet in Fig. 5 filters the football clubs to only those with players playing for this national team (see the new result set in Fig. 6).

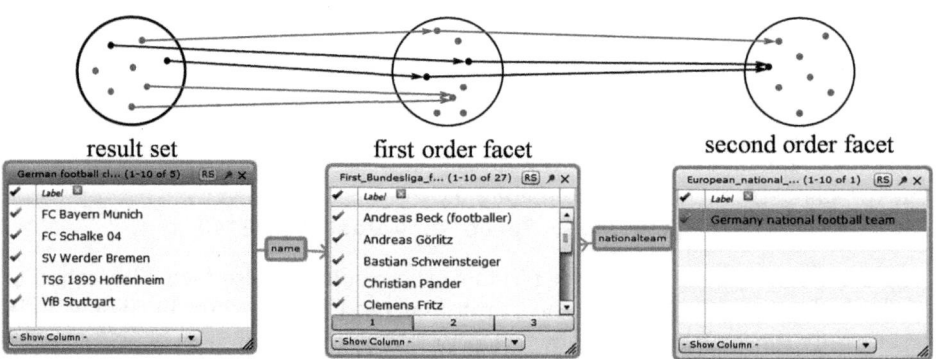

Fig. 6. Hierarchical facets can be used for filtering

To support traceability and sensemaking, we color-code the border of each node according to the current filters in effect for this node. If a facet object is selected, the selected object itself, all the filtered nodes and all the edges between them are marked with the same color (Fig. 6). When several filters are in effect for a node, several colored borders corresponding to the filters are shown. Nodes not affected by the filtering keep the normal border. The color coding provides an effective means to detect and understand the active restrictions on a node as well as the facet selections causing these restrictions.

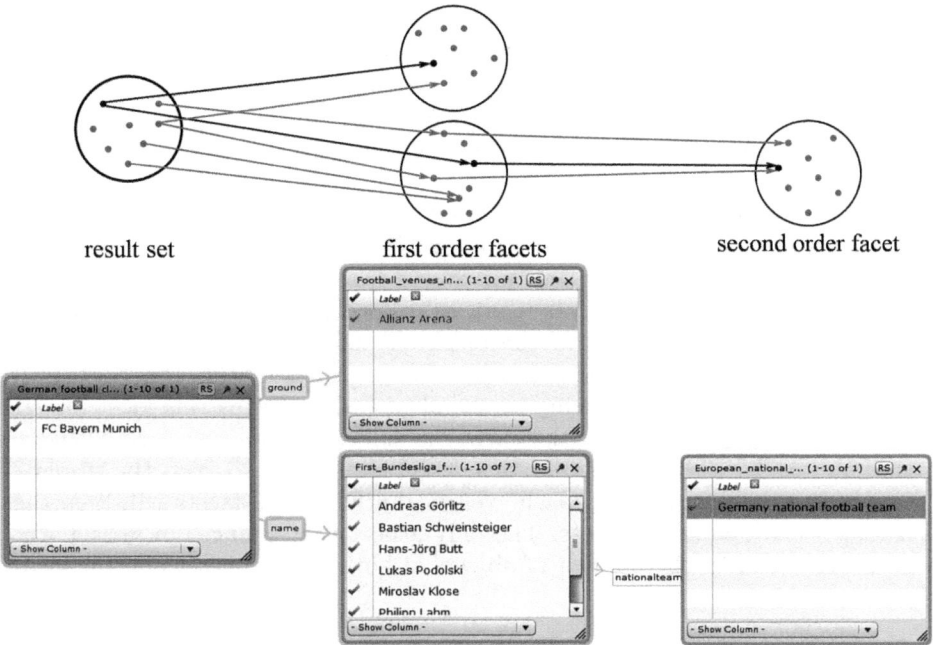

result set   first order facets   second order facet

Fig. 7. Multiple selections

As shown in Fig. 7, filtered nodes are surrounded by colored borders for each selection that affects them. New borders are added to a node like tree-rings when new filters come into effect. Deselecting the facet object that constrains the result also removes the corresponding border. In the current implementation, multiple filter selections represent a logical 'AND', constraining the result set to only those objects that are connected to all selections. Other logical operations would be possible, but have not yet been investigated for the current system.

4.3 Pivot Operation

While adding facets to the graph or filtering the result set in various ways, users may at any time change their minds about what they are interested in. gFacet supports such situated, exploratory behavior. When, for example, searching for 'German football clubs', users could become more interested in 'First Bundesliga footballers' and would like to explore which clubs they are playing for. They therefore might want to use clubs as a filter for footballers instead of the other way round. This operation is supported by a *pivot operation* which allows to change the perspective and direction of the filtering process. The pivot operation is known from the field of data drilling [15], where data are represented according to different dimensions.

The Nested Faceted Browser [12] and Humboldt [10] are the only tools mentioned in the related work section that allow users to perform a pivot operation and thus to change the focus of their search. In Humboldt, the user can replace the current result set displayed in the centre of the screen, by one of its visible facets, which are arranged on the right-hand side of the display. The chosen facet becomes the new result set and vice versa, the replaced result set becomes a new facet. In Humboldt, only directly related facets are shown next to the result set and thus hierarchical facets can only be reached by operating pivots. Whenever a pivot is operated and a new result set is shown in the centre of the screen, the list of directly related facets is updated accordingly. This way, information is partitioned over multiple pages, placing substantial cognitive load on the users to keep track of former result sets and facets, which are not visible yet.

Our graph-based approach, by contrast, allows a pivot operation to be performed without any changes of the displayed information structure and thus reduces the cognitive load to keep track of them. Clicking the 'RS'-Button (RS = result set) next to the pinning needle of any of the turns this facet into the new result set and vice versa the current result set into a new facet. Whereas other approaches have to rebuild their complete layout to keep the displayed facets up to date, in our approach even distantly related facets will keep their position while operating pivots. The only aspect that changes in gFacet when operating a pivot is the number of objects in both the result set and the visible facets.

5   User Study

To evaluate the usability of our approach, we conducted an initial user study that compared gFacet with Parallax [9], a tool that also uses a facetted approach to searching semantic data but which is not based on a graph visualization. For both tools we measured to what extent participants were able to solve the following three task types of different levels of difficulty:

1. Find two players who are playing for a certain club.
2. Find two cities where players who are playing for a certain club are born.
3. Find one player who is playing for a certain club and is born in a certain city.

We applied a 2x3 (*tool type x task type*) within-subject design. To control for learning effects, each participant was assigned to one of two groups which used the two tools in reversed order.. After completing all three tasks with one tool, the participants were asked to fill out an evaluation sheet to rate this tool. In a final questionnaire, participants had to directly compare both tool types with each other.

Ten participants took part in the study, with an average age of 28.3 (ranging from 24 to 31). Eight of them were male; two were female with all ten participants having normal or corrected to normal vision and no color blindness. Education level of the participants was at least general qualification for university entrance and they were all familiar with computers. The functionalities of both, gFacet and Parallax were introduced by videos in which sample tasks were solved.

5.1   Results

Overall, gFacet performed very well for complex tasks. However, it performed less well for more simple tasks that could also be accomplished by just following links.

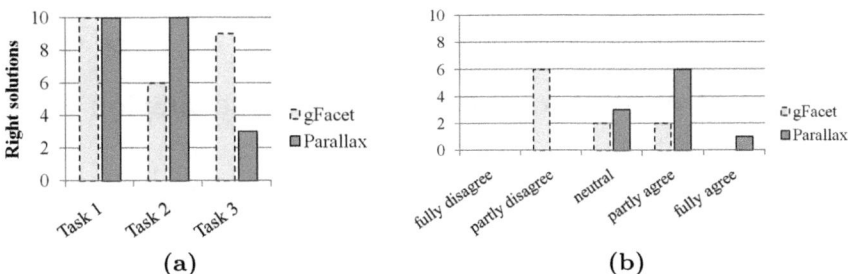

Fig. 8. a) Number of right solutions to the given tasks and b) comments to the statements 'It was difficult to understand the relations between the information'

The bar chart in Fig. 8a shows the number of correct solutions for each of the three different task types using the two different tool types. For task 1 and task 2, Parallax performed equally or even better than gFacet. This was mainly because in Parallax participants could accomplish both tasks just by following links and did not have to filter at all. In gFacet, by contrast, they had to filter despite the simplicity of the first two tasks and hence did not accomplish task 2 in four cases. The unfamiliar approach of graph-based facets seemed partly too complex to be properly used in average exploratory tasks. However, in order to find the right solution for more complex tasks, as for example for task 3, gFacet performed significantly better than Parallax. It was almost impossible so to find the right solution for task 3 just by following links in Parallax. All the links had to be checked in a trial-and-error method to actually find the player that is born in the given city. Since this is quite time-consuming, participants were forced to apply filters in Parallax as well.

To find the right solution to task 3, participants had to filter the list of all football players to only players that are playing for a certain club and are born in a certain city. Even though Parallax generally supports applying multiple filters, participants felt uncertain about the solutions they found. A reason for this is the strict separation in Parallax between exploration, which can be realized by clicking links on the right side of the content, and filtering, which can be done by clicking links on the left side (cp. Fig. 2a). If users explore a list of objects (e.g. cities where players are born) these objects cannot be used for filtering.

On the other hand, if users look at the filter options on the left side, they cannot further explore these options for hierarchical filters. To filter hierarchically, users first have to explore objects via links on the right side (e.g. cities where players are born) and then have to filter this list via links on the left side (e.g. to only cities located in Germany). Having to change from one side to the other can confuse users and thus can decrease their confidence in the found solutions. Moreover, clicking links to explore objects completely replaces the current content as well as the links at both sides. That way information gets partitioned over multiple pages and thus hampers users' understanding of the relations that exist between information (cp. bar chart in Fig. 8b). In gFacet, by contrast, all objects in all lists can be used for both filtering and the exploration of further facets and are all visible on one page.

6   Comparison of Tools Based on the Information Seeking Process

To discuss the advantages and limitations of our approach and to compare it with existing techniques, we use the general information seeking process (*ISP*) as described in [16] and determine to what extent existing tools support the different activities in the process. The ISP can be described in six stages: task initiation, selection, exploration, focus formulation, collection and presentation [16].. In the following, we propose a number of concrete requirements for each of these stages and analyze whether the tools fulfill the requirements (Fig. 9).

The first stage of the ISP, the *task initiation*, begins with awareness of lack of knowledge and leads to a concrete definition of the problem and its relation to prior experience and knowledge. Requirements are: A continuous support of the whole ISP including the problem definition (R1.1) and, based on this definition, suggestions on how to address the information need considering previously operated ISPs (R1.2).

The next stage, the *selection*, includes tasks like the identification and selection of the general topic to be investigated. Requirements are: An overview of all available topics (R2.1), for instance in form of a map that can be zoomed in and out, together with automatic suggestions of topics (R2.2) based on the entered problem description, entered keywords or an auto complete functionality. Both requirements aim at lowering the barrier to start an ISP.

The selection is followed by the *exploration* stage. It includes the investigation of the general topic, locating information and relating it to what is already known. Requirements are: A graphical representation of information that can be understood by the user (R3.1), interaction possibilities that are self-explanatory and easy to use (R3.2), the accessibility of details on demand (R3.3), sorting and paging techniques to handle large datasets (R3.4) and zooming functionalities that are capable of showing information in different levels of detail (R3.5).

The focus *formulation* includes tasks like the identification and the selection of hypotheses that result in the formulation of certain filters and thus allows a focused perspective of the topic. It is rather an iterative process than one that is strictly linear. Requirements are: The interactive and intuitive formulation and change of filters (R4.1), their immediate execution on the data (R4.2), the combination of different filters (R4.3), the possibility to build hierarchical filters (R4.4), the traceability of effects caused by each of them (R4.5) and a possibility to change the focus (R4.6).

ISP Stages	Task initiation		Selec -tion		Exploration					Focus formulation						Collec -tion		Presenta -tion
Require- ments	R1.1	R1.2	R2.1	R2.2	R3.1	R3.2	R3.3	R3.4	R3.5	R4.1	R4.2	R4.3	R4.4	R4.5	R4.6	R5.1	R5.2	R6.1
mSpace	-	-	-	-	+	+	-	-	-	+	+	+	-	-	-	-	-	-
Humboldt	-	-	-	-	/	-	-	-	-	+	+	+	+	-	+	-	-	-
Parallax	-	-	-	+	+	-	+	+	-	+	+	+	+	-	-	-	-	-
Tabulator	-	-	-	+	/	-	+	+	-	-	-	+	+	-	-	-	-	+
gFacet	-	-	-	+	+	+	+	+	-	+	+	+	+	+	+	-	-	-

Fig. 9. Comparison of existing systems with respect to requirements supporting a six-stage information seeking process

After the focus formulation, the *collection* takes place. Tasks are to gather and select information related to the focused topic. Requirements are: Easy mechanisms to select interesting findings (R5.1) and to export the selected information for further use in other systems (R5.2).

The last stage of the ISP, the *presentation*, consists of the task to present the found information. Requirements are: A broad range of opportunities to visualize the findings (R6.1).

From the pattern shown in Fig. 9 it becomes obvious that none of the tools supports the initial and the final stages of the ISP. gFacet apparently fulfills more requirements than any other tool. However, R3.5 is also not fulfilled by any of the tools. This is potentially problematic for the Facet Graph approach since extending the amount of information shown in the graph would result in very large images that are hard to overlook and handle. Introducing appropriate zooming techniques along with a better support for the initial and final stages are therefore possible extensions of the tool.

6.1   Conclusion and Future Work

In this paper we described Facet Graphs, a new approach for building semantically unique queries based on the concept of faceted search in combination with graph visualization. In addition to the general advantages of faceted search, the visualization of facets as nodes in a graph allows the direct representation of relationships between nodes by labeled edges and thus a connected presentation of the result set together with all relevant facets on one page. The user can add and remove facets to the graph to produce a personalized interface including even distantly connected and multiple facets that can be used to filter the result set from different user-defined perspectives. All caused filtering effects are color-coded in the graph making them better understandable and traceable for users.

We introduced gFacet, a prototypical implementation of our approach that can query arbitrary SPARQL endpoints (e.g. DBpedia) to access information

according to its semantics. We conducted a user study to compare gFacet with
Parallax and found out that our tool is especially applicable in scenarios where
multiple aspects from different domains need to be integrated in order to find certain information. Such scenarios seem to be particularly interesting for querying
the Semantic Web because of its huge variety of domains with each containing
large amounts of different classes, objects and properties. This opens up new and
outstanding opportunities for users to access information; however, controlling
such powerful opportunities remains a challenging task.

Future work includes the integration of appropriate zooming functionalities
in combination with a focus and context technique to foster users to retain an
overview even when using massive amounts of facets in one graph. Another interesting idea is to provide an opportunity to save especially helpful combinations
of facets and share such search interfaces with other users. This would further
lower the barrier of acceptance for using gFacet since users can load existing
search interfaces that are built by more experienced users and thus do not need
to start from scratch.

References

1. Berners-Lee, T., Fischetti, M.: Weaving the Web: The Original Design and Ultimate
   Destiny of the World Wide Web by its Inventor. Harper, USA (1999)
2. Auer, S., Bizer, C., Kobilarov, G., Lehmann, J., Cyganiak, R., Ives, Z.G.: DB-
   pedia: A nucleus for a web of open data. In: Aberer, K., Choi, K.-S., Noy, N.,
   Allemang, D., Lee, K.-I., Nixon, L.J.B., Golbeck, J., Mika, P., Maynard, D.,
   Mizoguchi, R., Schreiber, G., Cudré-Mauroux, P. (eds.) ASWC 2007 and ISWC
   2007. LNCS, vol. 4825, pp. 722–735. Springer, Heidelberg (2007)
3. Bizer, C., Heath, T., Kingsley, I., Berners-Lee, T.: Linked data on the Web. In:
   Proc. WWW 2008 Workshop: LDOW (2008)
4. Hearst, M., English, J., Sinha, R., Swearingen, K., Yee, P.: Finding the Flow in
   Web Site Search. Communications of the ACM 45(9), 42–49 (2002)
5. Hausenblas, M., Halb, W., Raimond, Y., Heath, T.: What is the size of the Semantic
   Web? In: Proc. I-SEMANTICS 2008, pp. 9–16. JUCS (2008)
6. Schraefel, M.C., Smith, D., Owens, A., Russell, A., Harris, C., Wilson, M.: The
   evolving mSpace platform: Leveraging the Semantic Web on the trail of the memex.
   In: Proc. Hypertext 2005, pp. 174–183. ACM Press, New York (2005)
7. Longwell RDF Browser, SIMILE (2005), http://simile.mit.edu/longwell/
8. Quan, D., Huynh, D., Karger, D.: Haystack: A Platform for Authoring End User
   Semantic Web Applications. In: Fensel, D., Sycara, K., Mylopoulos, J. (eds.)
   ISWC 2003. LNCS, vol. 2870, pp. 738–753. Springer, Heidelberg (2003)
9. Huynh, D., Karger, D.: Parallax and companion: Set-based browsing for the Data
   Web (2009)
10. Kobilarov, G., Dickinson, I.: Humboldt: Exploring Linked Data. In: Proc.
    WWW 2008 Workshop: LDOW (2008)
11. Berners-Lee, T., Hollenbach, J., Lu, K., Presbrey, J., Prud'ommeaux, E., Schraefel,
    M.C.: Tabulator Redux: Browsing and writing Linked Data. In: Proc. WWW 2008
    Workshop: LDOW (2008)
12. Huynh, D.: Nested Faceted Browser (2009),
    http://people.csail.mit.edu/dfhuynh/projects/nfb/

13. Heim, P., Ziegler, J., Lohmann, S.: gFacet: A Browser for the Web of Data. In: Proc. SAMT 2008 Workshop: IMC-SSW 2008, pp. 49–58. CEUR-WS (2008)
14. Fruchterman, T., Reingold, E.: Graph drawing by force-directed placement. In: Softw. Pract. Exper. 1991, pp. 1129–1164. John Wiley & Sons, Chichester (1991)
15. Gray, J., Bosworth, A., Layman, A., Pirahesh, H.: Data cube: A relational aggregation operator generalizing group-by, cross-tab, and sub-totals. In: Proc. ICDE 1996, pp. 152–159. IEEE Press, New York (1996)
16. Kuhlthau, C.C.: Developing a model of the library search process: cognitive and affective aspects. Reference Quarterly, 232–242 (1988)
17. Marchionini, G.: Information seeking in electronic environments. Cambridge University Press, Cambridge (1997)
18. Bates, M.J.: Where should the person stop and the information search interface start? Information Processing and Management 26(5), 575–591 (1990)
19. Heim, P., Ertl, T., Ziegler, J.: Facet Graphs: Complex Semantic Querying Made Easy. In: Aroyo, L., Antoniou, G., Hyvönen, E., ten Teije, A., Stuckenschmidt, H., Cabral, L., Tudorache, T. (eds.) ESWC 2010. LNCS, vol. 6088, pp. 288–302. Springer, Heidelberg (2010)

Fisheye Interfaces — Research Problems and Practical Challenges

Mikkel Rønne Jakobsen and Kasper Hornbæk

Department of Computer Science, University of Copenhagen
Njalsgade 128, Building 24, 5. floor
DK-2300 Copenhagen S, Denmark
{mikkelrj,kash}@diku.dk

Abstract. Fisheye interfaces give access to a large information structure by providing users with both local detail and global context. Despite decades of research in fisheye interfaces, their design and use are not well understood. To foster a discussion of fisheye views and their theoretical foundations, we identify five challenging areas in designing fisheye interfaces.

Keywords: Information visualization, fisheye interfaces, focus+context.

1 Introduction

A problem in many computer programs is that users can view only a small part of a large information structure. To make sense of a particular part, users may need to see that part in the context of the larger structure. Also, users may need to see details in parts of the structure that are not closely located. However, it is physically demanding to navigate an information structure in order to bring different parts into view (e.g., by scrolling) and cognitively demanding to assimilate the details that are viewed one at a time.

One user interface approach to addressing this problem is the fisheye view [12]. The fisheye view provides users with both local details and global context in a single view. According to the general formulation by Furnas [12], such a view can be generated by showing only those parts of the information structure that have a high degree of interest given the user's current focus.

Despite decades of research in fisheye interfaces (see [11] for a review), their design and use are not well understood. In his 2006 follow up paper on fisheye views, Furnas [15] noted that it is not clear what exactly we mean by focus and context and that essential questions about what information fisheye views should provide to users remain unanswered. Further, Lam and Munzner [27] remarked about focus+context interfaces that "we do not know when, how, or even if they are useful." Little advice is found in the literature on how to design fisheye interfaces. Designers are challenged with quantifying degree of interest and deciding how to distort the view without disrupting the user's work. Possibly because of these challenges, fisheye techniques are largely absent in

A. Ebert et al. (Eds.): HCIV (INTERACT) 2009, LNCS 6431, pp. 76–91, 2011.

widespread user interfaces. In short, fundamental research problems persist and fisheye interfaces remain very challenging to design.

In this paper, we describe these research problems and practical challenges concerning the design of fisheye interfaces. We hope to foster a discussion of fisheye views and their underlying concepts. One aim is to get away from point designs towards strong-hypothesis experiments [34]. Also, a long-term goal is the development of guidelines for the design of fisheye interfaces.

We first describe the background and motivation for fisheye interfaces and describe their design based on the current state of research so as to facilitate a discussion. Next, we describe our work on fisheye interfaces in programming in which the problems and issues that we discuss emerged. Last, we discuss the research problems and practical issues centered around five areas in the design of fisheye interfaces.

2   Related Work

Fisheye interfaces are one of several techniques for addressing the problem of working with information structures too large to fit within the display. Other techniques address the problem by providing information in multiple views separated either spatially (overview+detail) or temporally (zooming interfaces). By showing the parts simultaneously in a single view, fisheye interfaces aim to decrease the strain on memory associated with assimilating distinct views of the information structure, and thus potentially improve the user's ability to comprehend and manipulate the information structure [11].

Furnas [13] gave three motivations for balancing local detail and global context. First, local detail is needed for local interactions with a structure (e.g., editing a paragraph in a document). Second, global context is needed to interpret local detail. Third, global context is needed for navigation: "to tell the user what other parts of the structure exist and where they are".

Whereas Furnas [12] has mainly been concerned with what to show in the view, other research has focused on how to distort the view so as to seamlessly integrate focus and context. An early use of distortion is the Bifocal Display, in which a central 'close-up' region, showing items in full detail, is surrounded by 'demagnified' regions on either side showing all other items in less detail [37]. Similar distortion-oriented views were examined by researchers at Xerox PARC in the Perspective Wall [30] and the Document Lens [36]. Interest in fisheye views has not waned in recent years; in fact, explorations of fisheye views applied to web browsers [3], calendars [6], and programming environments [21,23] have been accompanied by empirical evaluations.

Below we describe fisheye interfaces and design aims mentioned in the literature. In describing fisheye interfaces, we distinguish between the *selection* of information, based on the degree of interest formalism originally proposed by Furnas, and the *presentation* of information. Earlier research has made a similar distinction [15,24,32].

2.1   Selection of Information

Based on the idea that users are not equally interested in all parts of an information structure, the degree-of-interest (DOI) function was suggested by Furnas for selecting information that should be shown in the fisheye view [12]. Furnas decomposed DOI into an *a priori* component—the global structural, intrinsic importance independent of the user's current interaction—and an *a posteori* component—the interest specific to the user's current interaction with the information structure. The DOI of some element x, given the current focus point $\cdot$, can be formally defined as

$$DOI(x|\cdot) = F(API(x), D(\cdot, x)), \qquad (1)$$

where $API(x)$ is the a priori importance of x, and D is the distance of x from the current focus. Using an additive function, a point's degree of interest thus increases with its a priori importance and decreases with its distance to the user's focus:

$$DOI(x|\cdot) = API(x) - D(\cdot, x) \qquad (2)$$

A Priori Importance. Elements in an information structure may be intrinsically more important than others, which Furnas [12] suggested may be particular to the global structure: "a notion of high versus low resolution, or degree of detail, or grossness of a feature, generality, etc." For instance, the heading of a document section may give a more general indication of the section's content than the paragraphs in the section, the first level headings are of less detail than second level headings, etc.—the outline view of Microsoft Word thus uses the global structure of a document to allow sections of the document to be hidden. To calculate the DOI of an element, some measure of a priori importance must be defined. As an example, for a tree structure with root node r, API of a node x can be formally defined as

$$API(x) = -d(r, x), \qquad (3)$$

where d is the distance measured as the number of edges between the node x and the root node r in the tree.

Distance To Focus. The second component of DOI is specific to the user's current interaction with an information structure—some elements may be closer to the user's focus and thus more important than others. Distance can be defined in different ways: for example, in a city map the distance might be defined geometrically (measured in meters) or as travel time (measured in minutes) either by walking, driving, or using public transit. For a tree structure, the distance $D(\cdot, x)$ can be defined as the number of edges between the node x and the node $\cdot$ (the focus point).

2.2   Presentation of Information

Several approaches have been investigated for the presentation of information in fisheye views.

Filtering. The fisheye view suggested by Furnas [12] used filtering to show only elements with a degree of interest above a given threshold c:

$$DOI(x|\cdot) > c \tag{4}$$

Distortion. Distortion-oriented techniques can be used to demagnify less interesting parts of an information structure to balance detail and context. Distortion can formally be described with a magnification function that determines how parts of the visual structure are magnified in the distorted view [29]. Fig. 1 shows the magnification functions for two fisheye views. The x axis represents one dimension of a visual structure (e.g., rows in a table). The y axis represents the degree of magnification of the visual structure in the given dimension. Fig. 1(a) shows a fisheye view where parts of the visual structure are entirely hidden (with magnification factor of 0), while Fig. 1(b) diminishes parts to a readable size with a magnification factor d_r. A magnification factor d_{ur} that diminishes parts to an unreadable size is shown with a dashed line in the figure.

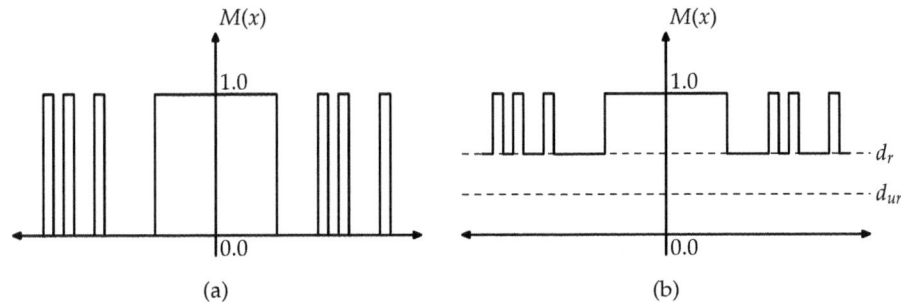

Fig. 1. Magnification functions for two fisheye views using discrete levels of magnification. (a) Less interesting parts of the visual structure are hidden by using a magnification factor of 0. (b) Less interesting parts are diminished by magnification factor d_r.

Some distortion-based techniques use non-continuous magnification (as in Fig. 1) where different parts of the information structure are magnified at discrete levels [10,19]. For example, Cockburn and Smith [10] compared source code views that demagnified blocks of code to levels that were 'just legible' and 'illegible'. Users preferred the 'just legible' magnification level, but performed better with the 'illegible' magnification level.

Other distortion-based techniques demagnify the content of dedicated context regions while leaving the content in a focal region undistorted [21,30,37]. For instance, the Perspective Wall [30] contains a center panel that shows an undistorted detail view with perspective context panels on either side that shows a demagnified view.

Still other distortion-based techniques use continuous magnification functions to the effect of a photographic fisheye lens by geometrically distorting the view of graphs or maps. For example, The Hyperbolic Browser [28] uses a hyperbolic geometry to uniformly embed an exponentially growing graph structure. Carpendale and Montagnese [9] have described the many possibilities for presentations provided by different types of lenses and distance metrics.

Semantic Zoom and Aggregate Representations. Demagnification can make an element unreadable at smaller sizes. With semantic zooming, popularized by Bederson et al. [4], alternative representations of an element are used at different sizes. A variant of semantic zooming, useful to reduce clutter in the view, is to show the individual elements in a group as one aggregate representation. For instance, DOI Trees [8] represent nodes that are distant from the focus point in aggregate form.

Resolution. Resolution can be used to filter information in the view without the use of elision or distortion [15]. For instance, Baudisch et al. [2] explored a focus+context approach in which a focus region in the center is shown in high resolution and the surrounding context region is shown in low resolution.

2.3   Design Aims

Specific goals in the design of fisheye views are discussed in the literature. One goal relates to one of Furnas' [13] motivations for fisheye views mentioned earlier, that is, to help the user navigate effectively in the information structure. Furnas [14] described two characteristics of effective navigation: First, the user must be able to traverse the structure in a small number of steps. Fisheye views can provide shorter paths to distant parts of the structure by including links to remote elements. Second, visual cues are needed to enable visual search for links in the view that lead closer to the information needed for the user's task. Pirolli et al. [33] suggested that strong information scent improves visual search, whereas crowding of targets in the context region of focus+context displays degrades visual search.

Munzner et al. [31] introduced the idea of 'guaranteed visibility' where highlighted areas of a structure that are important must remain visually apparent at all times. They find that guaranteed visibility relieves users from exhaustive exploration in identifying and comparing differences in large trees.

Zellweger et al. [38] considered different types of information about unseen objects that support different uses in City Lights: information about the existence of objects for *awareness*, physical or informational properties for *identification*, positional information for *navigation*, and abstract information for *interaction*.

In all, the appropriateness of different techniques for selecting and presenting information in a fisheye view depends on the user's tasks and how the fisheye view aims to support those tasks.

3 Fisheye Interfaces in Programming

The concerns we discuss in this paper emerged in the design and evaluation of fisheye interfaces that aim to support programming [21,23]. With the specific goal of helping programmers navigate and understand source code, we have integrated a fisheye view in the Java editor in Eclipse, an open source development platform. Basically, the fisheye view works by assigning a degree of interest (DOI) to each program line based on its a priori importance and its relation to the user's current focus in the file. Then, lines with a DOI below a certain threshold are diminished or hidden, resulting in a view that contains both details and context.

Below, we discuss the fisheye interface design used in an initial controlled experiment [21], and the design used in a later field study [23], arguing for the changes made to the initial design.

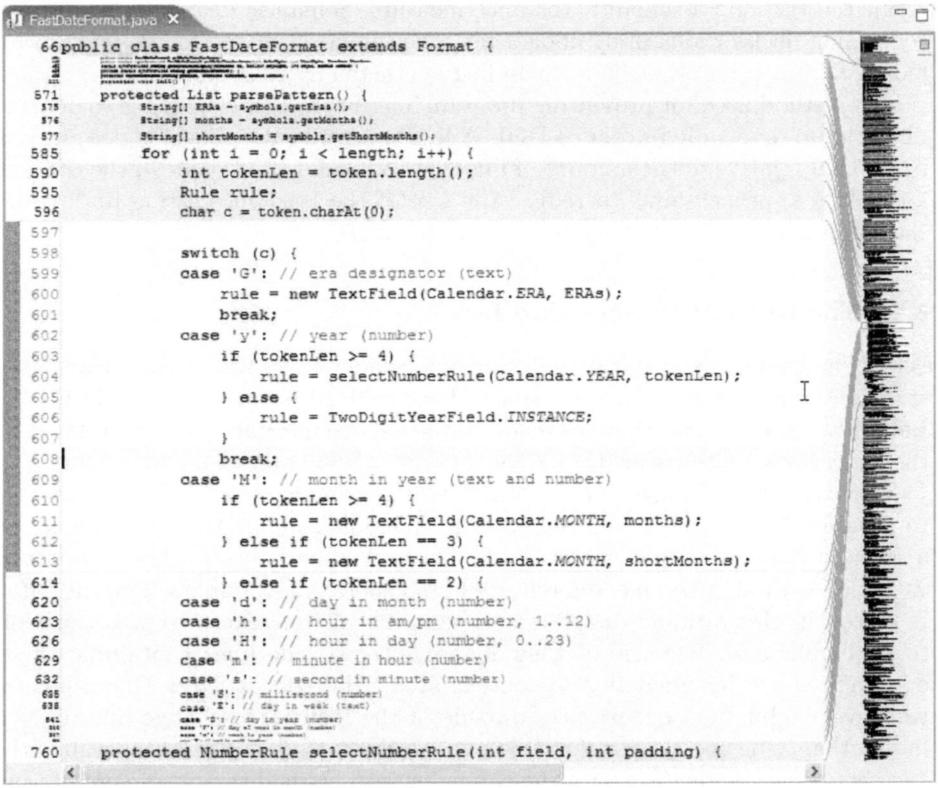

Fig. 2. The fisheye interface initially studied [21] contains an overview of the entire document shown to the right of the detail view of source code. The detail view is divided into a focus area and a context area (with pale yellow background color) that uses a fixed amount of space above and below the focus area. In the context area, program lines that are less relevant given the focus point are diminished or hidden.

3.1   The Fisheye Interface Initially Studied

In the fisheye interface we studied initially (shown in Fig. 2), the source code view is divided into a focus area and a context area. The editable part of the window, the focus area, is reduced to make space for a context area. The context area uses a fixed amount of space above and below the focus area. Parts of the source code that are less relevant given the focus point are diminished or hidden. The focus point is defined as all lines visible in the focus area. As a result, the context area is updated when the user scrolls the view, but remains unchanged when the user moves the caret within the bounds of the focus area.

A DOI function determines if and how much the lines are diminished in the context area. The API of a line is defined by its type (e.g., an indenting statement or a variable declaration) and indentation level. The distance component comprises both a syntactic distance measure similar to the tree distance described in [12] and a semantic distance measure. Semantic distance causes lines containing declarations of symbols that are referenced in the focus point to be more relevant than other lines, including syntactically close lines.

The method used for presenting program lines in the context area is to demagnify lines in descending order of DOI. A line's magnification level is determined by its DOI relative to the amount of lines yet to be allocated space in the context area. This approach aims to reduce the size of the least interesting lines while showing mainly readable lines in the context area.

3.2   The Evolved Fisheye Interface

Based on further experimentation and informed by lessons learned from user studies, the fisheye interface described above evolved into that shown in Fig. 3. Below, we describe two changes made to the fisheye interface that are related to the concerns we discuss next.

First, one of the changes made to the DOI function is to assign higher interest to program lines that contain annotations, including highlighted occurrences of a selected element. The occurrences allow programmers to see where a selected variable, method, or type is referenced. Fig. 3 shows an example where the caret is placed in the variable `dropShadows`, causing all references to that variable to be highlighted. Because of their higher interest, the lines containing these occurrences are included in the context area. The context area thus updates whenever highlighted occurrences outside of the focus area change due to user interaction. One motivation for this change was to allow the user to directly specify a semantic relation with the caret—we had learned that it was not always clear to users of the first fisheye interface what semantic relation that caused program lines to appear in the context area.

Second, we changed the presentation so that lines are always included in the context area if they have a degree of interest above a given threshold. All lines cannot be shown simultaneously in the fixed amount of space of the context area. However, instead of demagnifying lines prioritized by their DOI, which may result in some lines becoming unreadable or hidden, the context area can be

```
 DefaultGalleryItemRenderer.java  ✕
 12  package org.eclipse.nebula.widgets.gallery;
 37  public class DefaultGalleryItemRenderer extends Abs
 41      boolean dropShadows = false;
 78      public void draw(GC gc, GalleryItem item, int i
 95          if (itemImage != null) {
100              size = getBestSize(imageWidth, imageHeigh
101
102              xShift = (width - size.x) >> 1;
103              yShift = (useableHeight - size.y) >> 1;
104
105              if (dropShadows) {
106                  Color c = null;
107                  for (int i = this.dropShadowsSize - 1
108                      c = (Color) dropShadowsColors.get
109                      gc.setForeground(c);
110
111                      gc.drawLine(x + width + i - xShif
112                      gc.drawLine(x + xShift + dropShad
113                  }
114              }
115          }
152      }
154      public void setDropShadowsSize(int dropShadowsS
```

Fig. 3. The fisheye interface evolved for use in a field study [23]. Less interesting lines are hidden in the context area by using a magnification factor of 0. However, all lines with a degree of interest above a given threshold are included in the context area. In the example shown here, the bottom context area contains more lines than can be shown simultaneously. The context can be scrolled to view lines that are not initially shown.

scrolled. The motivation for this change is that all the lines may be important to the user. This design thus aims to guarantee users that the context area contains all the lines they expect to find (e.g., all the occurrences of a variable the user has selected).

3.3 Findings from User Studies

Overall, the results from our studies attest to the usefulness of fisheye interfaces to programmers. Participants in a controlled experiment preferred the fisheye interface to a linear source code interface [21]. Participants in a field study adopted and used the fisheye interface regularly and across different activities in their own work for several weeks [23]. The fisheye interface does not seem useful in all tasks and activities, however. Participants in the experiment completed tasks significantly faster using the fisheye interface, a difference of 10% in average completion time, but differences were only found for some task types. Although the results indicate usability issues, they also suggest that some tasks were less well supported by the fisheye interface. In addition, data from the field study showed periods where programmers did not use the fisheye interface, and debugging and writing new code were mentioned as activities for which the fisheye interface was not useful.

Specifically, the fisheye view enables programmers to perform some tasks with less physical effort compared with a normal linear view of source code. This was found in the controlled experiment by analyzing in detail how participants' performed tasks with a fisheye view compared with a linear view. Using a fisheye view, participants directly used information in the context area or navigated with sparse interaction; they read program lines in the context area or clicked in the context area to jump to a particular line. We saw this behavior also in observations of programmers using a fisheye interface in real-life work.

Consistently across our studies, we found that lines semantically related to the user's focus were the most important—such lines were the most frequently used and were the most often mentioned by participants as a benefit of the fisheye interface.

4   Research Problems and Practical Challenges

Several concerns came out of the studies of fisheye interfaces in programming that were described in the previous section. We discuss five areas that present both fundamental problems to research and practical challenges in the design of fisheye interfaces.

4.1   Is a Priori Importance Useful and If So, What for?

In an information structure, some information may be inherently important regardlessly of what the user is focusing on. For instance, significant landmarks in a map can provide useful context for navigation. However, the usefulness of showing a priori important information in a fisheye interface is not well understood. Further, the reasons why information is deemed a priori important may be confusing to users or may not be relevant in all contexts.

Evidence of the usefulness of showing a priori important information in fisheye interfaces is lacking. In our fisheye interface, lines are intrinsically interesting if they contain higher-level information, such as method declarations. Because lines that are directly related to the focus do not always fill the context area, lines that contain nearby method declarations, which are less directly related to the user's focus, are often shown (see Fig. 2). However, we found no clear indication that these lines improve performance in navigation and understanding tasks [21]. In real life, programmers did make use of lines containing nearby method declarations, but they seem less useful than lines directly related to the user's focus [23]. Also, Hornbæk and Hertzum [20] compared alternative fisheye menu interfaces, including one in which a priori important menu items outside of the focus region are shown at larger font sizes. Analysis of eye gaze fixations showed that the context region was used more than a fisheye menu interface without a priori important parts, but no performance differences were found. The authors suggest that the context region might have been used more because it contained more readable information. These findings indicate a use of a priori important information in fisheye interfaces. But neither these evaluations of fisheye interfaces, nor other studies we can think of, are able to link performance benefits to a priori importance.

There are practical challenges concerning a priori importance as well. One challenge is that users may become confused if information is important for no clear reason. The reason that section headings in a document are intrinsically important may be clear to users (ie., they give a general indication of the content of sections). In other cases, the reason why information is deemed important may be less clear. For instance, in a fisheye view of electronic documents, Hornbæk and Frøkjær [19] assigned higher a priori importance to the first and last paragraphs of document sections, which have been found to give better indication of the content of sections. Participants in their study spent less time on the parts of less a priori importance, but they lacked trust in the algorithm. Another practical challenge is that information may be a priori important for various reasons, but determining why it is useful to show in a fisheye view is difficult. A priori importance need not be given by intrinsic or structural properties such as level of detail. In programming, for instance, methods that are invoked many places in the program (a static indicator of importance) or methods that are frequently called (a dynamic indicator of importance) may be more important a priori. Also, dynamic data about the user's previous navigation patterns [18] or user-community popularity data [15] could indicate importance of information that could potentially make it useful to display. However, information that is important for one particular reason may not be relevant in all contexts of use of a particular interface.

In conclusion, research has yet to uncover how a priori importance contributes to the usefulness of showing information in fisheye interfaces. Also, as information may be important for many reasons, designers are challenged with determining a priori importance with respect to varied contexts of use and making clear to users why information is deemed important.

4.2   What Does the User Focus on?

Although focus is central to fisheye interfaces, very different notions of focus are used in the literature. We see issues concerning (1) how directly and predictably focus changes result in view changes, (2) how directly the user controls the focus, and (3) how the user's focus may depend on task or context.

First, fisheye interfaces that automatically balance focus and context depending on the user's focus can be distinguished from interfaces in which users manually balance focus and context. In Table Lens [35], for instance, the user has full control over which table cells are shown in detail by interacting directly with the cells using the mouse. The effect of the user's interaction on the presentation is relatively predictable. In fisheye interfaces that automatically change the view based on a DOI function, as formalized by Furnas [12], the effect of the user's interaction on the presentation is less direct: it depends on how the focus point is given by the user's interaction, how the distance component in the DOI function is defined, and how the presentation changes based on the DOI. As described in section 3.2, our fisheye design evolved to use a composite focus based on two forms of interaction: (1) a focus area spanning a range of program lines is used to determine which enclosing program structures that form the context to the code in focus; (2) the text caret gives the user explicit control for focusing on a specific variable, thus contributing as context those lines that contain occurrences of the variable. Consequently, the user can expect different types of information to change in the context area when moving the focus area (e.g., by scrolling) and when placing the caret in an element. We think this helps users control the focus and predict what information is shown in the view.

Second, very different mechanisms have been investigated in the literature for controlling the focus. Although a mouse or pointing device is probably the most frequently used for determining the user's focus [5,6,10,16,17,28], mechanisms range from tracking of eye gaze [1] to registering where the text caret dwells for a period of time [25]. It is unclear how different mechanisms compare (e.g., in directness or accuracy) in controlling the focus point in fisheye interfaces.

Third, a user's task and information needs may change during use of a fisheye interface. But information related to the user's focus may not be useful across tasks. Thinking of a user's focus in other terms than the DOI component, Mylar [25] builds a task context from multiple focus points by assigning DOI to elements in the view in which the text caret dwells for a period of time. Janecek and Pu [24] propose a DOI function composed of one or more weighted distance functions that the user can configure using sliders. However, the required effort of users in configuring the DOI function to meet changing information needs seems counter to the idea of fisheye interfaces that automatically change depending on the user's focus.

In conclusion, the user's focus—a central component in fisheye interfaces—is relatively indefinite and important problems are related to its use.

4.3   What Interesting Information Should Be Displayed?

A degree of interest function may result in varying amounts of interesting information as the user's focus changes. However, it is not trivial to visually present varying amounts of information in a view of a given size.

A specific instance of this issue in fisheye views of tree structures is the sibling overload problem where a tree node has many children all with the same DOI [26]. In answer to the problem, Koike [26] proposes fractal views in which the offspring of the nodes with lots of children will be the first to disappear. Fractal views may thus often, but not always, keep the information shown in the view constant. However, this approach may not be useful in all tasks and might confuse users about what information is left out of the view. In our study of fisheye interfaces, we found that programmers read lines directly in the context area, for instance to find a particular use of a variable. However, a large number of lines may contain occurrences of the variable that the user focuses on and not all can be shown simultaneously in a readable size. Using magnification would cause at least some of the occurrences to be unreadable. Our fisheye design thus allows users to scroll in the view of context information to access more lines than can be shown simultaneously. This design aims for predictability in that users can expect to access all information related to their focus in the context area—a scrollbar gives indication of the amount of lines in the context area. However, the scrollable context area adds complexity to the interface and does not strictly guarantee visibility of all related lines.

The issue of representing a varying amount of information may be further complicated when the fisheye interface balances different types of information that are useful in different tasks. If combined in one fisheye interface, visual representations of different types of information may conflict. Instead, a transient visualization, called up temporarily close to the user's focus, might show a representation of only the information needed to support a specific task without changing the permanent interface [22].

In conclusion, presenting varying amounts of information in a view of fixed size may be a problem if the information structure does not scale meaningfully to different sizes.

4.4   Do Fisheye Views Integrate or Disintegrate?

Fisheye interfaces distort the visual representation of information. When used in combination with applications that support rich interaction with the visual representation, distortion may interfere with those interactions. Research into the problems of integrating fisheye interfaces in real applications is, however, limited. With rare exceptions [6,23], fisheye interfaces explored in the literature are mainly designed as standalone systems. Table Lens [35], for example, demonstrates an innovative fisheye technique that facilitates exploratory analysis of large data tables. However, it is not clear how the functionality in Table Lens could be combined with the rich set of features in modern spreadsheet applications.

In our work on integrating a fisheye view in a source code editor, we tried to take into account the diversity of editor use in real-life programming work. In the fisheye interface that we initially studied, we used a static division of focus and context in a source code editor for at least two reasons. It provides stability in the context area, which changes only when scrolling the view, but remains stable when moving the caret within the focus area. Moreover, it allows users to interact with the editor as they normally do, including scrolling, searching, and editing. Even so, user study results suggest that the fisheye interface does not support all activities and that some users prefer a plain source code view in those situations. In the fisheye interface we deployed for real-life use, we thus provided an option for switching the fisheye interface on or off and a shortcut for transiently calling up the fisheye interface [23]. Other research support this approach: based on a study of web browser interfaces, Baudisch et al. [3] recommend allowing user's to call up a fisheye interface on demand for specific uses.

Although empirical insight in the adoption of fisheye interfaces in real-life applications is thus far limited, one lesson is that use of the visualization to improve performance for some tasks should not detract from performance for other tasks [6].

4.5   Are Fisheye Views Suitable for Large Displays?

A key motivation for using fisheye views is that many information structures are large, while the windows for viewing those structures are small [12,29]. With small windows, fisheye views can help by providing surrounding context to the local details currently looked at. However, it is not clear how the usefulness of fisheye views relates to window size. First, while small displays have motivated some uses of fisheye interfaces [6,7], small displays may detract from the usability of other fisheye views. In our study of a fisheye view of source code we learned that users' prefer a large view of local details, at least for some tasks, and that a larger display can mitigate the problems that the fisheye view causes. Work context is probably a key factor, but still we are curious: do large displays generally allow for fisheye views that are preferable and more usable compared to other techniques? Second, with wall-sized displays our view of a large information structure is limited mainly by the human visual system. Fisheye views may also in this context provide balance between contextual overview and local detail, but research in this area is lacking. With the rare exception of a study of focus+context screens [2], we are unaware of research in the use of fisheye techniques on large displays. In all, a better understanding of the effect of display size on design and usability of fisheye interfaces is needed.

5   Conclusion

We have discussed research problems and practical issues in the design of fisheye interfaces based on the degree of interest formalism of Furnas [12]. The concerns emerged in our empirical work on fisheye views in programming and we have related the concerns to fisheye research in the literature.

Five areas of concern have been discussed. First, a priori importance is central to the DOI formalism proposed by Furnas, yet its contribution to the usefulness of fisheye interfaces is not well understood. We have contrasted the usefulness of generally important information to that of information directly related to the user's focus. Second, concerning the user focus component of DOI we have discussed how the user controls the focus, the directness and predictability of the resulting view changes, and how the user's focus relates to the user's task. Third, we have called attention to the problem of determining what should be left out if not all important information fits in the view. Fourth, most fisheye techniques have been researched as standalone systems. We have discussed the challenges of integrating fisheye views in existing interfaces. Finally, we have questioned a key motivation for research in fisheye interfaces: that of viewing large information structures through small windows. However, large displays may potentially benefit from fisheye techniques as well. The effect of display size on the usefulness of fisheye interfaces needs investigation.

In sum, fisheye interfaces continue to present an intuitively attractive interface paradigm. However, as discussed in this paper several fundamental research questions and unsolved design challenges persist.

Acknowledgements

Many thanks to Miguel Nacenta and the anonymous reviewers for their constructive comments.

References

1. Ashmore, M., Duchowski, A.T., Shoemaker, G.: Efficient eye pointing with a fisheye lens. In: GI 2005: Proceedings of the 2005 Conference on Graphics Interface, School of Computer Science, University of Waterloo, Waterloo, Ontario, Canada, pp. 203–210. Canadian Human-Computer Communications Society (2005)
2. Baudisch, P., Good, N., Bellotti, V., Schraedley, P.: Keeping things in context: a comparative evaluation of focus plus context screens, overviews, and zooming. In: CHI 2002: Proceedings of the SIGCHI conference on Human factors in computing systems, pp. 259–266. ACM, New York (2002)
3. Baudisch, P., Lee, B., Hanna, L.: Fishnet, a fisheye web browser with search term popouts: a comparative evaluation with overview and linear view. In: AVI 2004: Proceedings of the working conference on Advanced visual interfaces, pp. 133–140. ACM Press, New York (2004)
4. Bederson, B.B., Hollan, J.D.: Pad++: a zooming graphical interface for exploring alternate interface physics. In: UIST 1994: Proceedings of the 7th annual ACM symposium on User interface software and technology, pp. 17–26. ACM, New York (1994)
5. Bederson, B.B.: Fisheye menus. In: UIST 2000: Proceedings of the 13th annual ACM symposium on User interface software and technology, pp. 217–225. ACM, New York (2000)
6. Bederson, B.B., Clamage, A., Czerwinski, M.P., Robertson, G.G.: Datelens: A fisheye calendar interface for PDAs. ACM Trans. Comput.-Hum. Interact. 11(1), 90–119 (2004)
7. Björk, S., Holmquist, L.E., Redström, J., Bretan, I., Danielsson, R., Karlgren, J., Franzén, K.: West: a web browser for small terminals. In: UIST 1999: Proceedings of the 12th annual ACM symposium on User interface software and technology, pp. 187–196. ACM, New York (1999)
8. Card, S.K., Nation, D.: Degree-of-interest trees: a component of an attention-reactive user interface. In: AVI 2002: Proceedings of the Working Conference on Advanced Visual Interfaces, pp. 231–245. ACM, New York (2002)
9. Carpendale, M.S.T., Montagnese, C.: A framework for unifying presentation space. In: UIST 2001: Proceedings of the 14th annual ACM symposium on User interface software and technology, pp. 61–70. ACM, New York (2001)
10. Cockburn, A., Smith, M.: Hidden messages: evaluating the efficiency of code elision in program navigation. Interacting with Computers 15(3), 387–407 (2003)
11. Cockburn, A., Karlson, A., Bederson, B.B.: A review of overview+detail, zooming, and focus+context interfaces. ACM Comput. Surv. 41(1), 1–31 (2008)
12. Furnas, G.W.: The FISHEYE view: A new look at structured files. Technical Report #81-11221-9, Murray Hill, New Jersey 07974, U.S.A., 12 (1981)
13. Furnas, G.W.: Generalized fisheye views. In: CHI 1986: Proceedings of the SIGCHI conference on Human factors in computing systems, pp. 16–23. ACM Press, New York (1986)

14. Furnas, G.W.: Effective view navigation. In: CHI 1997: Proceedings of the SIGCHI conference on Human factors in computing systems, pp. 367–374. ACM Press, New York (1997)
15. Furnas, G.W.: A fisheye follow-up: further reflections on focus + context. In: CHI 2006: Proceedings of the SIGCHI conference on Human Factors in computing systems, pp. 999–1008. ACM, New York (2006)
16. Gutwin, C.: Improving focus targeting in interactive fisheye views. In: CHI 2002: Proceedings of the SIGCHI conference on Human factors in computing systems, pp. 267–274. ACM Press, New York (2002)
17. Heer, J., Card, S.K.: Efficient user interest estimation in fisheye views. In: CHI 2003: CHI 2003 extended abstracts on Human factors in computing systems, pp. 836–837. ACM Press, New York (2003)
18. Hill, W.C., Hollan, J.D., Wroblewski, D., McCandless, T.: Edit wear and read wear. In: CHI 1992: Proceedings of the SIGCHI conference on Human factors in computing systems, pp. 3–9. ACM Press, New York (1992)
19. Hornbæk, K., Frøkjær, E.: Reading patterns and usability in visualizations of electronic documents. ACM Transactions on Computer-Human Interaction 10(2), 119–149 (2003)
20. Hornbæk, K., Hertzum, M.: Untangling the usability of fisheye menus. ACM Trans. Comput.-Hum. Interact. 14(2), 6 (2007)
21. Jakobsen, M.R., Hornbæk, K.: Evaluating a fisheye view of source code. In: CHI 2006: Proceedings of the SIGCHI conference on Human Factors in computing systems, pp. 377–386. ACM, New York (2006)
22. Jakobsen, M.R., Hornbæk, K.: Transient visualizations. In: OZCHI 2007: Proceedings of the 19th Australasian conference on Computer-Human Interaction, pp. 69–76. ACM, New York (2007)
23. Jakobsen, M.R., Hornbæk, K.: Fisheyes in the field: Using method triangulation to study the adoption and use of a source code visualization. In: CHI 2009: Proceedings of the SIGCHI conference on Human Factors in computing systems, pp. 1579–1588. ACM Press, New York (2009)
24. Janecek, P., Pu, P.: A framework for designing fisheye views to support multiple semantic contexts. In: International Conference on Advanced Visual Interfaces (AVI 2002), Trento, Italy, pp. 51–58. ACM Press, New York (2002)
25. Kersten, M., Murphy, G.C.: Mylar: a degree-of-interest model for ides. In: AOSD 2005: Proceedings of the 4th international conference on Aspect-oriented software development, pp. 159–168. ACM Press, New York (2005)
26. Koike, H.: Fractal views: a fractal-based method for controlling information display. ACM Trans. Inf. Syst. 13(3), 305–323 (1995)
27. Lam, H., Munzner, T.: Increasing the utility of quantitative empirical studies for meta-analysis. In: BELIV 2008: Proceedings of the 2008 conference on BEyond time and errors, pp. 1–7. ACM, New York (2008)
28. Lamping, J., Rao, R.: The hyperbolic browser: A focus + context technique for visualizing large hierarchies. Journal of Visual Languages and Computing 7, 33–55 (1996)
29. Leung, Y.K., Apperley, M.D.: A review and taxonomy of distortion-oriented presentation techniques. ACM Transactions on Computer-Human Interaction 1, 126–160 (1994)
30. Mackinlay, J.D., Robertson, G.G., Card, S.K.: The perspective wall: detail and context smoothly integrated. In: CHI 1991: Proceedings of the SIGCHI conference on Human factors in computing systems, pp. 173–176. ACM, New York (1991)

31. Munzner, T., Guimbretière, F., Tasiran, S., Zhang, L., Zhou, Y.: Treejuxta-poser: scalable tree comparison using focus+context with guaranteed visibility. In: SIGGRAPH 2003: ACM SIGGRAPH 2003 Papers, pp. 453–462. ACM, New York (2003)
32. Noik, E.G.: A space of presentation emphasis techniques for visualizing graphs. In: Proc. Graphics Interface 1994, pp. 225–233 (1994)
33. Pirolli, P., Card, S.K., Van Der Wege, M.M.: The effects of information scent on visual search in the hyperbolic tree browser. ACM Trans. Comput.-Hum. Inter-act. 10(1), 20–53 (2003)
34. Platt, J.R.: Strong inference. Science, New Series 146(3642), 347–353 (1964)
35. Rao, R., Card, S.K.: The table lens: merging graphical and symbolic representa-tions in an interactive focus + context visualization for tabular information. In: CHI 1994: Proceedings of the SIGCHI conference on Human factors in computing systems, pp. 318–322. ACM, New York (1994)
36. Robertson, G.G., Mackinlay, J.D.: The document lens. In: UIST 1993: Proceedings of the 6th annual ACM symposium on User interface software and technology, pp. 101–108. ACM, New York (1993)
37. Spence, R., Apperley, M.: Data base navigation: an office environment for the professional. Behaviour and Information Technology 1(1), 43–54 (1982)
38. Zellweger, P.T., Mackinlay, J.D., Good, L., Stefik, M., Baudisch, P.: City lights: contextual views in minimal space. In: CHI 2003: CHI 2003 extended abstracts on Human factors in computing systems, pp. 838–839. ACM, New York (2003)

Visualization of Workaday Data
Clarified by Means of Wine Fingerprints

Andreas Kerren

Linnaeus University
School of Computer Science, Physics and Mathematics (DFM)
Vejdes Plats 7, SE-351 95 Växjö, Sweden
kerren@acm.org

Abstract. More and more average users of personal computers, standard software, and web browsers come into contact with (information) visualization techniques. Depending on the task they have to perform, such visualizations are used for communication purposes, to provide a better overview of personal data, for instance pictures or emails, or to provide information of everyday commodities. After a brief outline about properties and characteristics of workaday data and their users, we focus in this paper on the visualization of wine attributes. The decision to buy a specific bottle of wine is a complex process that incorporates many different aspects from own experiences and current desires to various aromas and flavors that the wine promises to keep. We have developed two different visual representations for wine related data, which we call *wine fingerprints*. Both approaches are able to represent the most used wine attributes in literature and practice and can guide the purchase decision process of customers. Pros and cons of our wine fingerprints are discussed and compared with related approaches.

1 Introduction

Information visualization (InfoVis) for the masses, also called *casual information visualization*, has become an important new direction within the InfoVis community. In addition to the typical single-analyst, deep-dive analytical component of InfoVis, a growing focus of research is examining how to allow large numbers of people to produce, view and discuss information visualizations as well. The topic came up at the beginning of 2007 and was discussed during the first Dagstuhl Seminar on Information Visualization – Human-centered Issues in Visual Representation, Interaction, and Evaluation [11,12] in June 2007. It was a topic of special sessions at IEEE InfoVis Conferences in 2007 and 2008 too. Several researchers work on InfoVis approaches for the masses, often with a focus on collaboration, and have developed several systems, such as the ManyEyes project [28] or the Snap-together Visualization [19].

Workaday Data: In this paper, we illuminate the fact that more and more InfoVis techniques and approaches are slowly dropping in areas where the average

A. Ebert et al. (Eds.): HCIV (INTERACT) 2009, LNCS 6431, pp. 92–107, 2011.

customer comes in contact with them. A lot of different commercial and open-source products were developed and are available to those people [24]. However, either these visualization systems or libraries are too complex and difficult to use or they need at least fundamental programming knowledge to apply them. However, a few approaches are intuitive and can be used and understood by non-experts without large training efforts. This is, perhaps, not the final ultimate breakthrough of the broad usage of InfoVis tools in the population. But, it is one important step in showing the "value" of information visualization [4].

Without doing a serious evaluation of this last statement, one receives the impression that mostly "simple" and single techniques are used, such as treemaps, elementary node-link drawings, tag clouds, or bubble charts [6]. ManyEyes [28] offers many such techniques, which can be used by novice users as well. This impression is not astonishing because of at least two reasons. The first one is obviously located in the simplicity of the visualization methods. They are easy to understand and to explain to casual users. Their interaction possibilities are mostly straightforward, at least from our own perspective as visualization experts. This assumption is not well researched and needs more investigation in the future. The second reason lies, in our opinion, in the visualization aesthetics and metaphor. Often, a visually appealing visualization is more successful (relating to casual users) than a more "efficient" but unappealing visualization that presents the same data. A closer look into such phenomena could improve our vague understanding of this intersection of information visualization and visualization arts. Thus, it could also improve the success of information visualization techniques in practice.

Here, we focus on the visualization of wine attributes, such as vintage, aroma, or producer. Many customers come in contact with such attributes when deciding for a specific bottle of wine. Two different visual representations for wine related data were developed in our research group. Both can be subsumed under the term *wine fingerprints* and should not provide any interactions in order to give us the possibility to attach them to wine descriptions in actual wine shops. They are able to represent the most used wine attributes in wine literature and daily practice and can guide the purchase decision process of customers. A further aim of our developments is to get an aesthetically pleasing result.

The remainder of this paper is organized as follows. Section 2 gives a general overview about our understanding of workaday data and its potential users. Then, we discuss our sample data set, i.e., wine attributes, and present some related approaches that offer visual representations for subsets of these attributes in Section 3. Our own approaches to visualize wine attributes by using InfoVis techniques are presented in Section 4. First evaluation results are briefly outlined in this section too. We conclude in Section 5 and give an outlook to future work.

2   A Brief Look to Data and Users

By workaday data, we mainly mean data that is of individual interest to one person or a smaller group/community. In InfoVis, data is typically classified by its type, such as the number of attributes (dimensions) per data item or structural properties (hierarchy, graph, etc.). In the following, we employ a more user-guided categorization of data into *personal data* and *community data* as proposed by J. Heer et al. [7]. We restrict our discussion on people with basic computer knowledge (writing a text, sending/receiving email messages, using web browsers, ...), but no programming or visualization experiences. Thus, our target group in this paper usually acts as a customer, and the considered visualizations are used as information and communication medium in most cases.

Personal Data: This kind of data covers various types of information, which is important for the individual, for example, own financial situation, personal collection of pictures, address books, genealogical data, inventory of hobby collectors, and much more. An additional prominent example is managing emails. Data that is related to receiving and sending emails as well as message bodies were in the focus of different research projects. A. Perer and M. Smith visualized hierarchical, correlation and temporal patterns present in individual email repositories [22]. Users can identify interesting features in their repositories, e.g., how their own communication efforts look like. Another example in this context that focuses more on visualization metaphors is Anymails [8]. This tool visualizes received emails by using a microbe metaphor. Here, each email is a microbe of a specific type depending on whether the sender belongs to a specific group.

Other important data for the individual is data about specific goods, such as cars or wines (if someone is interested in to buy such goods), or communal/environmental information like crime statistics in his/her surroundings. As mentioned in Section 1, we will exemplify the application of InfoVis techniques for the visualization of workaday data by means of wine attributes and properties, i.e., our focus is on personal data in this paper.

Community Data: "Examples of community data include the content of political speeches, the number of users online in a World of Warcraft realm, or voting results per county" [7]. Thus, community data might be relevant for a group of persons who share similar interests or attitudes. Its importance is increasing due to the massive increase of social network applications, such as Facebook [3]. Our current work does not focus on community data.

3   Wine Attributes and Existing Visualization Approaches

If a consumer is buying a specific bottle of wine at the vineyard, at retailers in actual shops, or even web shops, then he/she may take different information sources into consideration for the final decision. Most people probably decide by watching the wine label on the bottle together with more or less detailed background knowledge of wines in general. Such average wine customers are interested in to know different properties or attributes of shortlisted wines, for instance, name of the wine, producer, complexity, producing country, region, grape type, color, taste, or price. Moreover, a more experienced wine consumer may also consider the storage type (e.g., steel cask or barrique), a rating by wine experts or other customers respectively, or the vintage of the wine. Among these properties, name, vintage, country, producer, etc. are textual attributes. The grape type, also called grape variety, is classified in two basic categories: red grapes and white grapes. Normally, red grapes are used for red wine and white grapes are used for white wine (however, a white wine can also be made from red grapes by only taking the flesh and not using their skin). The final color of a wine can be categorized into three types: red, white, and blush (rosé). In wine literature, one can find a richer color scale of about 12 different colors. All of these attributes are clear facts that can be collected from various data sources. One exception are the two most important attributes: taste and aroma. We will discuss this kind of data in Section 3.1. Note that pre-processing steps are usually needed to extract useful information from text files in idiosyncratic format. This process can be manually performed by human experts or automatically by natural language parsing techniques.

In contrast to the average wine consumer, more experienced people read wine notes (so-called tasting notes) written by wine experts, which are published in books or in the Internet. One popular source is Robert Parker's *Wine Advocate* [21] where tasting notes like the following one can be studied:

> "The medium ruby-colored 1997 Abadia Retuerta (a blend of 65% Tempranillo, 30% Cabernet Sauvignon, and 5% Merlot) exhibits an attractive spicy, cedary, tobacco, and berry fruit-scented nose. Herbaceousness makes an appearance in the mouth, but the wine is round, soft, and moderately concentrated, with fine cleanliness and accessibility. It should drink well for 5-6 years." Taken from [20].

Such tasting notes follow strict rules in their structure and diction. Even if—according to G. Morrot et al. [15]—humans have not developed an olfactory terminology to describe odors, there is a need to talk about different aspects of wines like smell or mouthfeel [13]. How can visualization techniques help to make such textual descriptions more clear or, perhaps, to replace them? To find a general answer is not straightforward as presented in the next subsection.

3.1   Related Works

We present three approaches that visually represent wine attributes from various perspectives. Each related work is accompanied by a screenshot to show its aesthetics and to explain the underlying idea of aroma visualization more efficiently.

Wine Aroma Wheels. In 1984, a new standard for a common wine aroma terminology was proposed in order to facilitate the verbal communication about wine aromas [18]. To support this terminology with a graphic representation, the so-called *Wine Aroma Wheel* was introduced by A. C. Noble et al. [17]. Meanwhile,

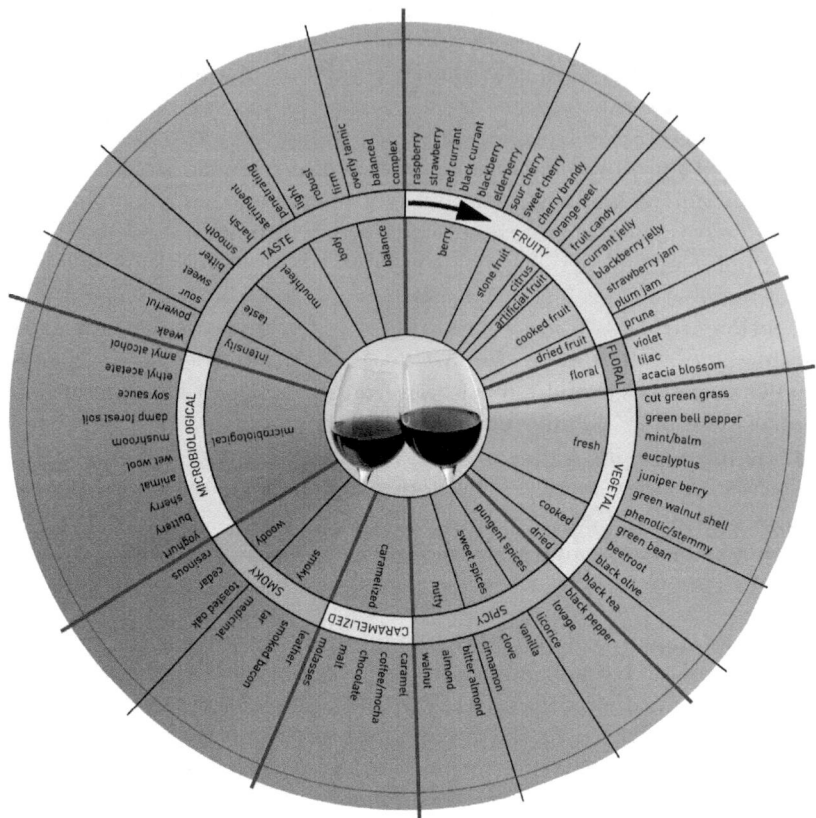

Fig. 1. Wine aroma wheel for German red wines [1]. *Image courtesy of Deutsches Weininstitut GmbH.*

different variants of this aroma wheel came up. Fig. 1 shows a modified version for German red wines. Its hierarchical structure for different aromas is clearly to identify. For example, the more general aroma "vegetal" at the first hierarchy level can be subdivided by "fresh", "cocked" and "dried" at the next level. Then, "cooked" can be further sub-classified into "green bean", "beetroot" and "black olive" at the third level. For the wheel's practical use, the German Wine Institute writes: "The aroma wheels for German white and red wines are subdivided into colored segments that describe seven characteristic aromas and one category for taste impressions. You work your way from a broad classification in the middle to the more detailed descriptions in the outermost circle. Let's begin at "fruity". Within the broad segment "fruity", for example, your more specific impression might be that of "berries". Now, through more intense sniffing, you can determine whether your wine smells more like currants or elderberries, or in some instances, perhaps both. From the individual aromas of a wine you can draw important conclusions about its grape variety and its region of origin. [...] Especially nice is the fact that this method of describing flavors and aromas enables everyone to follow experts' comments, and sooner or later, everyone can fully enjoy the pleasure of wine." [1].

For sure, such static graphics are used as a vehicle for a better communication and originally not for visualization purposes in terms of data analysis. But, the graphical representation is conceptually similar (with minor flaws due to the spatially mixed hierarchy levels) to some standard InfoVis representations for hierarchical data, such as SunBurst [25]. In this way, wine aroma wheels could serve as inspiring fundamentals for further investigations in wine visualization.

Aromicon. The German company Aromicon [2] uses Flash animations [5] to visualize different attributes of specific wines as shown in Fig. 2. Each animation consists of three areas. On the top, textural information is displayed, e.g., name of the wine, vintage and origin (area). On the right hand side, some additional attributes (sweetness and tannins) are represented by icons; for example, more sugar bits are shown if the tasted sweetness is high. The rest of the image is the main part for the taste representation and the wine color. The latter one is simply represented by the background color of the image. The taste is more complex, and the different flavors and aromas are shown by using animated "real-life" icons within a wine glass moving up from the bottom of the glass. Thus, our screenshot example conveys the flavor of cherries, coffee, black pepper and cinnamon to us. Even more complicated phenomenons, such as body or sustainability of the wine, are represented by the icons' sizes and transparencies

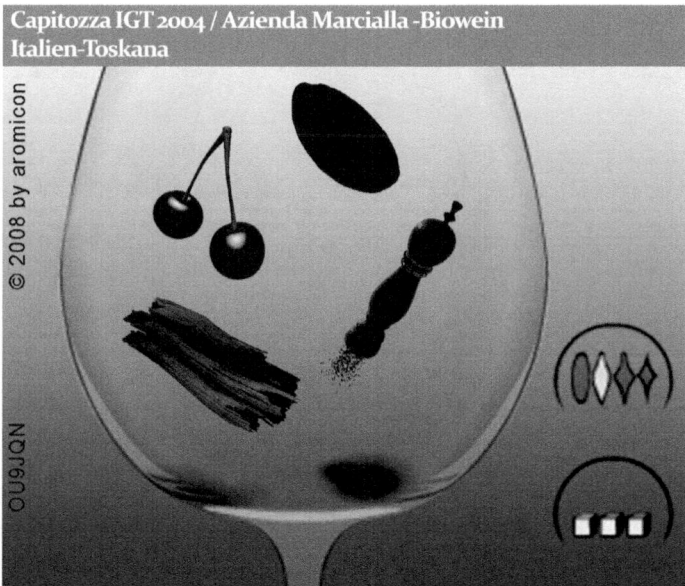

Fig. 2. Animated taste visualization of a red wine offered by the German company Aromicon [2]. *Image courtesy of Aromicon GmbH.*

respectively. Aromicon applies such animations to support customers in their decision to buy wines in a web shop.

This approach is very intuitive and visually appealing. A cherry aroma is represented by a real cherry image and not by an abstract visual representation or simple text. This is obviously a strong advantage, because wine tasting is a true sensory prescription based on vision, smell, taste, and mouthfeel. Another benefit is the usage of different animation features to represent additional information. For instance, a high velocity of the animated icons is used if the wine is tangy and fresh; a low velocity stands for a more aged wine. Animation frames (or time in general) are also used to preserve the available space in small images. Conceptual drawbacks are restricted possibilities to show many different types of attributes at the same time for comparisons as well as to support more advanced customers with the aroma hierarchy discussed above.

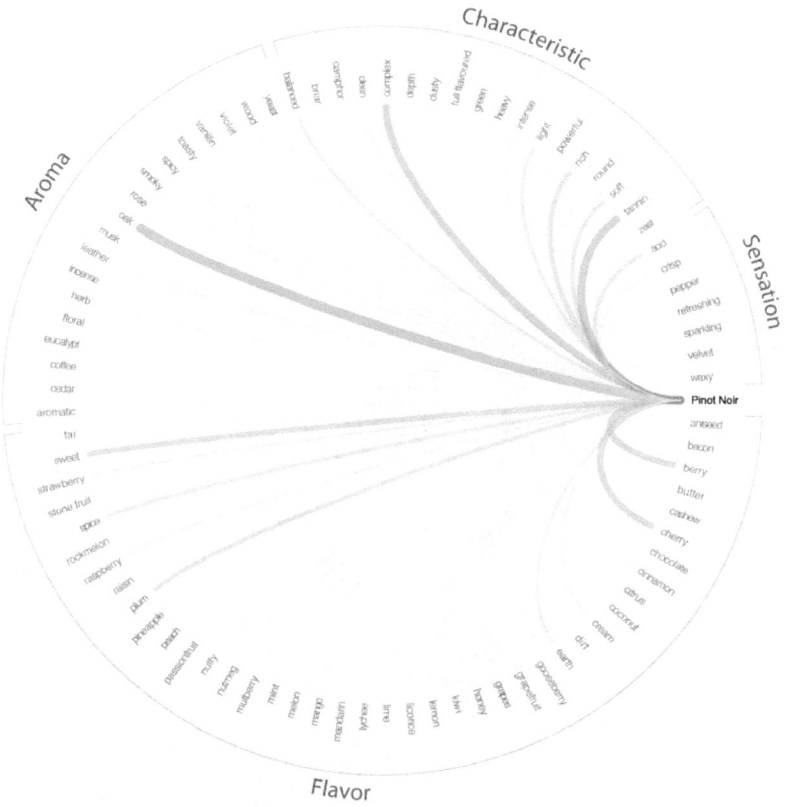

Fig. 3. Radial wine flavor visualization with regard to four different dimensions. Pinot Noir was chosen previously. Taken from the web page [26].

Wine Flavor Visualization. Fig. 3 shows a screenshot of a course work developed by C. Tashian at Tisch School of the Arts, New York [26]. This visualization focuses on the relationships between specific wine varieties and flavor components by using a radial hierarchical layout and arcs. The arc width represents the strength of these relationships between a wine variety itself and different attributes classified by four dimensions: sensation, characteristic, aroma, and flavor. Users can interactively choose between 11 different graphics for a small subset of varieties, i.e., no advanced interaction is provided. The underlying data set was gathered from about 5,000 wine tasting notes published over five years by a leading Australian wine magazine. In this figure, Pinot Noir was chosen as a sample wine variety. All arcs have their origin in the node on the right hand side representing this kind of wine. Thicker arcs give a hint of the most relevant properties of it. Thus, the line thickness represents the aggregated occurrences of a specific property over all tasting notes. In our case, the visualization shows that Pinot Noir has, in general, an aroma of oak with a sweet flavor of berry and cherry, a more acid sensation, etc.

This approach uses some well-known InfoVis techniques, especially a hierarchical, radial graph layout together with arcs. It is similar to M. Wattenberg's Arc Diagrams [27]. Advantages are its intuitive layout and its aesthetics. It could also be used for individual wines; not only for aggregated data. However, no nominal data (e.g., producer) or more general aroma levels can be smoothly included.

4   Visualization of Wine Attributes by Using InfoVis Techniques

Our idea is to use space-filling and aesthetically appealing InfoVis techniques to represent a variety of attributes that are related to a specific wine [14]. This data forms a multivariate data set as described in Section 3; a part of it can be hierarchically structured, such as the aroma hierarchy. Other attributes have a nominal, ordinal, or quantitative data type. For test reasons, we built up a MySQL database [16] to store a small test suite of wines together with their attributes. Currently, a wine can be attached with 14 different attributes (see Table 1). Four attributes stand out and need further explanations.

Wine Color: We distinguish between 16 different colors from Greenish Yellow to Garnet Red in ascending order. These colors are well-defined in the wine literature, such as in the *Wine Advocate* [21]. To prevent mistakes, we attached a unique integer ID to each color.

Rating: In practice, each professional tasting note is enhanced and complemented by a numerical rating. There are different rating systems depending on the individual wine expert or wine magazine. Parker's *Wine Advocate* [21] uses a 50-100 point quality scale, for example. In order to abstract from such individual systems, we restricted ourselves on an interval of integer values between 0 and 10. This could be easily changed in the future if needed.

Table 1. 14 wine attributes in our database together with their data type, range and visual mapping for both fingerprints (FPs). The fingerprints and their visual structures are explained in Section 4.1 and 4.2.

Attribute	Data Type	Range	Circular FP	Rectangular FP
Name	nominal	string	circle+label	rect.+label
Producer	nominal	string	circle+label	rect.+label
Country	nominal	13 IDs	circle+label	dot+label in a map
Region	nominal	any string	not used	not used
G. Variety	nominal	ID+string	circle+label	rect.+label
Complexity	nominal	3 values	circle+color	rect.+color
Barrel	nominal	2 values	circle+color	rect.+color
Category	nominal	3 values	together with *Color*	together with *Color*
Wine Color	ordinal	16 IDs+string	circle+color+label	rect.+color+label
Vintage	ordinal	1900–2008	circle+number	rect.+number
Viscosity	ordinal	any string	not used	not used
Rating	ordinal	0–10	circle+color+size	rect.+color+size+label
Price	quantitative	0–1000 SEK	circle+color+size	rect.+color+size+label
Aroma	hierarchical	three-digit	color+balloon tree	color+treemap

Grape Variety: This attribute differentiates between hundreds of numbered and textually labeled grape types, whereas a negative value of a grape type number means a white grape, a positive value means a red grape. Note that up to three different grape varieties can be combined in our data set, for example, if the wine is a blend between *170 Shiraz* and *35 Cabernet Sauvignon*.

Aroma: According to the aroma hierarchy, each aroma attribute value consists of a list of three-digit numbers as its related tree has three levels (the root node is at Level 0), cf. Fig. 4. The 100-digit is mapped to the first level of the aroma tree, the 10-digit is mapped to the second level, and so on. For example, looking at number 521, 5 means the fifth node of the first level that is "smoky" in our data model, 2 means the second node of the second level that is "woody", 1 means the first node of the third level that is "toastedOak". It is also possible to show the first and/or the second level only by resetting the appropriate digit to 0. Then, 500 means "smoky", for example. In this way, we can express more general and unspecified aromas, but we are theoretically restricted to nine different aroma values per level. Note that our aroma hierarchy is slightly different from the aroma wheel for German red wines in Fig. 1. The reason for this decision is that we would like to represent red and white wines, and thus, our aroma hierarchy is more generic compared to the presented one. The aforementioned restriction to nine different values is no issue in our current hierarchy.

To map this kind of data onto a visual representation, we developed two different visualizations, called *wine fingerprints*. They are described in the following subsections.

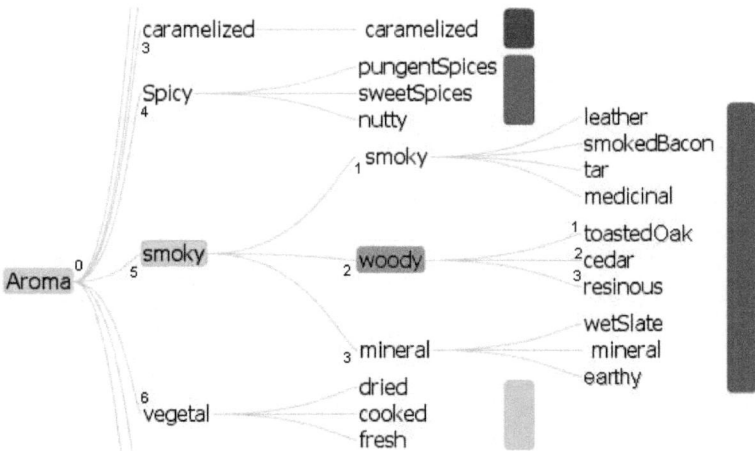

Fig. 4. A cutout of our own aroma tree structure realized in our database [14]. The complete subtree of the aroma "smoky" is unfolded. The colored bars at the right hand side of the subtrees stand for the used color coding in our wine fingerprints.

4.1   Rectangular Wine Fingerprints

Our first approach is based on a treemap layout for representing the aroma hierarchy as shown in Fig. 5. The most obvious difference to the second approach (see Section 4.2) is the use of a world map taken from ManyEyes [28] to represent the country attribute. It fits very well to the treemap, because they have both a rectangular shape. For space saving reasons, we decided to use only the upper and lower part of the world map according to the fact that wine grapes mostly grow between the 30th and the 50th degree of latitude in both the northern and southern hemisphere [29]. The space in between is then used for the treemap and other attribute representations.

We defined different saturated border colors and border thicknesses for the three levels of the aroma hierarchy to improve the perception of the tree structure. In the shown rectangular wine fingerprint, three different aromas and one specific taste for that specific wine are marked. The taste is colored in dark blue and corresponds to "sweet" at Level 3 of the hierarchy. The gray blue field represents "fresh" at the second level of the "vegetal" subtree etc. Remember, the deeper items are marked in the aroma hierarchy the more saturated the used colors, see the treemap area labeled with "fruity", for example.

The two map parts on the top and bottom symbolize wine-producing countries geographically. A red dot together with the country code locate the wine origin. On the right hand side besides the treemap, nine colored rectangles are used to visualize the remainder of the attributes. The vertical blue stripe displays the vintage, which is 2004 in this example. We used a slightly different representation for the vintage, because wine consumers typically have some knowledge about good and bad vintages. Thus, the pure date contains background information,

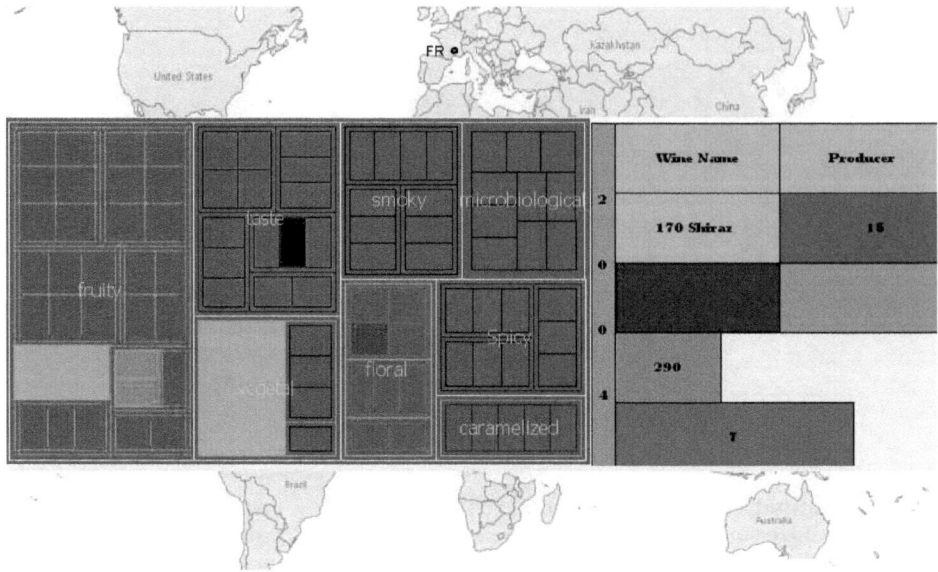

Fig. 5. A wine fingerprint using a rectangular drawing approach and a treemap layout [23] for the aroma hierarchy. The center area is divided into three rectangular areas with the treemap on the left hand side showing the complete aroma hierarchy with highlighted, individual flavors. Then, a small vertical stripe shows the vintage of the wine. On the right hand side, different areas represent nominal attributes (wine name, producer, and grape variety) by using text labels as well as ordinal/quantitative attributes (wine color, price, ...) by varying the color scale and/or widths like the two horizontal bar charts in the lower right corner. The background area indicates the origin (country) of the wine by a red dot on a world map.

which could be represented in the future too. The rectangles on the top represent from top to down and left to right the wine name, producer, grape variety (here *170 Shiraz*), color & category (white, rose and red together with the color ID; in this example, the color of the wine is *15 Brick Red*), followed by complexity (dark green represents a strong complexity) and barrel type (ocher represents a wood barrel). So far, this part of the fingerprint only shows nominal and ordinal attributes. The next two rectangles are horizontal bar charts to code ordinal and quantitative data of particular importance for the customer, such as price and rating. Consequently, they are double-coded by color and size: the higher the price the longer the bar and the color is more saturated.

4.2   Circular Wine Fingerprints

Fig. 6 shows a screenshot example of our second approach. It mainly consists of three concentric circles plus a center point, which represents the vintage by using a text label for the year. Then, the innermost circle shows five ordinal and quantitative data items: rating results, price, wine color, complexity, and barrel

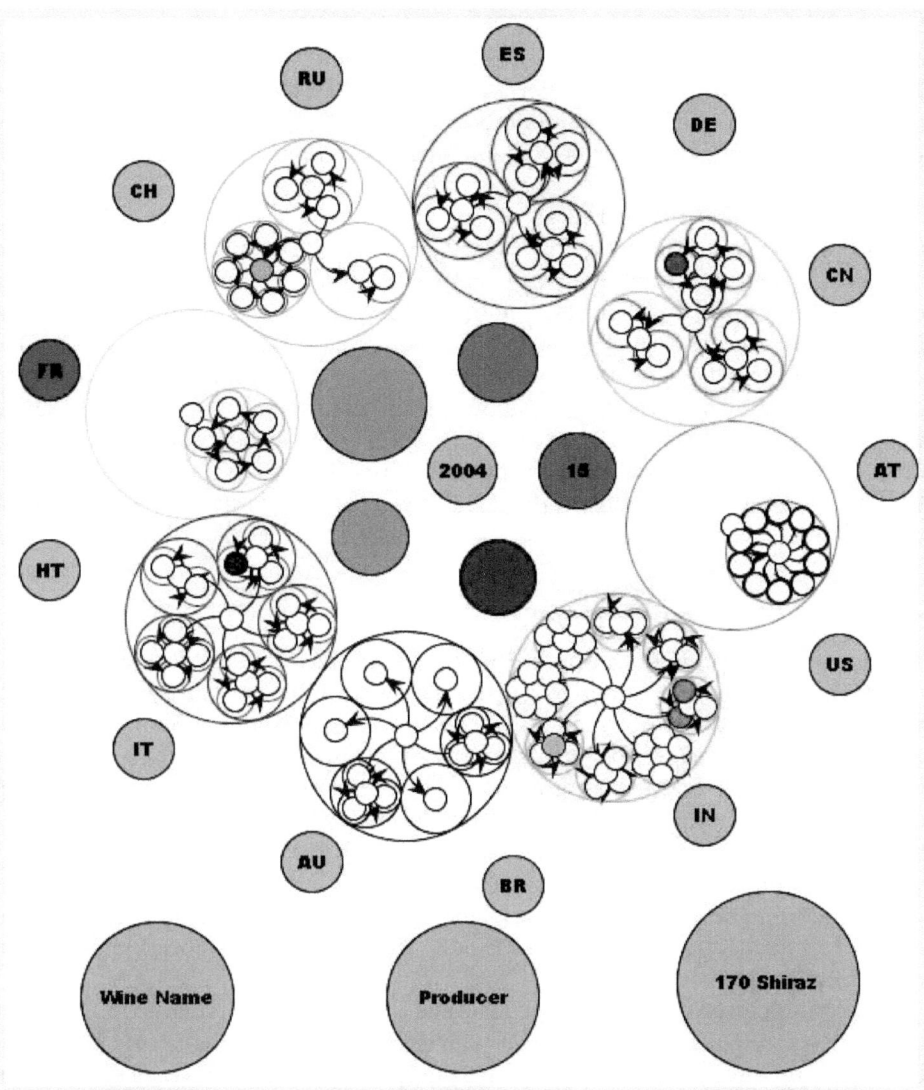

Fig. 6. Another wine fingerprint using a radial drawing approach (three layers) and a balloon tree layout for the aroma hierarchy. The midpoint of the fingerprint provides the vintage of the wine, the next circular layer represents ordinal/quantitative attributes, then the balloon tree shows the complete aroma hierarchy with marked, individual flavors. The outermost circular layer indicates the origin (country) of the wine in arbitrary order. At the bottom, nominal attributes are displayed, such as wine name, producer, and grape variety.

type. All of these attributes are double-coded in color and size or textual value respectively. The middle circle consists of a balloon tree layout (using the JUNG library [9]) for displaying the complete aroma hierarchy: each subtree represents a specific, color-coded aroma/flavor class as outlined in Fig. 4. Thus, the balloon tree visualizes our aroma hierarchy in a similar way as the treemap in the previous case. Looking at the concrete fingerprint examples, the color-coding is identical for of both the rectangular and the circular approach. Those tree nodes that fit to the current wine are filled with the corresponding color. All other nodes remain unfilled. The saturation of the node coloring is increasing the deeper we are in the aroma hierarchy. Note that the current aroma selection in Fig. 6 is identical to the current aromas in Fig 5. So, the reader can easily compare both wine fingerprints. The outer ring represents a (probably incomplete) set of countries that grow wine. Each country is represented by a circle and can be identified by its international country code. Similar as before, the current country where the wine was produced is marked in red color. The three circles at the lower part of this wine fingerprint represent nominal data: name of the wine, producer, and grape type. The circle for the grape variety is larger than the ones for name and producer in order to provide more space for up to three different varieties.

4.3   User Study and Discussion

We decided to develop both approaches to get a better feeling of which approach is better suited for the underlying wine data set. A first small user study with ten test persons was performed and yielded valuable hints for further improvements. The test design was straightforward. At first, the test persons should learn the different graphical components of the wine fingerprints with the help of an interactive user interface to become familiar with our ideas. For instance, they could select some flavors/aromas in the GUI and verify the resulting fingerprints immediately. After this learning phase, they had to compare various predefined wine fingerprints with a fingerprint based on a specific wine selection in order to identify the best match. Finally, they got a short questionnaire with rating and open questions.

Some results were surprising, for instance that our test persons did not understand the rectangular wine fingerprints using the treemap approach very well. Here, they had problems to identify the most appropriate fingerprint in the comparison task (62% correct answers). The results were better for the corresponding task with the circular approach (75% correct answers). Furthermore, seven of ten subjects would prefer our circular approach. Moreover, some test persons had the impression that the various circles within the circular fingerprints are a metaphor for wine grapes, which was originally not intended by us. Of course, the results of this user study are not significant and a more detailed study must be prepared.

If we compare our approaches to those discussed in Section 3.1, then we can identify pros and cons for them. Table 2 gives an overview of differences according to a set of features. As the Aroma Wheel is by definition restricted to represent aromas, tastes and flavors, it is only limited comparable to the other approaches, which can show more information about a wine. It is obvious that Aromicon and the light-weight Wine Flavor Visualization are strong with

Table 2. Comparison of related together with our own approaches

Feature	Aroma Wheel	Aromicon	Flavor Vis.	Circular FP	Rectangular FP
Accuracy	−	○	−	++	++
Extensibility	− −	○	+	++	++
Simplicity	+	++	++	+	○
Metaphor	○	++	○	+	○
Aesthetics	+	+	++	+	○
Perception	○	+	++	○	○
Intuitiveness	−	++	+	+	+
Training	−	+	+	−	−
Display	++	++	+	+	+

regard to intuitiveness, natural metaphor and aesthetics. Both cannot exactly show quantitative data and are hard to extend without destroying the overall layout. Our own approaches have their main benefit there: they are able to carry much more different types of data, and at least the Circular Fingerprint is aesthetically appealing and understandable. However, both are not easy to learn and are more difficult to perceive. One reason for this are the missing textual labels within the fingerprints to identify the graphical elements correctly. This was a conscious decision to reduce their visual complexity.

5   Conclusions

The aforementioned visualizations are only two examples for many applications of InfoVis techniques for workaday data. Other examples can be found in the visualization of community data [7], such as in Facebook [3] or similar services. To be successful, these visualizations must be easily perceivable, intuitive and understandable for the casual user, easy to produce in case a user plans to build an own visualization as well as follow meaningful metaphors. Our intention for this paper was not to provide a comprehensive survey on solutions for workaday data visualizations. Instead, we focused on one special application domain. We have developed two versions of *wine fingerprints* for specific wines and their attributes. Outgoing from a first evaluation, the circular wine fingerprint outperformed the rectangular wine fingerprint. Both approaches require some learning efforts of casual users, which is a clear drawback. Advantages are their accuracy to represent the underlying data and extensibility. We plan to perform a more detailed evaluation in the hope that the results can be used to improve the current realization of our ideas.

Describing sensory perceptions, such as vision, smell, taste, and mouthfeel, is a challenging task. Language researchers are interested in how humans talk about such sensory perceptions and what types of metaphorizations or lexical resources exist. Here, we are currently working together with Carita Paradis from the Center for Languages and Literature at Lund University. We plan to develop a visualization tool that can help to discover possible correlations or patterns in wine tasting databases in order to give linguists a better understanding of those (textual) descriptions. We are convinced that this research will also have a positive influence on the further development of our fingerprints.

Acknowledgments. I would like to thank Yuanxun Mei for implementing the wine fingerprint visualization as part of his Master's Thesis. Furthermore, I am thankful to Ilir Jusufi for his constructive comments that helped to develop and to improve our approach. Finally, I wish to thank Carita Paradis from the Center for Languages and Literature at Lund University, Sweden, to show us the need for visualizations of wine related data a well as to provide us with background information about this interesting field.

References

1. AromaWheel: Deutsches Weininstitut (2010), http://www.deutscheweine.de
2. Aromicon: Aromicon GmbH (2010), http://www.aromicon.com
3. Facebook: Facebook Webpage (2010), http://www.facebook.com/
4. Fekete, J.D., Wijk, J.J., Stasko, J.T., North, C.: The Value of Information Visualization. In: Kerren, et al. (eds.) [12], pp. 1–18
5. Flash: Adobe Flash (2010), http://www.adobe.com/de/products/flash/
6. Görg, C., Pohl, M., Qeli, E., Xu, K.: Visual Representations. In: Kerren, et al. (eds.) [10], pp. 163–230
7. Heer, J., van Ham, F., Carpendale, S., Weaver, C., Isenberg, P.: Creation and Collaboration: Engaging New Audiences for Information Visualization. In: Kerren, et al. (eds.) [12], pp. 92–133
8. Horn, C., Jenett, F.: Anymails Project Webpage (2007), http://www.carohorn.de/anymails/
9. JUNG: Java Universal Network/Graph Framework (2009), http://jung.sourceforge.net/
10. Kerren, A., Ebert, A., Meyer, J. (eds.): GI-Dagstuhl Research Seminar 2007. LNCS, vol. 4417. Springer, Heidelberg (2007)
11. Kerren, A., Stasko, J.T., Fekete, J.D., North, C.: Workshop Report: Information Visualization – Human-centered Issues in Visual Representation, Interaction, and Evaluation. Information Visualization 6(3), 189–196 (2007)
12. Kerren, A., Stasko, J.T., Fekete, J.D., North, C. (eds.): Information Visualization. LNCS, vol. 4950. Springer, Heidelberg (2008)
13. Lehrer, A.: Talking about Wine. Language 51(4), 901–923 (1975)
14. Mei, Y.: Visualization of Wine Attributes. Master's thesis, School of Mathematics and Systems Engineering, Växjö University, Sweden (October 2009)
15. Morrot, G., Brochet, F., Dubourdieu, D.: The Color of Odors. Brain and Languages 79(2), 309–320 (2001)
16. MySQL: An Open Source Relational Database Management System (2010), http://www.mysql.com/
17. Noble, A.C., Arnold, R.A., Buechsenstein, J., Leach, E.J., Schmidt, J.O., Stern, P.M.: Modification of a Standardized System of Wine Aroma Terminology. Am. J. Enol. Vitic. 38(2), 143–146 (1987)
18. Noble, A.C., Arnold, R.A., Masuda, B.M., Pecore, S.D., Schmidt, J.O., Stern, P.M.: Progress Towards a Standardized System of Wine Aroma Terminology. Am. J. Enol. Vitic. 35(2), 107–109 (1984)

19. North, C., Shneiderman, B.: Snap-together Visualization: A User Interface for Co-ordinating Visualizations via Relational Schemata. In: AVI 2000: Proceedings of the Working Conference on Advanced Visual Interfaces, pp. 128–135. ACM, New York (2000)
20. Paradis, C.: This Beauty Should Drink Well for 10-12 Years: A Note on Recommendations as Semantic Middles. Text & Talk 29(1), 53–73 (2009)
21. Parker, R.: Wine Advocate (2010), http://www.erobertparker.com
22. Perer, A., Smith, M.A.: Contrasting Portraits of Email Practices: Visual Approaches to Reflection and Analysis. In: AVI 2006: Proceedings of the Working Conference on Advanced Visual Interfaces, pp. 389–395. ACM, New York (2006)
23. Shneiderman, B.: Tree Visualization with Treemaps: A 2-d Space-filling Approach. ACM Transactions on Graphics 11, 92–99 (1991)
24. Shneiderman, B., Plaisant, C.: Designing the User Interface – Strategies for Effective Human-Computer Interaction, 5th edn. Pearson, London (2009)
25. Stasko, J., Zhang, E.: Focus+Context Display and Navigation Techniques for Enhancing Radial, Space-Filling Hierarchy Visualizations. In: INFOVIS 2000: Proceedings of the IEEE Symposium on Information Vizualization 2000, p. 57. IEEE Computer Society, Washington DC (2000)
26. Tashian, C.: Wine Flavor Visualization (2010), http://tashian.com/wine-flavors/
27. Wattenberg, M.: Arc Diagrams: Visualizing Structure in Strings. In: INFOVIS 2002: Proceedings of the IEEE Symposium on Information Visualization (InfoVis 2002), p. 110. IEEE Computer Society, Washington DC (2002)
28. Wattenberg, M., Kriss, J., McKeon, M.: ManyEyes: A Site for Visualization at Internet Scale. IEEE Transactions on Visualization and Computer Graphics 13(6), 1121–1128 (2007)
29. Wikipedia: List of Wine-Producing Regions (2010), http://en.wikipedia.org/wiki/List_of_wine-producing_regions

Staying Focused: Highlighting-on-Demand as Situational Awareness Support for Groups in Multidisplay Environments

Olga Kulyk[1], Tijs de Kler[2], Wim de Leeuw[3],
Gerrit van der Veer[4], and Betsy van Dijk[1]

[1] Human Media Interaction, University of Twente, The Netherlands
[2] SARA Computing and Networking Services, Amsterdam, The Netherlands
[3] Integrative Bioinformatics Unit, University of Amsterdam, The Netherlands
[4] Open University, The Netherlands

Abstract. User interfaces and visualisations are part of group problem solving. Technology is already a part of daily decision-making in multidisplay environments, both as communication tools and information devices. As these devices, such as large displays and visualisation tools become more accessible, there is an increasing opportunity to develop applications that enhance group decision-making abilities, rather than restrict them. This chapter presents the results of the empirical user study on the effect of the Highlighting-on-Demand concept on situational awareness and satisfaction with the group decision-making process in a real multidisplay environment. Highlighting-on-Demand interface enables a team member who is currently controlling the shared large display to draw attention of the other team members by highlighting certain visualisation. Displaying all alternatives on a shared large display fosters information sharing and the Highlighting-on-Demand interface enables group members to draw attention to certain visualisation, while keeping the other alternatives still in view.

The results suggest that when group members use the Highlighting-on-Demand interface during the discussion, the satisfaction with the final group decision increases. Participants expressed willingness to use the Highlighting awareness support for visualising real data (e.g., biomedical, omics experiments) and manipulating how the data is visualised to discuss the experiment results with other team members in real project discussions.

1 Introduction

The complexity of communication processes in a co-located decision-making environment requires the combination of several approaches to support situational awareness. This, in turn, requires a practical method to capture and analyse the dynamics of technology-mediated interactions in context. The nature of the interfaces as well as the physical characteristics and affordances of the environment influence the way in which interactions occur [Fruchter and Cavallin, 2006].

A. Ebert et al. (Eds.): HCIV (INTERACT) 2009, LNCS 6431, pp. 108–126, 2011.

Therefore our approach for data analysis includes a combination of behaviour, interaction and environment analysis.

We will assess shared situational awareness of team members when we provide supportive visualisations on a shared large display. We aim at reducing disturbing factors that are considered a distraction from the primary group decision-making task. We intend to establish an indication of the relations between situational awareness, team satisfaction, group processes like decision making and the perceived task performance. Video recordings from several viewpoints will enable us to analyse several simultaneously ongoing interactions. In addition to observations, post-interviews and questionnaires are carried out to obtain subjective judgments of the team members, for example, on group satisfaction, awareness and distraction from primary tasks [Cadiz et al., 2002; Kulyk et al., 2007; Olaniran, 1996]. Group satisfaction will be assessed by a combined validated post-task questionnaire featuring the group process and decision making [Olaniran, 1996]. We apply these questions to assess the perceived usefulness and impact of the Highlighting-on-Demand interface on the shared situational awareness of team members, on distraction from the primary task, and on team satisfaction with the group process and decision-making process.

2   Theory Grounding

2.1   Situational Awareness

Situational awareness is expected to be an important determinant of team performance [Bolstad et al., 2005; Endsley, 1995a]. SA provides the *"primary basis for subsequent decision making and performance in the operation of complex, dynamic systems..."* [Endsley, 1995a]. At its lowest level the team member needs to perceive relevant information (in the environment, system, self, etcetera), next integrate the data in conjunction with task goals, and, at its highest level, predict future events and system states based on this understanding [Endsley, 1995a].

Situation Awareness theory primarily focuses on how visual information influences the ability of groups to formulate a common representation of the state of the task, which in turn allows them to plan and act accordingly [Endsley, 1995b, 1993]. Visual information helps team members assess the current state of the task and plan future actions [Endsley, 1995b; Whittaker, 2003]. This awareness supports low-level coordination for tightly-coupled interactions.

The most commonly cited definition of SA is one suggested by Endsley [1995b] who states that situational awareness *"...is the perception of elements in the environment within a volume of time and space, the comprehension of their meaning, and the projection of their status in the near future"* (p. 36, more elaborated 3-levels definition of SA is presented in [Kulyk, 2010]). Despite the frequency of its citation, many researchers do not accept this definition of SA. For example, Wickens [1992] suggests that SA is not limited to the contents of working memory, but it is the ability to mentally access relevant information about the evolving circumstances of the environment. Crane [1992] provides a very different conceptualization of situational awareness by focusing on inadequate performance and suggests that SA is synonymous with expert-level performance.

In this research, we define situational awareness as: (1) *detection* and *comprehension* of the relevant perceptual cues and information from the environment; (2) *understanding* of the situation, based on individual *previous knowledge*; and (3) *interpretation* of these and reconfiguration of understanding and knowledge in a continuous process during the *group collaboration effort*. This allows *awareness of changes in the environment*, knowing what team members are doing and have done regarding current events in the environment, and keeping track of work progress.

Especially in multidisciplinary settings situational awareness information is affected by the abilities of individual members, their interaction with other team members, and the environment in which they collaborate [Bolstad et al., 2005]. Various factors affect individual situational awareness formation: environmental (physical location, display arrangement and size, etcetera) and group aspects (communication, use of collaboration tools, team processes, etcetera). In order to assess SA during evaluation of collaborative interfaces or awareness displays, specific factors need to be identified relevant to a particular domain. Applying an iterative user-centered design approach, we need to analyse the actual work context in order to design technology that supports team members in their primary task. Thus, this leads teams to communicate and interact in a collaborative environment with prolonged involvement and, hopefully, better results. It will also help us to find out how new technology in collaborative environments, such as large shared displays, influences daily work and team coordination [Hallnass and Redstrom, 2002]. This and other aspects of situational awareness theory are extensively addressed in [Kulyk, 2010].

Based on the theory of situational awareness [Endsley, 1995a] and on the results of our previous user study and task analysis study [Kulyk, 2010], displaying all alternatives on a shared large display should foster information sharing and the Highlighting interface should enable group members to draw the attention of the group to a certain visualisation, while still keeping the other alternatives in view. The Highlighting-on-Demand concept supports level 1 of situational awareness, perception. The detailed description of the Highlighting-on-Demand interface, as well as results of the user evaluation are presented in section 5 of this chapter.

2.2   Social Psychology of Groups and Technology

Research in social psychology has demonstrated that our ability to make group decisions is frequently flawed because we overly rely on social cues during a group discussion [McGrath, 1984; McGrath and Hollingshead, 1993]. Conversations held by groups for the purpose of making decisions are fraught with complications. Social psychologists have demonstrated that individuals allow the presence of the other people in the group to influence their behavior to such a degree that through the process of exchanging opinions, the group is led to a lower quality decision, as compared to aggregating individual decisions [Bray et al., 1982; Hackman, 1992; Janis, 1982; Myers and Bishop, 1971; Whyte, 1991].

While groups have flawed decision processes, Raven [1998] describes a well-known experiment that aptly illustrates the difficulty in universally stating that groups hinder decision-making. The results of his experiment show that the groups that reached a unanimous decision felt more satisfied with their decision than those that did not, even if they were shown to be incorrect in their judgment. This experiment illustrates that individuals rely on the opinion of others as an indicator of the accuracy of their judgments, but this reliance can occasionally lead to an error in judgment. Yet, as a corollary to this, if a criterion of decision success is satisfaction with the outcome, then individuals' use of this decision-making strategy may be beneficial even in cases where their judgment is wrong.

With this understanding of the complexity of our limitations, what can we do to limit the harm and harness the benefits of groups? By altering its decision-making process, a group can avoid the above communication flaws and over-reliance on others. According to DiMicco et al. [2004] and based on the related studies on the psychology of groups, there are three possible areas that should be examined to enhance decision-making processes with technology. First, determine ways to encourage vigilance in considering choice alternatives in the discussion [Janis, 1982]. Second, limit the effects of group polarisation (a group's tendency to shift towards risk or caution) [Brown, 1986]. And third, increase the sharing of information between individuals [Stasser and Titus, 1987].

For example, vigilance can be fostered by a system that keeps all the alternative ideas in front of the group, and makes the infrequently mentioned alternatives re-appear within the discussion. Group polarization can be limited with a reframing of decisions in terms of gains, not losses, and an interface or tool that enables a group to reframe questions from different points of view. Information sharing can be encouraged within a group by allowing the documentation and presentation of individual decisions that will later be shared with the group.

Technology is already a part of daily decision-making environments (e.g., smart meeting rooms and multidisplay environments), both as communication tools and information devices. As these devices (e.g., large displays) and tools become more accessible, there is an increasing opportunity to develop applications that enhance group communication abilities, rather than restrict them. If tools can be designed such that the satisfaction with the group decision-making process increases, then the potential for achieving more gains of group interaction increases.

3   Objectives and Hypotheses

Based on the results of the exploratory user study and task analysis results [Kulyk, 2010], we have come up with a number of situational awareness (SA) concepts to explore various alternative solutions [Kulyk et al., 2008] in order to support group decision making in co-located collaborative environments, presented in [Kulyk, 2010]. One example is a Highlighting-on-Demand interface, which enables a team member who is currently controlling the shared display to draw the attention of the other team members by highlighting a certain visualisation, for example, using a slider on a shared display or a personal interaction device.

The goal of this experiment is to perform a controlled comparative case study in order to measure the effect of the Highlighting-on-Demand concept on: a) satisfaction with the final group decision and b) satisfaction with the group decision-making process in a multidisplay environment. We will assess satisfaction with the decision-making process of team members, providing supportive visualisations on a shared large display. We aim at reducing the distraction from the primary decision-making task, and increasing the group member's satisfaction, with the decision-making process and group communication, as well as satisfaction with the perceived task performance (individual decision versus group decision).

Based on theories on the formation of shared situational awareness [Kulyk, 2010] and social psychology of groups [Janis, 1982; Brown, 1986; Stasser and Titus, 1987], displaying all alternatives on a shared large display should foster information sharing and the highlighting interface should allow group members to draw attention of the group by highlighting a certain alternative, while keeping the other alternatives still in view. Therefore, by presenting all alternatives on a shared large display and enabling highlighting on a shared touch screen, it is hypothesized that satisfaction with the group decision-making process will increase. These predictions are summarized as two hypotheses:

H1 — In the condition with the Highlighting-on-Demand interface, participants' satisfaction about group process and decision-making process will be higher.

H2 — Participants' satisfaction about the final group decision, in relation to their individual decision, will be higher in the condition with the Highlighting-on-Demand interface.

Next section presents the experiment design and procedure.

4   Setting and Procedure

Within-group design is applied in this experiment, which means that each group of participants performs a group decision-making task in both conditions: one Without (N) and one With (Y) the Highlighting interface. The conditions are balanced (See Table 1 below).

Table 1. Experiment design

Group Session	Condition (N/Y)	Image (A/B)	Set	Questionnaire (*see Section 4.5 below*)
1	N	A		Part I
	Y	B		Part I & II
2	Y	B		Part I & II
	N	A		Part I
3	N	B		Part I
	Y	A		Part I & II
4	Y	A		Part I & II
	N	B		Part I

Legend, Table 1:

Conditions:

N (=NO): Without Highlighting

Y (=YES): With Highlighting

Image Sets:

Set A = 7 various large paintings (landscape, portrait, abstract, fantasy etc.) – Figure 1.

Set B = a set of 7 other various large paintings – Figure 2.

4.1   Target Group

The chosen target group for this experiment is ad-hoc small groups of four to five members. Group members are scientists who might be colleagues working together at the same faculty at the university, or in the same research group (e.g. human-computer interaction or visalisation research group), with multidisciplinary backgrounds. We mixed-up group members to create balanced small groups. As a result, some of the participants knew each other well beforehand, and others have never worked in one team together.

4.2   Group Task Scenario

In this study we address the domain of the group decision making which involves group discussion and review of the arguments prior to making a final decision. The goal of the group task in this study was to initiate a group discussion on a topic of joint interest and motivate the team members to develop an individual and a group decision-making strategy. Since it was not feasible to find several life science teams to participate in the study, we decided to choose a general task for group decision making, not related to omics experimentation or life sciences. Taking into account that ad-hoc groups consist of group members from different disciplines, we picked a general task, which would be of interest to each participant and to the whole group at the same time.

Fig. 1. Paintings: set A

Fig. 2. Paintings: set B

A group decision-making scenario was presented as a group task, where a group had to discuss seven paintings and then pick three of them to put it in the shared coffee room. After discussing each painting with the whole team, and the pros and cons of putting it in the shared coffee room, each group member had to pick a maximum of three favourite paintings individually. After that,

Fig. 3. Paintings: test set 0

Table 2. Session planning - group session 1 (see Table 1)

Time duration (Total: 60 min.)	Activity
7 min.	Intro & Example (interaction via plasma touch screen) – Image **Test Set 0** (Figure 3)
10 min.	**Task** (N = No Highlighting, only moving) – Image **Set A** (Figure 1)
5 min.	**Pre-Q**uestionnaire (**Part I**)
3 min.	Intro & Example (Highlighting & resizing) – Image **Test Set 0** (Figure 3)
10 min.	Task (Y = With Highlighting & resizing) – Image **Set B** (Figure 2)
10 min.	**Post-Q**uestionnaire (**Part I & II**)
5 min.	Illustrate extra function: Highlight one image, fade out the rest automatically
10 min.	**Debriefing**: post group interview

Legend, Table 2:
Set 0 = a set of 7 different large paintings (Figure 3) used only for the introduction.

participants were asked to play a ranking game, where everybody had to share their individual choice with the rest of the group by dividing 3 points between three, two or one painting. Finally, a group had to reach a decision by picking three paintings only, either by summing up the individual scores or by agreeing on the mutual group decision.

Each group had a limited time of ten minutes to reach a group decision. The main goal for the group was to reach a group decision that each group member would agree with. Each participant received a €8 gratuity coupon for their participation.

Instructions to the group
Your faculty at UvA has received 7 paintings as a present from students of Utrecht Art Academy. Only 3 paintings can be put in the coffee room of your research group. Your goal is to discuss these 7 paintings (presented on a large tiled display in front of you) as a group and choose 3 paintings for the coffee room of your research group. After discussing each painting (pros/cons, why you like it, why does it suit in the coffee room etc.) in a group, you will have to score them to make a group decision. Each of you will have 3 points that you can choose to either divide between 2 (e.g.: Painting 3 = 2 points, Painting 5 = 1 point) or 3 paintings, or you can give all 3 points to just one painting of your personal choice. You have to announce your group choice of favorite 3 paintings after 10 minutes. Please use a blank A4 page or a whiteboard (on your right) to put your personal and group scores.

4.3   Pilot Test

Before the actual experiment, a pilot session was conducted in order to test the procedure, the experiment design, the prototype, the position of the paintings on the shared tiled display and the displays setting. Several technical problems were found and solved during the pilot test. We only name a relevant one here:

Namely, the 'Highlight one image - fade the rest' checkbox (Figure 5, right bottom) was removed due to the distraction caused by the flashing effect on the Plasma Touch Screen. Since the Highlighting prototype was running on a Windows platform via SAGE interface, it was not possible to solve the flashing and therefore it was decided to ask the participants about the usefulness of this feature during a post group discussion and in the post-task questionnaire instead. The sliding bar (Figure 5, bottom) was left visible on the Highlighting interface. A user could highlight or fade a selected painting (or any projected window on the Tiled Display) by moving the slider left or right via direct touch or using a mimio pen on a Plasma Touch Screen (Figure 4, left). The effect was immediately visible on the Tiled Display (Figure 4, right).

4.4   Multidisplay Environment Setting

The experiment took place in the E-BioLab multidisplay meeting environment (see Figure 4). In all conditions, images were displayed on the central Tiled Display (5x4 lcd-monitors, resolution 1600x1200, 38 Megapixels) in the middle of the lab (Figure 4, right image).

In condition N (No Highlighting interface), only a moving feature (via direct touch or using a mimio pen on a 63-inch Plasma Touch Screen with a resolution of 1360x768, Figure 4, left) of the interface was shown to the participants. That

Fig. 4. Group session, Highlighting-On-Demand Experiment: group member interacting with the Highlighting interface on a plasma touch screen (*left*); group members discussing paintings displayed on the shared tiled display (*right*).

Fig. 5. Highlighting-On-Demand pilot

means that group members were only able to move and rearrange images on the Tiled Display (Figure 4, right), using the Highlighting-on-Demand interface version without a sliding bar below (Figure 6).

In condition Y (Highlighting interface), in addition to a moving feature as in N condition, participants were able to highlight or fade paintings (via direct touch or using a mimio pen on a Plasma Touch Screen, Figure 4, left). Interaction with the Highlighting interface was logged in a text file with time stamps. All sessions were captured with four video cameras from four different angles.

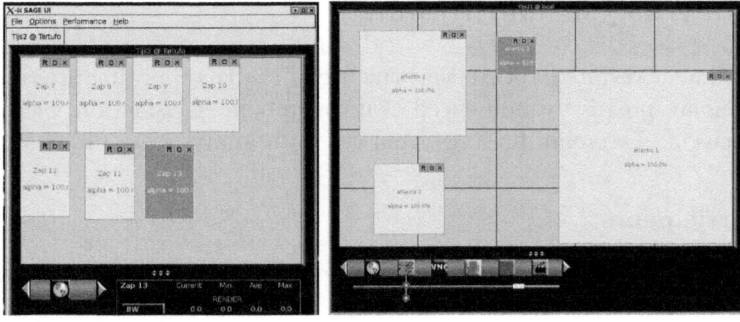

Fig. 6. Highlighting-On-Demand prototype: desktop version (*left*), image courtesy of Tijs de Kler, SARA; a touch screen version (*right*).

4.5   Measures

Two dependent variables were measured: group process and decision making, and satisfaction. By keeping the team composition balanced and the task case constant in all groups, the effect of this variable was diminished. Likert scale questionnaires were applied to access the perceived group process quality [Olaniran, 1996], satisfaction with the decision-making process [Kulyk et al., 2006; Paul et al., 2004], and the perceived agreement with the final group decision. All questionnaires used 5-point Likert-scale, where '1' meant 'Strongly agree' and '5' – 'Strongly disagree'. Group process and decision making questionnaire was administered to team members in both N and Y condition.

Direct self-rating techniques, such as SART [Taylor, 1989], have a potential limitation that participants may experience difficulties rating low periods of SA [Salmon et al., 2006]. In view of the rather short duration of the study, we predict that SART measure might not be sensitive enough for our case. Instead, we use perceived agreement with the final group decision as an indirect measure of shared situational awareness [Bolstad and Endsley, 2000; Wickens, 1992].

An additional set of questions addresses participants' subjective judgments about satisfaction with and usefulness of the Highlighting-on-Demand interface (including distraction and awareness) [Cadiz et al., 2002; Kulyk et al., 2006; Paul et al., 2004]. Post-task usefulness questionnaire was administered to team members only in Y condition. The overview of all measurements and techniques is given below.

- Questionnaires:
    1. Satisfaction with group process and decision making (Part I)
    2. Perceived agreement (Part I)
    3. Usefulness and satisfaction with the Highlighting-on-Demand interface; awareness and distraction (Part II)
- Observations (observation protocol)
- Post-session group interviews
- Video capturing (4 cameras)

5   Data Analysis and Results

The experiment results indicate that the use of the Highlighting interface on the shared display positively influenced team members' satisfaction with the final group decision. The main findings from the data analysis are discussed below.

5.1   Participants

In total 18 participants (15 male and 3 female, age range 25-31 years) were recruited from the university community and assigned in 4 groups (2 groups of 5 members each, and 2 groups of 4 members each). Gender was split so that 3 groups out of 4 had members of both genders. Participants were mostly students, scientific programmers and postdoc researchers from three different research groups at the same university (University of Amsterdam, UvA) and had various scientific backgrounds (e.g., computer science, physics, computational biology, mathematics, engineering). None of the participants had experience with group discussion in the multidisplay environment before.

5.2 Questionnaires

Group Process, Decision Making and Situational Awareness

Wilcoxon Signed Ranks test was conducted to compare group members' satisfaction with the decision-making process in Y (Highlighting - condition 2) and N (No Highlighting - condition 1) conditions. There was a significant difference in the scores on the satisfaction with the final group decision, in relation to the personal preference, for the Y-Highlighting (M^1 =4.67, SD^2=0.48) and N-No Highlighting (M=4.11, SD=0.83) conditions; p^3=0.02 (z^4=-2.33). Table 3 shows the results of a Wilcoxon Signed Ranks test only for the significant result – satisfaction with the final group decision. There was no significant difference found in the scores on the satisfaction with the group process and the decision-making process (Wilcoxon Signed Ranks test).

Table 3. Wilcoxon signed ranks test for the differences between N (*No Highlighting*) and Y (*Highlighting*) condition

Questions: Decision Making Process	N: Mean (SD)	Y: Mean (SD)	Sig.
Overall, I am satisfied with the final decision of the group, in relation to my personal preference.	4.11 (0.83)	4.67 (0.48)	0.02

These results suggest that the Highlighting-on-Demand interface really does have an effect on the satisfaction with the final group decision. Specifically, our results suggest that when group members use the highlighting interface during the discussion, the satisfaction with the final group decision increases. In this manner, H2, stating that participants' satisfaction about the final group decision, in relation to their individual decision, will be higher in the condition with the Highlighting interface, is confirmed. On the other hand, H1, stating that in the condition with the Highlighting-on-Demand interface participants satisfaction about the group process, and the decision-making process will be higher, is not confirmed.

Perceived agreement with the final group decision is an implicit measure of shared situational awareness [Bolstad and Endsley, 2000; Fjermestad, 2004;

---

[1] M - Mean

[2] SD - Standard Deviation

[3] p - probability value

[4] z - critical value for a 95% confidence interval (or a 5% level of significance); a shortcut to the hypothesis testing of the Wilcoxon signed rank-test.

Wickens, 1992]. This suggests that in the condition with the Highlighting-on-Demand support, the situational awareness was higher in terms of the perceived quality of group decisions and level of consensus. As the study of Wickens [1992] also indicates the ability of group members to accurately perform probabilistic diagnosis (situational awareness) coupled with the assigned values of different alternatives (ranking game), results in more satisfactory group decisions.

Usefulness, Awareness and Distraction
We balanced the valence of our satisfaction questions. For negatively phrased questions (marked with an asterisk in Table 4 and Table 5), we reversed the rating so that higher was always positive. The rating for the ability to focus the attention of others on certain information on the large display was above the average but not high enough. One of the reasons could be the difficulty to self-report the allocation of attention of oneself and others. More objective measures like eye gaze might be more efficient in this case, though there is still no eye-gaze tracking system applicable for dynamic group settings. Counting the number of times a participant attends to a certain display or a part of the display is another option, though it is burdensome and requires at least one observer per participant.

Ratings on awareness and distraction were also mostly neutral to positive (see Table 5). Awareness and distraction ratings indicate that the Highlighting interface did not distract participants from group discussion, but did not make then more aware of the information on the large display.

Ratings on usefulness and satisfaction with the Highlighting interface were mostly neutral to positive (see Table 4). From the ratings, it is clear that participants had no difficulty understanding the Highlighting interface and did not need more training to understand the interface. Group members also stated that they had confidence in the information provided by the Highlighting interface.

Table 4. Questionnaire results: usefulness and satisfaction

	Question	Average Rating (SD)
1.	I have difficulty understanding the highlighting interface.*	4.7 (0.5)
2.	Highlighting interface is easy to use.	3.3 (1.4)
3.	Highlighting interface is reliable.	3.0 (1.4)
4.	I have confidence in the information provided by the highlighting interface.	4.0 (0.9)
5.	I need more training to understand the highlighting interface.*	4.8 (0.4)
6.	I find the information provided by the highlighting interface informative.	3.3 (0.8)
7.	The information provided by the highlighting interface is comprehensible.	3.6 (0.8)
8.	Overall, I am satisfied with the highlighting interface.	3.1 (1.1)
9.	I would be happy to use the highlighting interface in the future.	3.3 (1.3)

Table 5. Questionnaire results: awareness and distraction

	Question	Average Rating (SD)
1.	I found the highlighting interface distracting.*	3.6 (1.1)
2.	Highlighting interface helped to grab my attention at the right time.	3.0 (1.2)
3.	Highlighting interface interrupted me during the group discussion.*	4.1 (0.9)
4.	Highlighting interface helped me to be aware of information on the large display.	3.0 (1.3)
5.	Highlighting interface helped me to focus the attention of others on certain information on the large display.	3.3 (1.2)
6.	I would rather have the highlighting interface displayed only privately.*	2.1 (1.0)

User Preferences on the Highlighting Interface Features

Three additional questions in the post-task questionnaire addressed the user preferences of the various features of the Highlighting interface, as well as the interaction preferences. The results indicate that 12 out of 18 participants found highlighting an image the most useful feature. Participants mentioned that the highlighting was helpful when eliminating choices: *"...so that we could quickly/efficiently move on to a decision. Visually removing eliminated options aided my group focus on the remaining choices"*. It was also used to emphasize, select an image, and to fade away the painting that didn't pass the vote. Among other mentioned useful features were: fading an image (7 of 18) and moving an image (4 out of 18).

Concerning the interaction preferences, 11 out of 18 participants preferred to interact with the highlighting interface via the touch screen. Tablet PC or a private PC screen was preferred by 6 out of 18 group members. Among other mentioned preferred means of interactions were, the direct manipulation on a tiled display (2 out of 18), interaction via speech (2 out of 18) and multitouch (2 out of 18).

User Comments

Most participants had very positive responses about the highlighting interface:

- *"I liked the intuitive interaction, you can directly manipulate things and everyone can see the changes right away"*;
- *"Intuitive and fast. Would use it for spatial positioning"*;
- *"I would like to use this for visualising data and manipulating how the data is visualised and discuss the data with others"*.

This first comment points to the ongoing awareness of changes in the environment. Several group members also mentioned that a feature to highlight one image and fade the rest would be useful. The wish-list features for the future highlighting interface is the multi-user and multitouch gesture interaction on the large display. Some participants complained about the black lines on the tiled display (2 out of 18), and about the reaction time of the touch display when resizing an image (1 out of 18).

Next, we discuss the qualitative results of the observations and the post-session discussions with the teams.

5.3 The Use of Large Shared Display

At the beginning of the discussion, group members would discuss each painting, why it would or would not be good to put it in the shared coffee room.

N condition: No Highlighting Interface
In N condition, participants used the Plasma Touch screen less intensively. If the whole group would eliminate a certain painting, a group would ask one member interacting with the plasma screen, to move that painting below or to the side of the Tiled display. In this way, participants were free to rearrange the screen as they wished, putting the most preferred paintings, or 'to be discussed' paintings in the middle or at the top of the tiled display.

Y Condition: Highlighting Interface
While going through each painting, in Y condition one of the participants would highlight or enlarge[5] the discussed painting. Spontaneous interactions also occurred frequently, when one group member would approach the plasma touch screen and would start interacting with the highlighting interface during the discussion, intuitively following the requests of the other team members as to which painting to highlight or to fade.

N & Y Conditions
The results of our previous observations [Kulyk, 2010] and video analysis of scientific team discussions in the multidisplay e-BioLab environment showed that life scientists tend to walk to the shared tiled display to inspect a specific detail of a visualisation. This indicates that, unlike a static projection in the meeting room, a large shared display plays an important role in engaging the group members in the discussion. This points to the dynamic nature of interactions as reported in other studies [Tan et al., 2006]. Even though in this experiment only paintings were displayed and there was no need to inspect specific details of each painting during the group task, in both conditions participants still tended to gather around the display while discussing the alternatives and making the group decision. Participants tended to point at the shared large display when referring to one painting, also referring to it by a given name, such as a 'boy', or 'flowers' (Figure 2, paintings set B).

---

[5] Despite that only the Highlighting feature was encouraged to use in the Y condition, and moving in N condition, users also discovered the resizing feature during the test session as it was fairly intuitive. Even though resizing was not very easy, it was still used by some participants.

5.4   Interaction with the Highlighting-on-Demand interface

The majority of participants liked interacting with the Highlighting interface via the shared Plasma Touch Screen as it helped the other group members to follow what was being changed on the shared large screen during the discussion. Some participants also mentioned that they would also like to interact with the Highlighting interface on a private Tablet PC.

Next to using the Highlighting-on-Demand in Y condition, and moving feature in N condition, users also discovered the resizing feature during the test session as it was fairly intuitive. One of the shortcomings of the particular touch screen used in this study was the response delay when resizing an image, also caused by the fact that the SAGE user interface was originally designed for the Tablet PC. Precision was hard to achieve when resizing an image by hand on a Plasma Touch Screen. Even though resizing was not very easy, it was still used by some participants. Therefore resizing might have effected the results. Since a resizing feature was a standard SAGE interface option, and in this experiment we focus only on the Highlighting interface, we did not focus on the redesign of the SAGE interface.

Several participants who were previously very familiar with touch screens, missed the multitouch feature on the Plasma Touch Screen. On the other hand, though the Plasma Touch Screen allowed only one person to interact at a time, it helped other group members to constantly stay aware of who was in control of the shared large display during the discussion. We did not observe any conflicts between group members concerning the interaction with the Plasma Touch Screen.

5.5   Individual and Group Decision Making Strategies

Most groups used the individual ranking approach to come up with the group decision, by summing up the individual ranks after they had made their personal choice. One of the group members would usually use a whiteboard to write down the ranks, or alternatively one by one each group member would write his/her personal rank on the whiteboard.

Some of the groups tended to discuss the strategy of the individual ranking for longer than 10 minutes. For instance, one very active participant in the fourth group changed the personal ranking of paintings in order to influence the final group decision in his favour.

6   Reflections and Future Work

The results of the observations and post-session group discussions indicate a high involvement of group members in the discussion while interacting with the highlighting interface on the shared display. This effect could be partially caused by the novelty of touch displays.

One of the shortcomings of the study is that it was hard for the participants to make a clear distinction between the Highlighting interface and the rest of the touch screen's features such as moving and resizing. Some of the participants even mentioned that, if they had not been being told clearly, they would refer to all interfaces and displays in the environment while filling in the usefulness questionnaire on the usefulness of the Highlighting interface.

Previous studies by van Nimwegen et al. [2006] and O'Hara and Payne [1999] discuss a counterproductive effect of the interfaces that present information externally on the display and fade out irrelevant information. On one hand, when information is externalized on the display (for example, by graying out momentarily unavailable buttons), users might quickly perform a problem solving task in a short run. On the other hand, the strong reliance on a visual display may have negative consequences for knowledge acquisition and task performance in the long run. We believe that giving users control over what parts of the information should or should not be externalized might be an alternative solution to the automatic information externalization. Although we did not study the long-term learning effects on the perceived performance (satisfaction with the final group decision), the results of our study suggest that providing the Highlighting-on-Demand support might help to prevent the counterproductive effects named above on the group performance in problem solving tasks.

As for the role of a large display compared to just having paintings printed as large posters on the wall, we believe that interaction played an important role in our experiment. Besides the presence of a shared visual representation and the awareness of the fact that the team members can refer to the same visual representation, being able to perform simple interaction like fading, resizing and hiding the painting played a certain role in the group decision-making strategy. One of the other points on our research agenda is to study the long-term effects of shared large displays on situational awareness and decision-making strategies between co-located and distributed groups.

7   Summary

This chapter presented the results of the first empirical user study on the effect of the Highlighting-on-Demand concept on satisfaction with the group decision-making outcome in a real multidisplay environment. The Highlighting-on-Demand interface enables a team member who is currently controlling the shared display to draw the attention of the other team members by highlighting a certain visualisation by using a slider on a touch display. The results suggest that when group members use the Highlighting-on-Demand interface during the discussion, the satisfaction with the final group decision increases. Participants expressed willingness to use the Highlighting awareness support for visualising data and manipulating how the data is visualised to discuss the data with other team members in real project discussions.

References

Bolstad, C., Cuevas, H., Gonzalez, C., Schneider, M.: Modeling shared situation awareness. In: Proceedings of the 14th Conference on Behavior Representation in Modeling and Simulation (BRIMS 2005), Los Angles, CA, USA (2005)

Bolstad, C.A., Endsley, M.R.: The effect of task load and shared displays on team situation awareness. In: Proceedings of the 44th Annual Meeting of the Human Factors and Ergonomics Society, pp. 189–192. The Human Factors and Ergonomics Society, Santa Monica (2000)

Bray, R., Johnson, D., Chilstrom, J.: Social influence by group members with minority opinions: A comparison of hollander and moscovici. Journal of Personality and Social Psychology 43, 78–88 (1982)

Brown, R.: Group polarization. In: Brown, R. (ed.) Social Psychology, pp. 200–248. Free Press, New York (1986)

Cadiz, J.J., Venolia, G., Jancke, G., Gupta, A.: Designing and deploying an information awareness interface. In: Proceedings of the 2002 ACM Conference on Computer Supported Cooperative Work (CSCW 2002), pp. 314–323. ACM Press, New York (2002)

Crane, P.: Theories of expertise as models for understanding situation awareness. In: Proceedings of the 13th Annual Symposium on Psychology in the Department of Defense, pp. 148–152 (1992)

DiMicco, J., Pandolfo, A., Bender, W.: Influencing group participation with a shared display. In: Proceedings of the ACM conference on Computer Supported Cooperative Work (CSCW 2004), pp. 614–623. ACM Press, New York (2004)

Endsley, M.: A survey of situation awareness requirements in air-to-air combat fighters. International Journal of Aviation Psychology 3(2), 157–168 (1993)

Endsley, M.: Measurements of situation awareness in dynamic systems. Human Factors 37(1), 65–84 (1995a)

Endsley, M.: Toward a theory of situation awareness in dynamic systems. Human Factors Special Issue: Situation Awareness 37(1), 32–64 (1995b)

Fjermestad, J.: An analysis of communication mode in group support systems research. Decision Support Systems 37(2), 239–263 (2004)

Fruchter, R., Cavallin, E.: Developing methods to understand discourse and workspace in distributed computer-mediated interaction. AI and Society 20(2), 169–188 (2006)

Hackman, J.R.: Group influences on individuals in organizations. In: Dunnette, M.D., Hough, L.M. (eds.) Handbook of Industrial and Organizational Psychology, vol. 3, Consulting Psychologists Press, Palo Alto (1992)

Hallnass, L., Redstrom, J.: From use to presence: On the expressions and aesthetics of everyday computational things. ACM Transactions on Computer-Humon Interaction 9(2), 106–124 (2002)

Janis, I.: Groupthink: Psychological studies of policy decisions and fiascos. Houghton Mifflin, Boston (1982)

Kulyk, O.: Do You Know What I Know? Situational Awareness of Co-located Teams in Multidisplay Environments. PhD thesis, University of Twente (2010)

Kulyk, O., van Dijk, E., van der Vet, P., Nijholt, A.: Do you know what i know? situational awareness and scientific teamwork in collaborative environments. In: Nijholt, A., Stock, O., Nishida, T. (eds.) Proceedings Sixth Workshop on Social Intelligence Design (SID 2007). CTIT Workshop Proceedings Series, vol. WP07-02, pp. 207–215. Centre for Telematics and Information Technology, University of Twente, Enschede, The Netherlands (2007)

Kulyk, O., van der Veer, G., van Dijk, E.: Situational awareness support to enhance
teamwork in collaborative environments. In: Proceedings of the 15th European Conference on Cognitive Ergonomics (ECCE 2008), pp. 18–22. ACM Press, New York
(2008)
Kulyk, O., Wang, J., Terken, J.: Real-time feedback on nonverbal behaviour to enhance
social dynamics in small group meetings. In: Renals, S., Bengio, S. (eds.) MLMI 2005.
LNCS, vol. 3869, pp. 150–161. Springer, Heidelberg (2006)
McGrath, J.E.: Groups: Interaction and Performance. Prentice Hall College Div., En-
glewood Cliffs (1984)
McGrath, J.E., Hollingshead, A.B.: Groups Interacting with Technology: Ideas, Evi-
dence, Issues and an Agenda. Sage Publications, Inc., Thousand Oaks (1993)
Myers, D., Bishop, G.: The enhancement of dominant attitudes in group discussion.
Journal of Personality and Social Psychology 20, 385–391 (1971)
van Nimwegen, C.C., Burgos, D.D., van Oostendorp, H.H., Schijf, H.H.J.M.: The para-
dox of the assisted user: guidance can be counterproductive. In: Proceedings of the
SIGCHI Conference on Human Factors in Computing Systems (CHI 2006), pp. 917–
926. ACM Press, New York (2006)
O'Hara, K.P., Payne, S.J.: Planning and the user interface: the effects of lockout time
and error recovery cost. International Journal of Human-Computer Studies 50(1),
41–59 (1999)
Olaniran, B.A.: A model of group satisfaction in computer-mediated communication and face-to-face meetings. Behaviour and Information Technology 15(1), 24–36
(1996)
Paul, S., Seetharaman, P., Ramamurthy, K.: User satisfaction with system, decision
process, and outcome in gdss based meeting: An experimental investigation. In:
Proceedings of the 37th Hawaii International Conference on System Sciences (HICSS
2004). IEEE Computer Society Press, Los Alamitos (2004)
Raven, B.: Groupthink, bay of pigs, and watergate reconsidered. Organizational Be-
havior and Human Decision Processes 73(2/3), 352–361 (1998)
Salmon, P., Stanton, N., Walker, G., Green, D.: Situation awareness measurement:
A review of applicability for c4i environments. Applied Ergonomics 37(2), 225–238
(2006)
Stasser, G., Titus, W.: Effects of information load and percentage of shared information
on the dissemination of unshared information during group discussion. Journal of
Personality and Social Psychology 53, 81–93 (1987)
Tan, D., Gergle, D., Scupelli, P., Pausch, R.: Physically large displays improve perfor-
mance on spatial tasks. ACM Transactions on Computer-Human Interaction 13(1),
71–99 (2006)
Taylor, R.M.: Situational awareness rating technique (sart): The development of a
tool for aircrew system design. In: Proceedings of the Symposium on Situational
Awareness in Aerospace Operations, AGARD-CP-478 (1989)
Whittaker, S.: Things to talk about when talking about things. Human-Computer
Interaction 18(1), 149–170 (2003)
Whyte, G.: Decision failures: Why they occur and how to prevent them. Academy of
Management Executive 5, 23–31 (1991)
Wickens, C.: Workload and situation awareness: An analogy of history and implications.
In: Insight: The Visual Performance Technical Group Newsletter, pp. 1–3 (1992)

Using Gaze Data in Evaluating Interactive Visualizations

Harri Siirtola and Kari-Jouko Räihä

Visual Interaction Research Group (VIRG)
Tampere Unit for Computer-Human Interaction (TAUCHI)
Department of Computer Sciences
FIN-33014 University of Tampere, Finland
{harri.siirtola,kari-jouko.raiha}@cs.uta.fi

Abstract. Evaluations have long been missing or imperfect in a publication presenting a new visualization technique, but proper evaluations are now becoming a standard. There are many reasons for the reluctance of evaluating visualization techniques, including the complexity of the task and the amount of work required. We propose a simple evaluation approach that consists of a set of tasks carried out in an experimental setting coupled with eye tracking to approximate the focus of the user's attention. In addition, we discuss three methods to visualize the gaze data to gain insight into the user's attention distribution, and show examples from a study where a parallel coordinate browser was evaluated.

1 Introduction

Evaluation of interactive visualizations is a challenging task. This is easy to verify by observing the attention it is given in the literature, and the number of workshops, panels, sessions, and keynote speeches dedicated to it. The complexity of evaluation comes from the large number of factors that affect how a particular technique performs. These factors include interplay of the user's internal models, perceptive processes, interpretations, and cultural elements [1]. It is often difficult to cancel out even some of these factors which leads to hard-to-analyze experimental results.

The lack of evaluation is a serious problem in visualization research. Often the published ideas are visually or technologically interesting, but the lack of evaluation leaves it open if they are actually useful. Ellis and Dix [2] did in 2006 a survey of 65 papers describing a new visualization application or technique, and found that only 12 of them had any kind of evaluation at all, and of those 12 evaluations only two were of any use! This is clearly a problem for the visualization community since development of visualization techniques should be based on experiences from prior work.

The proposed evaluation methods for interactive visualizations vary a great deal. In one end we have recommendations to perform longitudinal and extensive in-depth user studies, and in the other end there is an exasperated demand to

A. Ebert et al. (Eds.): HCIV (INTERACT) 2009, LNCS 6431, pp. 127–141, 2011.

"try it at least by yourself." Somewhere, between these two extremes, there must be an approach that is both practical and acceptable to the community.

In recent years the eye tracking technology has become affordable and is now considered as standard in usability testing [3]. When the early usability methods used video taping of the computer screen and test participant in analysis, it is now possible to overlay the screen recording with the test participant's gaze path. This is immensely useful in analyzing interactive visualization techniques as well, because when a person maintains her gaze on a single location for a certain period of time, it can be used as an approximation of the person's focus of attention [4]. Without this information it is really hard to say if the user's attention is drawn to the relevant, task-specific parts of the visualization.

The main hindrance in using eye trackers in evaluation is the sheer volume of data they produce. Unless the analyst is willing to watch all the gaze-overlaid videos and transcribe the events, the data must somehow be abstracted, summarized and visualized to allow the analysis. Analyses of usability tests often abstract the data into heatmaps that do reveal the highly useful overview of gaze behavior, but abstract away much of the gaze data. In the evaluation of interactive visualizations a bit more detail is often desired.

In this paper we consider a number of methods to abstract the gaze data for the analysis of interactive visualizations. The following approaches to represent the gaze data are explored:

- Heatmaps of fixations
- Proportion of time spent on Areas-Of-Interest (AOIs)
- Transitions between AOIs

Each of these approaches provide a different view of how a visualization performs. In Section 4 we introduce a parallel coordinate browser and its evaluation data that is used as material in examples.

2   Related Work

Saraiya et al. [5,6] discuss the limitations of using a short-term controlled experiment to study interactive visualizations and present an "insight-based longitudinal method" for evaluation. They argue that the evaluation should cover the entire analysis process from a raw data set to the insights sought from the data. In similar vein, Shneiderman and Plaisant [7] propose a method titled "multidimensional in-depth long-term case study (MILC)" which is based on a vast array of methods applied in a longitudinal study.

Isenberg et al. [8] propose a "grounded evaluation" method that uses qualitative data to "ground" the evaluation to the correct context of the intended use of the visualization technique. They advocate application of qualitative methods early on and through-out the entire development life cycle, and greater sensitivity to context.

In addition to the MILC approach, the other publications and position statements from the BELIV workshops ("Beyond time and errors: novel evaluation methods for information visualization") [9,10] are relevant as well. Andrews [11] gives a clarification of different flavors of evaluation and discusses which method is applicable in which phase of the development cycle. O'Connell and Choong [12] stress that the evaluation should be based on large, realistic data sets and tasks, and advocate the user-centered approach to evaluation. Robertson [13] stresses the importance of ecological validity, both in tasks and in the choice of participants.

Eye tracking has a long history in evaluating eye movements for a variety of visual inspection tasks [14]. The richness of the data brings with it an added challenge: which metrics to use for evaluating the data and the interaction with the application? Jacob and Karn [15] list more than ten possibly useful metrics, each fit for and used in for various purposes in varying contexts. For a researcher mainly interested in the interactive visualization and not on the analysis tool, finding the right analysis metric can be a challenge. Systematic, standardized approaches would be desirable.

In keeping with the tradition of the visualization community, to make sense of the gaze data one should naturally try to find suitable visualizations of it. Ramloll et al. [16] address the challenges and opportunities in designing gaze data visualization tools. Various tools have since been produced by eye tracker vendors and by researchers (e.g., [17]). This paper builds on the existing tools by proposing a method suitable for analyzing interactive visualizations.

3   Evaluation Method

The proposed evaluation approach can be seen as an extension of what North [18] suggested in his column about measuring "insight generation." Our approach has two elements:

1. Artificial tasks that simulate the true tasks;
2. Approximation of visual attention by eye tracking.

North suggested that (1) should include both simple benchmarking tasks and more complex, open-ended tasks. The former allow us to check the performance of low-level mechanics of the visualization, and the latter bring at least some ecological validity to the evaluation. The open-ended tasks are highly useful as post-test interview material as well. The "artificiality" of tasks means that they can be real tasks, if possible, but often we need to resort to something that is only mechanically close to the real ones.

The second element (2) proposes that we use eye tracking data to inspect where the user is looking at while using a visualization. An eye tracking device captures participants' gaze data, especially their fixation targets and lengths. A *fixation* occurs when the person maintains his or her gaze on a single location for a certain period of time, and it can be used as an approximation of the person's focus of attention. The rapid transition between fixations is called a *saccade*, and no visual percepts accumulate during the saccades.

These elements are combined in a controlled experiment that provides both quantitative (task execution time, correctness, gaze distribution) and qualitative (observation, think-aloud protocol, interview) data about the visualization. While this data may often be quite noisy, it is highly useful when comparing two designs or when trying to understand why a certain visualization performs as it does.

We believe that the "light-weight" or "discount" evaluation method proposed here might be a good tradeoff which reveals enough about the evaluation target to draw informed conclusions. Depending on whether the main interest is in quantitative or qualitative information, the elements (such as think-aloud and eye tracking) may be combined in different ways [19], lending flexibility to the approach.

4 Evaluating Parallel Coordinate Explorer

Evaluation of *Parallel Coordinate Explorer (PCE)* [20,21] is used as an example to illustrate how gaze data helps in studying interactive visualizations. This particular implementation was chosen because there are several studies of it, its strengths and weaknesses are well known, and we recently redid one of the studies by adding gaze tracking to the experimental setup [22]. The implementation of PCE is available on the web [23] as well.

PCE is a parallel coordinate browser that allows users to interact with a parallel coordinate plot by creating and modifying persistent selections. These selections highlight the lines that fulfill the constraints that can be combined with logical connectives (AND, OR, XOR).

Figure 1 shows a typical interaction with PCE. Suppose the task is to find the most powerful four-cylinder car in the data set (i.e., its engine having the highest horsepower value). The four-cylinder cars have been highlighted (constraint on axis CYL), another constraint on axis HP focuses the selection on the cars with high engine horsepower, and one of the cars in the selected set has been drilled down (the values are displayed under the axis bottom labels in red). The end-points of an axis show normally the minimum and maximum values of the corresponding variable, but change to display in red the minimum and maximum of a constraint if there is exactly one range selection on the axis.

The details of the experimental setup and the results are presented in Siirtola et al. [22] and only the nine tasks are given here:

0. How many American cars are there in the data set?
1. How many cars have a four or six cylinder engine?
2. What is the average mileage for the six-cylinder cars?
3. How would you describe the cars that weigh over 4500 pounds?
4. What is the origin of the six-cylinder cars that were manufactured in 1971?
5. Which Japanese cars have the best acceleration?
6. What else is common to the most powerful, best accelerating, and heaviest cars in the data set?
7. How many non-American cars are there in the data set?
8. What is the most common number of cylinders for cars manufactured in 1973?

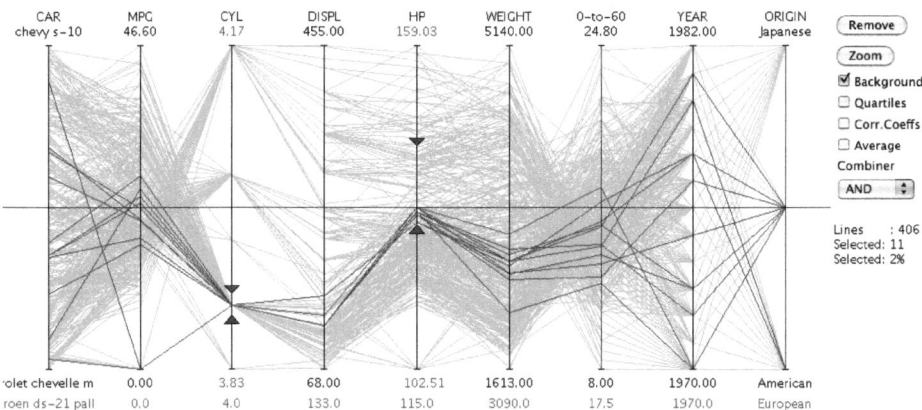

Fig. 1. Interacting with Parallel Coordinate Explorer: finding the most powerful engine among the four-cylinder cars

There are three distinct task types: simple selections, complex selections, and explorative tasks. All tasks except 3 and 6 had an unambiguous answer. Task 0 was always performed first as a practice task but the participants did not know about this.

Here we will focus on the approximation of visual attention by visualizing gaze data. The other elements of evaluation mentioned in Section 3 (task execution measurements, live observations, think-aloud, and interviews) are similar as in any usability test [24], and an example of applying them in the evaluation of an interactive visualization can be seen, e.g., in Siirtola et al. [25].

The following sections will show what kind of observations about an interactive visualization tool can be made by abstracting and visualizing the fixations and saccades of evaluation participants. In the following, the gaze data is represented as heatmaps of fixations, as balloon plots of attention proportions, and as gaze transitions between areas of interest.

5   Heatmap-Based Observations

The most popular approach to visualize fixation data is to ignore the order of the fixations completely and to base the analysis on how long the gaze has been fixated on different areas of the screen. Here "long" can mean either number of fixations or total duration of fixations in the area. Long fixations are usually an indication of increased cognitive processing, and a high number of fixations suggests problems in the visual search. By smoothing the data appropriately and encoding it with different levels of gray or color, the interest or attention can be visualized in a style familiar from maps. Such visualizations have been called "attentional landscapes" [26] and "fixation maps" [27]. The most common term for this concept nowadays is "heatmaps" or even "attention heatmaps".

Figure 2 shows the heatmap of task 4 for a single participant where the objective was to find the origin of six-cylinder cars manufactured in 1971. Solving the task requires making a selection with two constraints, one on the CYL axis that selects the six-cylinder cars, and another on the YEAR axis that further prunes the selection to cars that were manufactured in 1971. With this selection it is easy to verify that those cars were manufactured in the U.S.A. In (the color version of) the figure the number of fixations is encoded ranging from green to red via yellow, green being the lowest number of fixations observed and red being the highest.

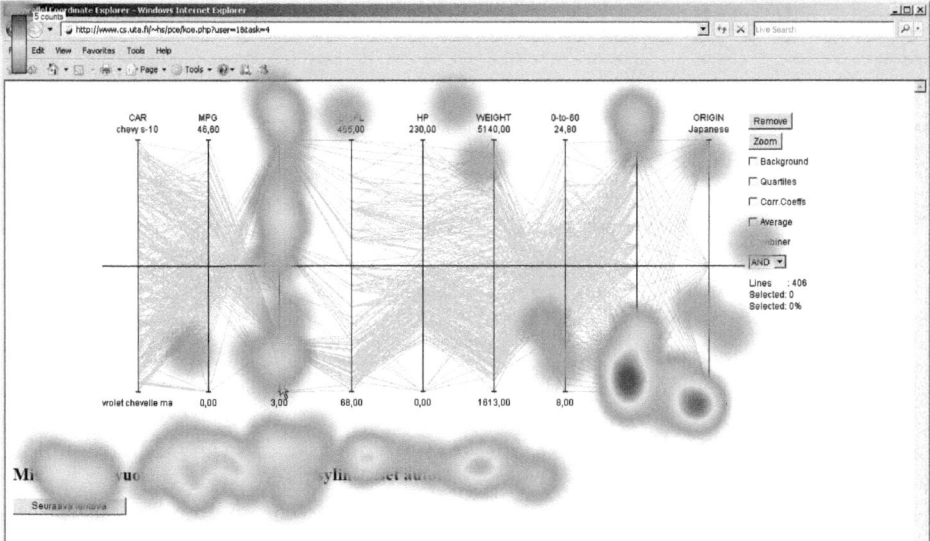

Fig. 2. Heatmap of fixation counts for task 4 for a single participant ("What is the origin of the six-cylinder cars that were manufactured in 1971?")

There are two red "peaks" in this landscape in the bottom of axes YEAR and ORIGIN (appearing darker in grayscale). One might expect that there should be three peaks, one for each selection and one for reading the result. It appears that this particular participant had problems making the selection for year 1971 and also spent a relatively long time verifying the result. Making the selection from the YEAR axis is more difficult than making the selection from the CYL axis because of the higher number of items which translates into lesser space to mouse the selection.

Figure 3 shows the heatmap of task 4 for all participants. The overall situation appears more like expected – there are three distinct peaks for the task-critical areas, and the trickiest selection has received most of the attention. In addition, it seems that the participant of Figure 2 remembered the location of axes CYL and ORIGIN, but some of the participants had to scan the axes names to locate them (indicated by the light green color over the axis names).

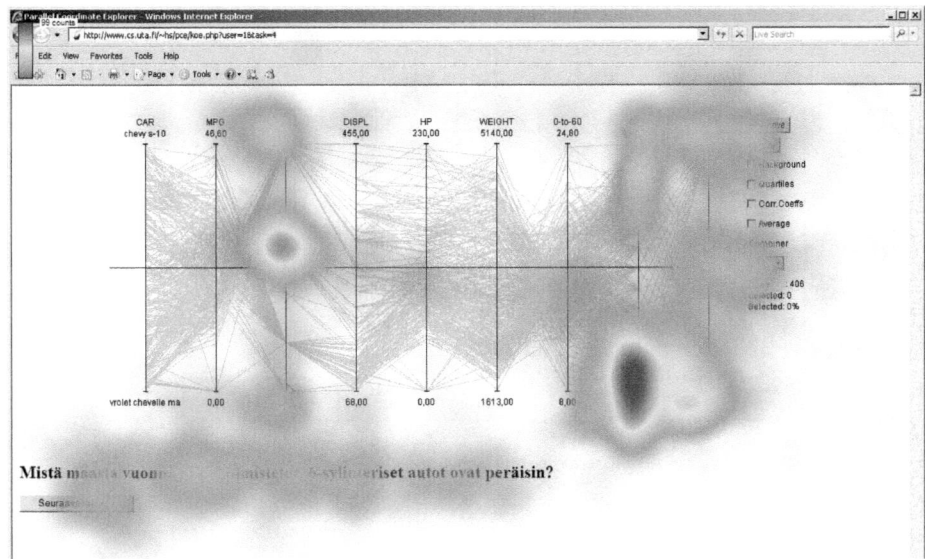

Fig. 3. Heatmap of fixation counts for task 4 over all users

Heatmaps are good for summarizing large quantities of data that would be next to impossible to gain insight into if presented numerically. Sometimes, as in the example above, heatmaps may give useful insight into the distribution of users' attention, especially if the task at hand is focused and simple enough.

Heatmaps are typically used in single-condition situations, or in multi-condition experiments without tests for statistical significance. Therefore heatmaps should primarily be used for data visualization instead of data analysis [28]. In addition, the heatmaps often do not come with all the relevant metadata, and being unaware of it can lead into false interpretations. Another issue is the attractiveness and apparent intuitiveness of heatmaps which can lead into over-interpretation.

6 Proportion of Time Spent on Areas-of-Interest

The heatmap-based analysis of fixations can be made more detailed if we divide the underlying visualization into "Areas of Interest (AOI)", basically by naming the parts of the visualization that are of interest. In many visualizations we have at least some static elements in the interface that allow to track when the user's gaze is fixated into them. If the visualization does not have any static elements at all, it is still possible to compute the fixations for dynamic elements, but it will be a technical challenge. In PCE, the only dynamic parts of the visualization are the selection constraints, making it easy define the AOIs. Figure 4 shows the AOI definitions that were used in the experiment [22].

Each area is named in Figure 4 after the axis and divided into three parts: top of the axis (1), axis itself (2), and bottom of the axis (3). For instance, for the first vertical axis from the left (CAR), CAR.1 refers to the area enclosing

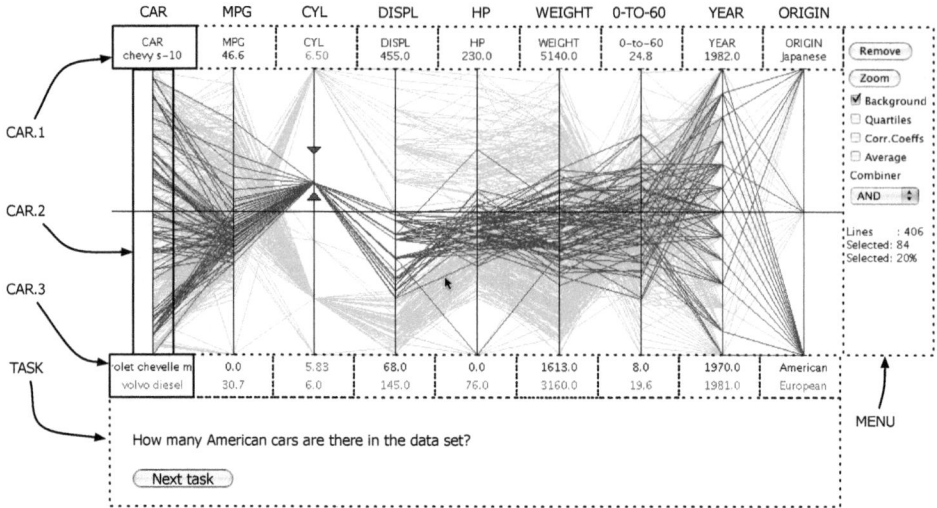

Fig. 4. Areas Of Interest (AOI) used in the analysis and their naming conventions

axis label and the maximum value, CAR.2 to the axis itself, and CAR.3 to the mimimun value and the selected value, if one polyline is chosen. Figure 4 shows in addition a visual query where all the six-cylinder cars have been highlighted (triangles at the CYL axis) and the one with the smallest engine displacement has been selected (a Volvo diesel, values shown in red below the labels of the axes).

Dividing the user interface of PCE into AOIs allows to list the areas that must be attended to solve a task. For example, solving task 0 ("How many American cars are there in the data set?") requires looking into the areas TASK (to read the task), ORIGIN.2 and ORIGIN.3 (to find and select "American" cars), and MENU (to read the number of selected cars). This is the optimal course of events which is rare in a real first-use situation. However, the comparison makes it easier to evaluate the design and implementation of a visualization by revealing which proportion of fixations is spent on the areas that are relevant in carrying out the task.

Figure 5 shows two balloon plots of the fixation data (produced with the package *gplots* of statistical system R [29]). In a balloon plot each cell contains a dot whose size reflects the relative magnitude of the corresponding component. The left-hand side plot shows the medians of fixations before entering an AOI, and the right-hand side plot shows the fixation duration means in an AOI. On the left, the grey background in a cell indicates an AOI that must be first attended to solve a task, and on the right the grey background shows all the cells that must be attended in a course of the task. Therefore, to approach the optimal solution, on the left a smaller value on grey background is "better" and on the right a bigger value on grey background is "better".

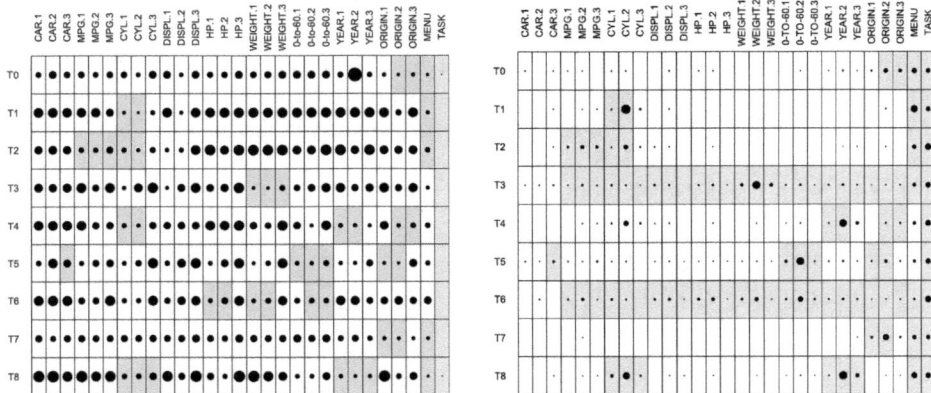

Fig. 5. On the left: balloon plot for AOI by Task: Medians of fixations before entering an AOI. On the right: Balloon plot for AOI by Task: Fixation duration means in an AOI. The mandatory AOIs for a task have a grey background.

In the experiment [22], the percentage of time spent on task-specific AOIs varied between 53% and 92%. The lowest percentages were observed on two open-ended tasks (3 and 6, 53% and 58%, respectively) and on the task with a complicated selection (task 4, 55%). The left balloon plot in Figure 5 shows the medians of fixations before entering the respective AOI and indicate that the important areas were found quickly (the balloons with grey background are small). The right side of Figure 5 plots the duration means in an AOI, and shows that the middle part of the axes drew longer fixations than either the top or bottom area. This is caused by the fact that the interactive part in the middle required more intense attention than the (mostly) static values at the ends.

7   Transitions between Areas-of-Interest

Both the heatmap and the AOI-based visualizations of fixation data ignore the order of fixations completely, which may leave important aspects of interaction unnoticed or even skew the observations. In this third method to visualize fixation data the focus is on the *transitions* between the Areas-of-Interest. This is a piecewise representation of gaze paths and does not show them as continuous objects as in a video overlay. Instead, the idea is that the relevant parts of the interaction should "pop out" as having more inter-area transitions, providing better insight to the course of events.

The following visualizations were produced by extracting the AOI transitions from eye tracker log files with an AWK [30] script that transformed the AOI data into a transition graph defined in the language DOT (part of the Graphviz project [31]). The DOT compiler was then used to lay out and produce an image of the transition graph.

The initial, plain versions of the graphs were hard to read because of the automatic layout. It completely broke the resemblance to the user interface, trashing the mental model for the UI, and made it hard to interpret the transitions. To force the axis AOIs to stay together, they were placed in the same subgraph. Now the Graphviz layout engine may move the subgraphs around, but not the nodes inside them. Figure 6 shows a transition graph for the AOIs shown in Figure 4 with its static elements, without any transitions.

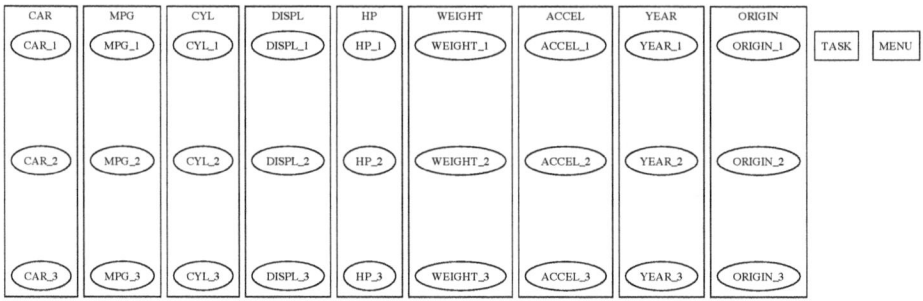

Fig. 6. Area-of-Interest elements in a transition graph. The subgraph structure constrainsts the nodes inside an axis area to stay together and in the correct order.

As seen in Figure 6, the period in axis names is replaced by underscore to allow indexing of associative arrays with the AOI names. Another change related to the AOIs is that the gaps between the axis AOI's (as defined in Figure 4) were removed to prevent frequent transitions to and from the AOIs to areas that do not belong to any AOI.

To reduce visual clutter in the transition graphs two additional encodings were introduced. Repeated transitions between two AOIs are represented as a single connection line and the number of transitions is encoded into the line width. In addition, the overall fixation time of an AOI is encoded into the line width of a node symbol. A dashed line is used to indicate a single transition and an AOI without any fixations.

Figure 7 shows a single user's transition graph for task 4. The focal point of attention is in the middle part of the YEAR axis, YEAR_2, which has the highest duration of fixations as indicated by the bold border of the node. As noted previously, it is a challenge to select one of the twelve items from a crowded YEAR axis. A similar selection from the five-value CYL axis is easier, and this participant does not even bother to check the lower limit of selection at all (no fixations in CYL_3).

The inter-AOI transitions are mainly between ORIGIN, YEAR, and TASK. This participant chose first the six-cylinder cars, then the year 1971, and finally read the selection from the ORIGIN axis. There are several confirmatory YEAR-ORIGIN and ORIGIN-TASK transitions. Overall, the attention is where it is supposed to be when solving this task.

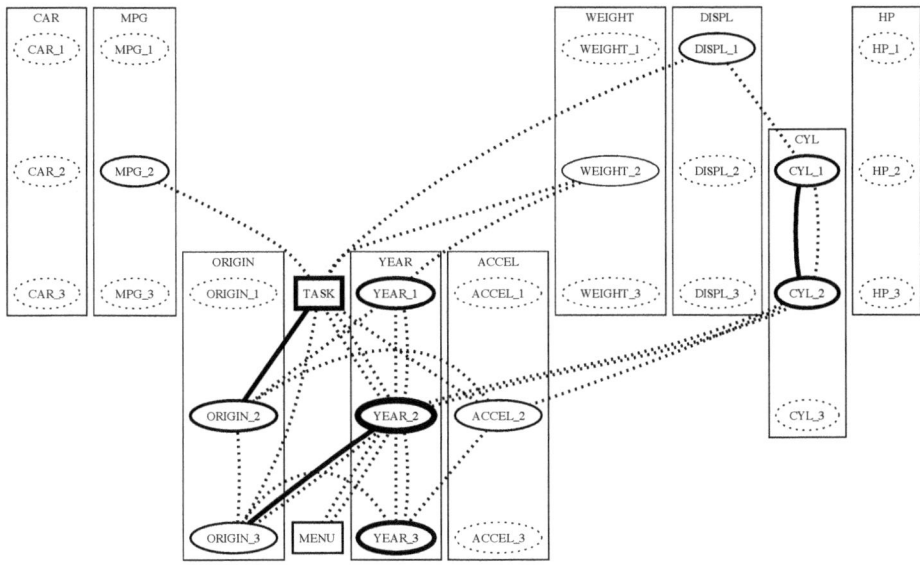

Fig. 7. Transition graph for a single user's task 4, "What is the origin of the six-cylinder cars that were manufactured in 1971?"

Figure 8 shows a transition graph of task 4 for all participants. Overall, the selection problem on the YEAR axis receives the most of the attention, but beyond that the situation is quite even. However, it is clear that the axes CYL, YEAR, and ORIGIN are in the focus as the layout sets them next to each other.

Figure 9 shows a typical single participant's transition graph for an exploratory task, which is here task 3: "How would you describe the cars that weigh over 4500 pounds?" The strategy is to select the cars having WEIGHT over 4500 and then scan the other axes in search of patterns. AOIs WEIGHT and TASK receive most of the attention and transitions. The middle parts of the axes are then attended and occasional drill-down hits the lower part of the axes. No attention is devoted to the axis labels, indicating that this participant knows the variable positions by now.

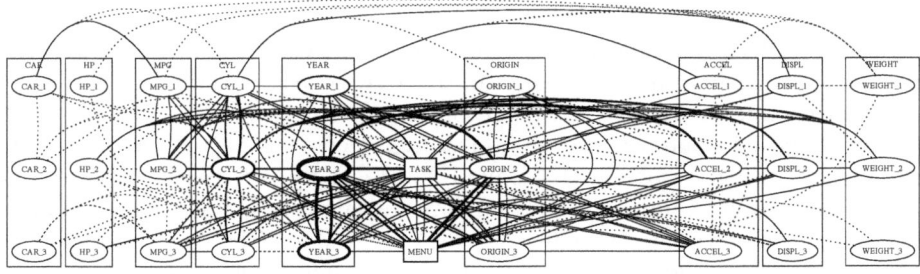

Fig. 8. Transition graph for task 4 over all participants

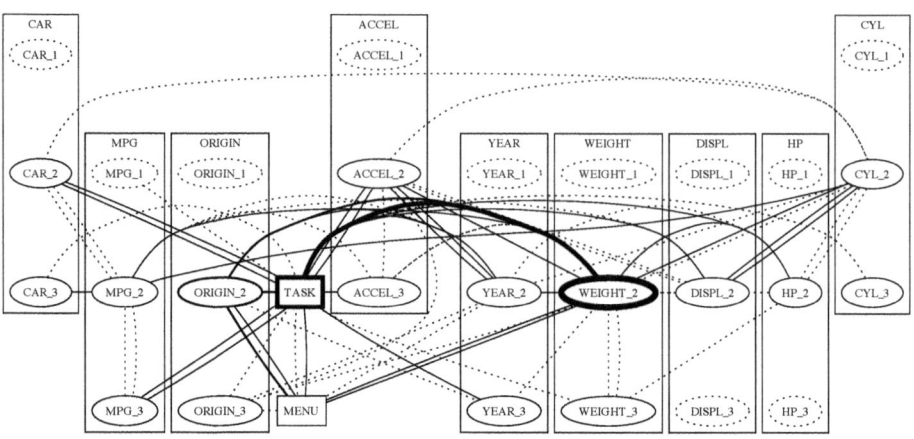

Fig. 9. Transition graph for task 3: "How would you describe the cars that weigh over 4500 pounds?"

8   Discussion

The proposed light-weight evaluation method is proposed as a trade-off between complex methods involving an array of qualitative and quantitative methods applied in a longitudinal study, and simple controlled experiments. The goal is to separate data collection and data interpretation as much as possible, and make the evaluation easier to repeat. When the AOIs are documented and the percentages are printed, the experiment is fairly easy to repeat and verify.

Instead of studying the participants' focus of attention by observation and interviewing, we advocate to use the eye tracking technology for it. What is really needed is "brain tracking", but eye tracking is a substitute while this technology matures. The problem with eye tracking is the amount of data collected even for a modest experimental setting. We discussed three approaches that avoid viewing all the video footage and provide useful visualizations of gaze data instead: heatmaps, AOI-based balloon plots, and AOI-based transition diagrams. These correspond roughly to three more general problem solving approaches: acquiring general overview, working top-down, and working bottom-up. Heatmaps are good for giving an overview of how an interface is really used, but on a high level only. The AOI-based balloon plots give a bit more fine-grained insight into how an interactive visualization is used, and the AOI-based transition graphs reveal the most common paths taken while using the visualization.

The proposed approach has the advantage that it is repeatable and, with some practice, can become a technique that is fast for a researcher to use. Eye tracking is, however, no panacea. There are caveats that a researcher should be aware of, such as the inherent inaccuracy of gaze data (the combined effect of tracker inaccuracy and the perceptual span of the human eye can yield offsets of up to 2 degrees of visual angle) and the sensitivity of the results on the algorithm used for estimating fixations [32]. The inaccuracy makes it difficult to apply eye tracking for visualizations that have densely packed information, such as those in Figure 5, though even there focusing on the areas of interest (the grey areas) can make the approach usable. And in many other cases the areas of interest are more sparsely located, such as in our example, or in many timeline visualization.

The proposed evaluation approach is simple and not a substitute to a longitudinal study with real users and tasks. However, we believe that the approximation of users' focus of attention with gaze data analysis is highly useful in revealing the issues that should certainly be addressed before a proposed visualization method is acceptable. The gaze data cannot prove that a certain method is a success, but it is impeccable in pointing out the major design flaws.

In this paper we have applied the proposed evaluation approach into one visualization method and repeated an earlier experiment. In the future, we plan to refine the evaluation method further, do additional experiments, and develop a software tool to streamline the gaze data visualization. In such a tool we could link the two gaze data visualizations which would allow rapid movement between the two views, i.e., spotting an interesting cell in a balloon plot would be a link into the corresponding transition graph and vice versa. One should be able to select and unselect included participants and tasks, and adjust thresholds for the diagrams. This clearly calls for a conventional multiple-view interface with dynamic controls and brushing.

Acknowledgements

We thank Tuuli Laivo for collecting the gaze data that was used in our example visualizations. This work was supported by the Academy of Finland (project 1129300). The work of the second author was supported by the Academy of Finland grant 1130044. The paper was written while he was visiting the University of Canterbury in Christchurch, New Zealand.

References

1. Spence, R.: Information Visualization – Design for Interaction. Prentice-Hall Europe, Pearson Education Ltd., Harlow, England (2007)
2. Ellis, G., Dix, A.: An explorative analysis of user evaluation studies in information visualisation. In: BELIV 2006 - Beyond Time and Errors: Novel Evaluation Methods for Information Visualisation (AVI 2006 Workshop). ACM Press, New York (2006)
3. Nielsen, J., Pernice, K.: Eyetracking Web Usability. New Riders Press, Indianapolis (2009)
4. Posner, M.I.: Orienting of attention. Quarterly Journal of Experimental Psychology 32, 3–25 (1980)
5. Saraiya, P., North, C., Duca, K.: An insight-based methodology for evaluating bioinformatics visualizations. IEEE Transactions on Visualization and Computer Graphics 11(4), 443–456 (2005)
6. Saraiya, P., North, C., Lam, V., Duca, K.A.: An insight-based longitudinal study of visual analytics. IEEE Transactions on Visualization and Computer Graphics 12(6), 1511–1522 (2006)

7. Shneiderman, B., Plaisant, C.: Strategies for evaluating information visualization tools: multi-dimensional in-depth long-term case studies. In: BELIV 2006: Proceedings of the 2006 AVI Workshop on Beyond Time and Errors, pp. 1–7. ACM, New York (2006)

8. Isenberg, P., Zuk, T., Collins, C., Carpendale, S.: Grounded evaluation of information visualizations. In: BELIV 2008: Proceedings of the 2008 Conference on Beyond Time and Errors, pp. 1–8. ACM, New York (2008)

9. Bertini, E., Plaisant, C., Santucci, G.: Beliv 2006: beyond time and errors; novel evaluation methods for information visualization. Interactions 14(3), 59–60 (2007)

10. Bertini, E., Perer, A., Plaisant, C., Santucci, G.: Beliv 2008: Beyond time and errors: novel evaluation methods for information visualization. In: CHI 2008: CHI 2008 Extended Abstracts on Human Factors in Computing Systems, pp. 3913–3916. ACM, New York (2008)

11. Andrews, K.: Evaluation comes in many guises. In: BELIV 2008: Beyond Time and Errors: Novel Evaluation Methods for Information Visualization (revised position paper; CHI 2008 workshop) (April 2008)

12. O'Connell, T.A., Choong, Y.Y.: User-centered evaluation methodology for interactive visualizations. In: BELIV 2008: Beyond Time and Errors: Novel Evaluation Methods for Information Visualization (position paper; CHI 2008 workshop) (April 2008)

13. Robertson, G.G.: Beyond time and errors – position statement. In: BELIV 2008: Beyond Time and Errors: Novel Evaluation Methods for Information Visualization (position paper; CHI 2008 workshop) (April 2008)

14. Goldberg, J.H., Kotval, X.P.: Computer interface evaluation using eye movements: methods and constructs. International Journal of Industrial Ergonomics 24, 631–645 (1999)

15. Jacob, R.J.K., Karn, K.S.: Eye tracking in human-computer interaction and usability research: Ready to deliver the promises. In: Hyona, J., Radach, R., Deubel, H. (eds.) The Mind's Eye: Cognitive and Applied Aspects of Eye Movement Research, pp. 573–605. Elsevier Science, Amsterdam (2003)

16. Ramloll, R., Trepagnier, C., Sebrechts, M., Beedasy, J.: Gaze data visualization tools: Opportunities and challenges. In: International Conference on Information Visualisation, pp. 173–180 (2004)

17. Špakov, O.: iComponent - Device-Independent Platform for Analyzing Eye Movement Data and Developing Eye-based Applications. In: Dissertations in Interactive Technology, vol. 9, University of Tampere (2008)

18. North, C.: Visualization Viewpoints: Toward measuring visualization insight. IEEE Computer Graphics and Applications 26(3), 6–9 (2006)

19. Hyrskykari, A., Ovaska, S., Majaranta, P., Räihä, K.J., Lehtinen, M.: Gaze path stimulation in retrospective think-aloud. Journal of Eye-Movement Research 2(4), 1–18 (2008)

20. Siirtola, H.: Direct manipulation of parallel coordinates. In: CHI 2000: CHI 2000 Extended Abstracts on Human Factors in Computing Systems, pp. 119–120. ACM, New York (2000)

21. Siirtola, H.: Direct manipulation of parallel coordinates. In: IV 2000: Proceedings of the International Conference on Information Visualization, pp. 373–378. IEEE Computer Society, Los Alamitos (2000)

22. Siirtola, H., Laivo, T., Heimonen, T., Räihä, K.J.: Visual perception of parallel coordinate visualizations. In: IV 2009: Proceedings of the Thirteenth International

Conference on Information Visualization, pp. 3–9. IEEE Computer Society Press, Los Alamitos (2009)
23. Siirtola, H.: Parallel Coordinate Explorer (2000),
    http://www.cs.uta.fi/~hs/pce/
24. Nielsen, J.: Usability Engineering. Academic Press, Inc., London (1993)
25. Siirtola, H., Räihä, K.J.: Interacting with parallel coordinates. Interacting with Computers 18(6), 1278–1309 (2006)
26. Pomplun, M., Ritter, H., Velichkovsky, B.: Disambiguating complex visual information: Towards communication of personal views of a scene. Perception (25), 931–948 (1996)
27. Wooding, D.S.: Fixation maps: quantifying eye-movement traces. In: ETRA 2002: Proceedings of the 2002 Symposium on Eye Tracking Research & Applications, pp. 31–36. ACM, New York (2002)
28. Bojko, A.: Informative or misleading? Heatmaps deconstructed. In: Jacko, J.A. (ed.) Human-Computer Interaction, HCII 2009, Part I. LNCS, vol. 5610, pp. 30–39. Springer, Heidelberg (2009)
29. R Development Core Team: R: A Language and Environment for Statistical Computing. R Foundation for Statistical Computing, Vienna, Austria (2010) ISBN 3-900051-07-0
30. Aho, A.V., Kernighan, B.W., Weinberger, P.J.: The AWK programming language. Addison-Wesley Longman Publishing Co., Inc., Boston (1987)
31. Graphviz: Graphviz – graph visualization software (2008),
    http://www.graphviz.org/
32. Salvucci, D.D., Goldberg, J.H.: Identifying fixations and saccades in eye-tracking protocols. In: ETRA 2000: Proceedings of the 2000 Symposium on Eye Tracking Research & Applications, pp. 71–78. ACM, New York (2000)

Giga-Scale Multiresolution Volume Rendering on Distributed Display Clusters

Sebastian Thelen[1], Joerg Meyer[2], Achim Ebert[1], and Hans Hagen[1]

[1] University of Kaiserslautern, Kaiserslautern, Germany
{s_thelen,ebert,hagen}@cs.uni-kl.de
[2] University of California, Irvine, U.S.A.
jmeyer@uci.edu

Abstract. Visualizing the enormous level of detail comprised in many of today's data sets is a challenging task and demands special processing techniques as well as a presentation on appropriate display devices. Desktop computers and laptops are often not suited for this task because data sets are simply too large and the limited screen size of these devices prevents users from perceiving the entire data set and severely restricts collaboration. Large high-resolution displays that combine the images of multiple smaller devices to form one large display area have proven to be an adequate solution to the ever-growing quantity of available data. The displays offer enough screen real estate to visualize such data sets entirely and facilitate collaboration, since multiple users are able to perceive the information at the same time. For an interactive visualization, the CPUs on the cluster driving the GPUs can be used to split up the computation of a scene into different areas, where each area is computed by a different rendering node.

In this paper we focus on volumetric data sets and introduce a dynamic subdivision scheme incorporating multi-resolution wavelet representation to visualize data sets with several gigabytes of voxel data interactively on distributed rendering clusters. The approach makes efficient use of the resources available on modern graphics cards which mainly limit the amount of data that can be visualized. The implementation was successfully tested on a tiled display comprised of 25 compute nodes driving 50 LCD panels.

Keywords: High-Resolution Displays, Large-Scale Data Sets, Volume Rendering.

1   Introduction

Many data sets that are acquired in today's applications exceed the computational capabilities of desktop PCs or workstations. The Visible Human Project [34], for instance, provides 40GB of data for the female cadaver, thus asking for techniques to process an enormous amount of information. A lot of research has focused on developing methods for handling such large data sets. Solutions include the parallelization of the render process or the invention of

A. Ebert et al. (Eds.): HCIV (INTERACT) 2009, LNCS 6431, pp. 142–162, 2011.

level-of-detail or data compression techniques. The benefits of these methods are undeniable, however, one limitation remained for a long time: the visualization of large amounts of information and the advantage of having high-resolution data sets also require a large amount of screen real estate.

The pixel count of regular computer monitors is usually too low to display complex data sets at their full level of resolution. For three-dimensional data sets, the gap between the amount of information contained in a partially transparent volume and the available screen space becomes even more obvious.

Zooming+panning (e.g., Google Earth navigation) or focus+context (i.e., a high-resolution focus view and a low-resolution context view) approaches offer ways to deal with this problem but for some data sets these methods are not appropriate. For instance, such data sets can only be fully perceived when they are displayed entirely. In the last couple of years tiled high-resolution displays have become more and more popular due to advances in display and hardware technology. Tiled high-resolution displays combine the resolution of multiple devices to form one large display area. Two basic approaches have emerged: *projector-based* and *monitor-based* tiled displays. Multiple projectors can be combined to form a projector-based tiled display. The challenge is to calibrate the system, as projector images are usually distorted and non-uniform in terms of color and luminance. LCDs represent the most affordable way to build a large high-resolution display. LCD-based systems are easier to set up since they usually require less space, and problems like lens distortions or mismatches of color temperature and luminance are limited to a minimum. Further, the resolution of today's average LCDs is higher than the one of most projectors, so that it is relatively easy to build systems with a resolution of several hundred megapixels.

In this paper we focus on the development of a volume rendering application for large scalar data sets on tiled displays. The display system we work with is a tiled wall consisting of fifty 30 inch LCDs arranged in a 10×5 grid. Instead of the traditional isosurfaces, i.e., regions representing a constant scalar value within the data set, we use a direct volume rendering approach based on 3D texture mapping for visualization. The size of data sets that can be visualized on a computer is mainly limited by the available amount of video RAM on the graphics card. Therefore, the main contribution of this paper is the description of a technique that fully exploits the resources of a render node in the display cluster. We combine octree-based out-of-core frustum clipping with a wavelet-based multi-resolution representation of the data to increase the visual quality of the renderings.

The rest of the paper is structured as follows: Section 2 gives a brief overview of current literature relevant to our work. Section 3 describes the data structure we employ, while section 4 deals with software- and hardware related aspects. In section 5, we introduce the actual method that allows us to visualize high-resolution data sets on large displays, followed by a description of implementational aspects in section 6. Section 7 discusses the results we achieve on our system that are more deeply analyzed in section 8. Section 9 compares our system to other distributed rendering systems. The paper ends with a conclusion and an outlook on future work.

2   Related Work

In its simplest form, 3D texture mapping is limited by the fact that the original data has to fit entirely into the texture memory of the graphics card. To overcome this limitation, LaMar et al. [20] describe a multi-resolution approach that is based on octree subdivision. The leaves of the octree define the original data and the internal nodes define lower-resolution versions. Artifacts are minimized by blending between different resolution levels. Weiler et al. [48] extend this approach. Their hierarchical level-of-detail representation allows consistent interpolation between resolution levels. The described methods are relevant to our work since we also produce multi-resolution images of the data set. However, in our case multi-resolution refers to the detail levels of tiles within the display wall and not to regions of different resolution within the resulting picture. The techniques above are able to handle data sets that do not fit into the texture memory of the graphics hardware. Nonetheless, data still has to fit into the computer's main memory.

The data structure we exploit in this paper has been described by Meyer et al. [31]. The authors use a dynamic subdivision scheme that incorporates space-subdivision based on octrees and wavelet compression. It has been used to implement a network-based rendering application that is able to visualize data sets between 20MB and 76GB size by first transferring low-resolution versions of the data via network and then gradually refine them [30]. Plate et al. [38] developed the Octreemizer, a hierarchical paging scheme that uses octrees to deal with data sets that exceed the size of RAM. The Octreemizer however only exploits the octree subdivision characteristics without incorporating any data compression scheme.

Various attempts have been made to parallelize rendering on a cluster of computers by image-order [37,2,3], object-order [13,16] or hybrid approaches [14]. The aim of these methods is to achieve a speed-up in the rendering process by combining the computational power of a set of computers. Far less research though has focused on utilizing clusters to generate high-resolution results of volume rendered images on high-resolution displays.

Vol-a-Tile [46] was able to visualize seismic data sets on the 5×3 GeoWall2 [15] display grid at EVL. The authors present a master-slave prototype that uses an MPI-based rendering library and an OptiStore data streaming server. Application specific implementation details are not given. The TeraVoxel project [23] founded at the California Institute for Technology was able to interactively render a $256 \times 256 \times 1024$ data set on a 3840×2400 display using four VolumePro 1000 cards by employing pipelined associative blending operators in a sort-last configuration, contrary to our sort-first approach. Schwarz et al. [45] describe an octree approach for frustum clipping to make better use of system resources without exploiting the power of a multi-resolution wavelet representation and give a comparison of various parallel image- and object-order as well as hybrid volume rendering techniques. QSplat [43] is a multi-resolution rendering system for displaying isosurfaces out of point data sets. It also uses a progressive refinement technique but generates images using a splatting approach (see section 5.1). Despite the increasing popularity of high-resolution displays, until today the ultimate general purpose software solution for driving all different types and configurations of displays is still missing. Various commercial and non-commercial software solutions are available, differing mainly in the way they perform distributed rendering and the display configurations they can handle. Distributed rendering strategies were first analyzed and classified by Molnar et al. [33]. The authors identified three classes of rendering algorithms, characterized by the stage in which geometry is distributed among the nodes (sort-first, sort-middle and sort-last). Alternatively, distributed rendering can be classified by the execution mode of applications on the cluster [9]. In master-slave mode, an instance of the application is executed on each node of the cluster, while in client-server mode a client node issues rendering tasks to the render servers via network. A good survey on distributed rendering software was given by Ni et al. [36] and Raffin et al. [39]. Some of the best known software packages include CAVELib [8], VRjuggler [5], Syzygy [44], AnyScreen [10], OpenSG [40], Chromium [17], NAVER [18], Jinx [47] , and CGLX [11].

3   Data Structures

Rendering of large data sets in real time requires data reduction techniques and hierarchical subdivision of the data set. This chapter describes a space- and time-efficient, combined space subdivision and multi-resolution technique for volumetric data [30].

3.1   Adaptive Octree

Large volumetric data sets, which are typically arranged in a regular Cartesian grid, are often too complex to be rendered in real time on today's hardware for cluster nodes and with current 3D texture-based rendering techniques. Therefore, they must be reduced to a reasonable size, so that each node can quickly access the appropriate section of the 3D volume and render this portion of the data almost instantaneously. The slice format in which volume data often comes is not suitable for this purpose, because too many files need to be opened in order to display a 3D volume from cross-sections. Opening large numbers of files has proven to be prohibitively slow.

Therefore, an octree space subdivision algorithm is employed. Instead of using a database, the Unix file system and an efficient indexing scheme are used to access the right block of data instantly. The octree method is illustrated in Fig. 1. Three simple binary decisions (left or right, front or back, and top or bottom) are necessary at each level to determine the position of a voxel in an octree. Each decision corresponds to a two bit index, which can take on $2^3 = 8$ states (0-7),

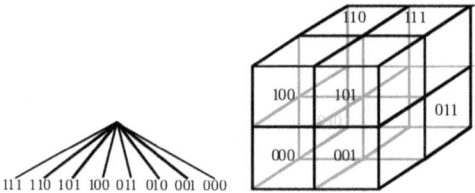

Fig. 1. Octant indexing scheme used to represent paths in the octree

i.e., the eight child nodes of the octree. The number represents the file name, and several numbers in a file name indicate an octree traversal path. With this fast indexing scheme, it is possible to traverse the tree almost instantaneously in order to get to the leave of the tree which carries the data.

The main advantage of the octree data structure is the early termination of the traversal in branches that are empty. It works best for data sets where the object is located near the center of the data cube and has an empty or nearly empty background (e.g., for CT or MRI scans), but it also works for sparse data sets. The information is determined in a preprocessing step when creating the octree data structure. Empty areas are not stored, saving a significant amount of disk space and RAM.

Several space subdivision algorithms have been implemented in order to compare their performance and scalability [32] with the octree approach. Binary Space Partition (BSP) trees, for example, are based on a binary subdivision of three-dimensional space. A root node is recursively subdivided in alternating directions, in a cycle of several subdivisions (one for each dimension). Empty regions are marked, so that they can be skipped in order to speed up the rendering procedure.

A statistical analysis based on typical data sets (CT and MRI scans) has been conducted, and it was found that for the same data set size the octree technique consistently outperformed other techniques like the BSP tree both in terms of preprocessing time and, more importantly, traversal time during rendering [31].

At this point, depending on the depth of the octree, the data block to be read from the octree may still be too large to fit into the texture buffer of a rendering node's graphics card. For this reason, the leaves are stored in a multi-resolution wavelet format, which is described in the next section.

3.2 3D Non-standard Haar Wavelet Decomposition

We use a 3D non-standard Haar wavelet decomposition method to store the leaves. The benefit of using this method is the fact that low-resolution information can be stored at the beginning of the file, and if more detail is desired, more data in the form of detail coefficients can be loaded in order to refine the image. Depending on the number of wavelet levels, a tremendous reduction of data can be accomplished with acceptable visual artifacts in the rendered image. On the first level, only 1/8th of the data needs to be rendered, on the second

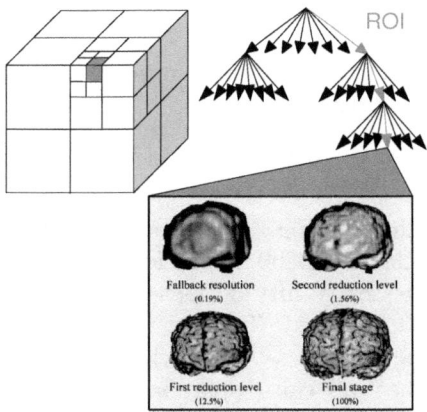

Fig. 2. Octree space subdivision uses multi-resolution wavelet representation for the leaves

level 1/64th (less than 2% of the total data set), and so forth. This exponential reduction leads to a significant acceleration and memory savings.

The volume pyramid can be compressed by removing small coefficients. A threshold determines whether a coefficient can be set to zero or not. Real numbers with fractions can be quantized, e.g., by removing the fraction part, and low-frequency coefficients could be stored at higher precision than high-frequency coefficients. However, one of the most important advantages of the wavelet approach is the fact that we can use the same amount of memory to store the hierarchy as to store the original volume. Typically, we would use float as the data type to store detail coefficients. We can replace this data type by integers with no loss of precision, and therefore we can make use of the fact that integer arithmetic is much faster than floating point arithmetic [7].

In our implementation, we use the following method: Volume data is represented as a three-dimensional array of scalar values. The resolution is 8 bits, which allows for 256 different gray levels. For the wavelet transformation, we use an unsigned integer (32 bits) to store coefficients, which is the same size as a float (4 bytes). Initially, our data is stored in bits 23...30. The leftmost bit 31 is usually unused. Only when the algorithm computes the sum of two data items in order to determine the reduced pixel, i.e., their representation in the lower resolution image, the intermediate result can become temporarily larger than 255, which causes an overflow into this unused bit. For the computation of reduced pixel values and detail coefficients, a division by two is involved, which corresponds to a bit shift to the right, i.e., an underflow. Since we have three dimensions per cycle, we can have a 3 bit underflow. We have 22 bits available. This means that we can apply the algorithm 7 times before we run out of bits. This is sufficient, since the data set is then already reduced to $(1/8)^7 = 4.77 \times 10^{-7}$. This means, for instance, that a typical data set of $256^3 = 16,777,216$ voxels is then already reduced to 8 voxels.

4   System Details

The following section discusses hard- and software related aspects of the display cluster used for the visualizations.

4.1   Cluster Display Wall

Our visualization cluster (see Fig. 3) consists of 25 PowerMac G5 computers, equipped with nVidia GeForce 6800 and nVidia Quadro FX4500 graphics cards. These 25 compute nodes drive fifty 30 inch Apple Cinema Displays that have been arranged in a 10 × 5 grid. Together they form a 200 megapixel tiled display wall which measures 23 × 9 ft. Each screen has a native resolution of 2560 × 1600 pixels. The wall can display scenes at a maximum resolution of 25,600 × 8,000 pixels. A designated front-end node processes user input and launches applications. The current operating system on the cluster is Mac OS X Tiger.

Fig. 3. 200 megapixel tiled display cluster measuring 23 × 9 ft

4.2   CGLX

As mentioned in section 2, there exists a variety of different distributed rendering libraries. Our implementation of the volume renderer is based on CGLX [11], a Cross-Platform Cluster Graphic Library. CGLX was developed at the California Institute for Telecommunications and Information Technology at UC San Diego and is a flexible and transparent OpenGL-based graphics framework for distributed visualization systems in a master-slave setup. Master-slave architectures run an instance of the application on each compute node of the cluster. Communication between nodes is realized through a light-weight, thread-based network communication protocol. Attempting to be as transparent as possible to the developer, CGLX offers a GLUT-like (OpenGL Utility Toolkit) interface, which allows the library to intercept and interpret OpenGL calls, providing a distributed large scale OpenGL context on tiled displays.

Theoretically, existing applications can be ported to CGLX by just changing the includes from `GL/glut.h` to `clgX.h` and calling `cglXOrtho`, CGLX's equivalent to `glOrtho`. However, in practice things like synchronized access to global variables or shared resources (e.g., files) require some more tweaking.

5   System Design

When doing volume rendering of large-scale data sets on desktop computers, the limited resources of the system pose restrictions to the visualizations. Above all, the available amount of video RAM determines the size of data sets that can be visualized on a given system. The same restrictions apply when designing cluster applications, where each node computes the entire scene. The waste of system resources is enormous, since nodes allocate memory for the entire scene, but only display a small part of it. Often however, this approach is favored by distributed rendering libraries. Since libraries try to be transparent, programmers write code almost as if they are developing applications for desktop PCs. The library lets each node compute the entire scene and sets viewport and viewing frustum according to the location of its screens within the grid. While this is a clear advantage for the developer, it leads to a waste of system resources, which we try to avoid with algorithm described in the following section.

5.1   Rendering Algorithm

Different methods have been developed to visualize volumetric data sets by approximating the volume rendering equation [29]. As opposed to isosurface algorithms [24], these techniques simulate the propagation of light in a transparent light emitting and absorbing medium.

Raycasting [21,19,42] is an image-order method that casts rays through each pixel of the viewing plane into the volume and samples along the ray. The method is able to yield high-quality results but is computationally expensive. In order to be interactive, it requires sophisticated adaptive sampling schemes, empty space skipping, and early ray termination. Their implementation is partly supported by today's modern programmable GPUs. However, even though raycasting is able to produce the best optical results, it generally means having to trade speed for image quality. We decided that raycasting is not going to pay off when the goal is to achieve interactive framerates on a fifty tile display wall.

Splatting [50,49,43] is a rendering approach in which voxels of the volume are projected in back-to-front order onto the 2D viewing plane. Splat kernels, e.g., Gaussian kernels, are used to blend splats and generate smooth images. Splatting in general is faster than raycasting, but the implementation is tricky and results depend on the choice of the splat kernel. Therefore, splatting was not our first choice rendering algorithm.

Texture mapping [51,6,41] treats volumetric data as 3D textures that are
mapped to sets of proxy geometry. The general approach is to map data
sets to a stack of view-aligned planes via trilinear interpolation. Afterwards,
blending of adjacent planes generates a continuous three-dimensional visualization of the volume. Texture mapping is very efficient on modern GPUs,
since trilinear interpolation is hard-wired on today's graphics cards. Furthermore, the technique is easy to implement and produces good-quality results.
Therefore, we decided to implement a rendering algorithm that is based on
this approach.

It is worth pointing out that our prototype could theoretically be adapted to
use any of the other rendering approaches. Most changes would concentrate on
the main render loop and not on the data structure employed in our algorithm.
We want to make full use of the resources of each rendering node and determine
which parts of a scene its monitors are going to display. The rendering node
allocates resources only for a portion of the data set and uses the available video
memory to display its subvolume at the highest possible quality. For doing so, we
make use of the data structure described in section 3. The volume subdivision of
the octree is well suited for being used in a frustum clipping step (see section 6.1).
It allows rendering nodes to disregard parts of a scene that do not have to be
displayed. These parts do not need to reside in RAM and do not need to occupy
precious texture memory. The wavelet representation of the octree data allows
rendering nodes to determine a compression level for the subvolumes, so that
they still fit in their graphics card's texture memory and at the same time provide
the highest possible level of detail.

As a result we end up with a scene in which each LCD of the grid displays
a portion of the volume at an individual but maximal quality. For large-scale
data sets this quality can differ by a factor of $8 - 64$ (which corresponds to $1 - 2$
wavelet levels) from the results that can be achieved on a desktop PC.

5.2   Progressive Refinement

When transforming the volume (by translation, rotation or scaling operations)
frustum clipping has to be rerun because parts of the data set might fall into a
different region of the display wall. Frustum clipping can slow the system down
because it implicates time consuming file operations to load new data chunks
from hard disk into main memory. Therefore, it is impossible to clip at interactive rates. Our solution to this bottleneck is a fallback texture. The fallback
texture permanently resides in the graphics card's texture memory and contains
the entire data set which is loaded only once at start-up time. Whenever the
volume is transformed, i.e., when the user uses the mouse to change the current position or scaling factor of the volume, we switch from the individually
computed subvolumes of a node to the fallback texture. The size of the fallback texture is chosen in a way that each rendering node maintains a predefined

minimum frame rate. That way we keep the system responsive and guarantee that the volume is displayed at any given time in its current position. Because the fallback texture contains the entire data set and has to be stored once on each node, its detail level is usually lower than the ones that result from the clipping process.

When the mouse is released, i.e., when user interaction is paused, the system gradually increments a counter, which determines the detail level. As a consequence, the image is gradually refined up to the maximum level of detail each graphics card can display.

Data sets can comprise several gigabytes and are stored in the octree-wavelet format. The size of the octree bricks is determined by the octree depth - a parameter that is specified by the user. The deeper an octree is, the more brick files there are and the smaller the brick files will be. However, loading the required information from these files in just one step may take too long. The data organization of the brick files allows a rendering node to load the content incrementally. The content of the files is organized in such a way that the data of the highest wavelet compression appears at the beginning of a file and is followed by the detail coefficients of lower wavelet levels (see section 3). Thus, it is possible to first load the lowest detail level and then gradually refine by sequentially loading detail coefficients for the reconstruction. In practice this means, that we start at a level i, display the data set at that resolution and then, triggered by a timer, switch to level $i - 1$, $i - 2$ and so forth. This way, after having interacted with the volume, the user is provided with instantaneous visual feedback.

Progressive refinement including fallback textures keeps the system responsive and enables users to explore data sets interactively. For small movements through the volume, where only parts of a scene change, the user experience could in the future be improved by loading additional high-resolution data around a hull of the frustum.

Synchronization between nodes is achieved through the render library's built-in synchronization mechanism. Before OpenGL render buffers are swapped, a barrier synchronization lets the system stall until all threads reach the barrier. While this means having to wait for the slowest node in the cluster, it gives us a way to switch synchronously between wavelet levels during progressive refinement and to reduce artifacts. Note, that within a tile the wavelet level is always constant, in contrast to the method that was presented by LaMar et al. [20]. Their algorithm generates regions of varying resolution within the final image.

6   Implementation

This section discusses implementation details of the frustum clipping and texture mapping stage.

6.1   Out-of-Core Frustum Clipping

During the clipping stage each rendering node determines for each of its monitors (i.e., two in our case) which parts of the data set they are going to display depending on the current view. This yields a subvolume for each screen for which the according files are loaded at the node. The subvolume is loaded at the maximum possible resolution, so that it still fits into a predefined portion of the texture memory. As a result, frustum clipping yields a partial copy of the entire data structure from hard disk in a node's main memory, ready to be visualized by 3D texture mapping.

To determine if an octree brick is going to be displayed by a monitor, we calculate where on the tiled display the eight corners of an octree brick are going to appear, i.e., we project them into 2D space and calculate their window coordinates. Determining the window coordinates (wx, wy) of a given point $v = (ox, oy, oz, 1.0)$ in object space under a modelview matrix M, a projection matrix P and viewport V can be accomplished via OpenGL's `gluProject` method. `gluProject` first computes $v' = P \cdot M \cdot v$. The actual window coordinates are obtained through

$$wx = V[0] + V[2] \cdot (v'[0] + 1)/2 \qquad (1)$$
$$wy = V[1] + V[3] \cdot (v'[1] + 1)/2. \qquad (2)$$

wx and wy specify the window coordinates of point v. The viewport V of course is defined by the size of the tiled display, i.e., $25,600 \times 8,000$ in our case. The projection matrix P is the matrix that orthogonally projects the viewing frustum to the viewport V. Since we transform the volume by manipulating OpenGL's texture matrix T, we use its inverse T^{-1} as an input to `gluProject` instead of the modelview matrix M (inverse, because T manipulates texture coordinates and not the texture image).

Once the window coordinates of the eight brick points are known, their bounding box is tested for intersection with the area of each LCD in the grid. The intersections with the screen of a node define a rectangular subvolume whose content we load from hard disk. The wavelet representation of the octree bricks allows us to load the subvolume at a detail level, that will not exceed a predefined number of voxels n. The wavelet level for a subvolume of dimensions dx, dy, dz is calculated as follows:

$wavelet\_level = 0;$
$cMod = 1;$
while $(dx/cMod) \cdot (dy/cMod) \cdot (dz/cMod) > n$ **do**
    $wavelet\_level + +;$
    $cMod = 2 \cdot cMod;$
end while

We limit textures to $n = 16.7 \times 10^6$ voxels. A three-dimensional RGBA texture containing that many voxels has a size of 64MB. Notice, that we have to store three textures at each node: One high-resolution texture for each of the two monitors that are connected to a node and one common low-resolution fallback texture containing the entire data set.

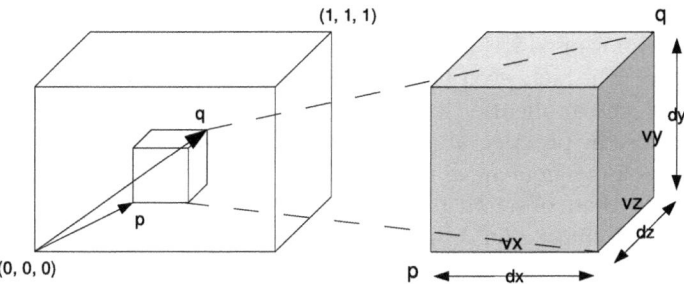

Fig. 4. Mapping information

6.2 Assembling the Volume

Now that we have buffers containing different regions of the data set at different levels of resolution, the next step is to render them using the texture mapping approach discussed in section 5.1. Therefore, data chunks have to be assembled to form the entire volume. Since buffers represent 3D textures, one can think of two approaches to assemble them: The first approach maps each subvolume to its own stack of view-aligned proxy geometry, whose size and position within object space depends on the particular subvolume. The second approach maps each subvolume to the same (full screen) stack of view-aligned proxy geometry but scales and translates each texture so that it appears at the right position when being mapped. We chose the second approach, because it can easily be realized with the meta information that comes with each buffer and is provided by the data structure that implements the wavelet-octree (see Fig. 4).

The following facts are known about each subvolume: vx, vy and vz denote the buffer's axis dimensions. As explained above, $vx \cdot vy \cdot vz \leq 16.7 \times 10^6$ holds. Further, the rectangle's two diagonal points $p = (px, py, pz)$ and $q = (qx, qy, qz)$ are known. Their coordinates are normalized with respect to the full size of the data set, so $(0, 0, 0)$ and $(1, 1, 1)$ span the entire volume. p and q allow us to compute the actual portion of the data set, that is represented by all $vx \cdot vy \cdot vz$ voxels through $dx = qx - px$, $dy = qy - py$ and $dz = qz - pz$. Furthermore, p provides us the normalized offset within the entire volume with respect to the origin $(0, 0, 0)$.

Now, the calculation of appropriate scaling factors and translation vectors to place the texture at the right location in the volume is straight forward.

7 Results

Limiting the size of textures to 16.7×10^6 voxels, i.e., 64MB for an RGBA texture, does not seem logical considering the fact that each graphics cards is equipped with 256MB VRAM. However, each node maintains three textures, all with a maximum size of 64MB, resulting in a total of 192MB. Another 31.25MB are used for the framebuffer of each display supporting a resolution of 2560×1600

pixels. Thus, only 32.75MB remain for additional operations. The calculation shows that a limit of 64MB per texture results in an optimal use of the available video resources. In fact, even the main memory workload of a node is kept low. Theoretically, the application only needs to allocate main memory for all three texture buffers. In practice about twice the amount of memory is needed due to the internal management of data. If more physical memory was added to the graphics cards, these observations would scale accordingly, and the visual quality of the displayed image would further improve. A variety of factors influence the quality of visualizations:

- Data sets themselves influence quality in that their dimensions partly determine the level-of-detail. Data sets consisting of many slices and therefore having a large extension in z-direction will not be displayed at the same detail level as data sets with fewer slices.
- The octree depth has a big influence on the final result. An octree of depth one partitions the entire volume into eight bricks, resulting in a rather coarse subdivision for the clipping process. An octree of depth two, however, produces 64 bricks and increases the quality since frustum clipping is able to extract smaller subvolumes that better represent the actual portion of data to be displayed.
- Last but not least, the current view has a strong effect on the detail level. Zooming-in maps fewer octree bricks to a tile and can therefore increase the level-of-detail. Rotations and translations have a similar influence.

Fig. 5(a) depicts a typical multi-resolution scene, where each monitor displays at its own tile-specific wavelet level. Note, that multi-resolution in this case refers to potentially different wavelet levels between tiles and that the level of detail within a tile is constant. The data that is visualized is a histology data set of a human cadaver brain. In order to illustrate the wavelet distribution within the wall, screens have been color coded in Fig. 5(b). Tiles marked red correspond to regions of wavelet level 2, meaning that these LCDs display the data set at $1/64 = 1.5\%$ of the original resolution. Green tiles correspond to areas of wavelet

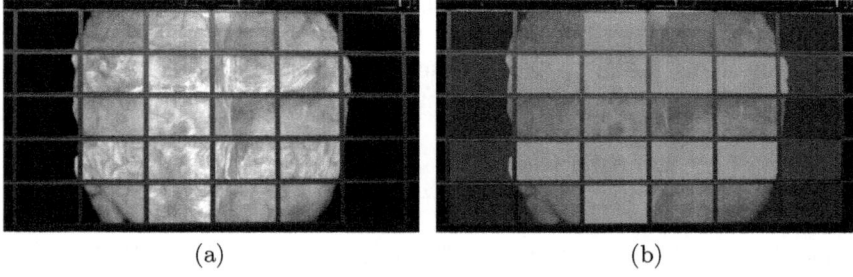

(a)   (b)

Fig. 5. (a) Multi-resolution rendering of the Toga data set. (b) Wavelet level distribution. Red corresponds to tiles of level 2 ($1/64 = 1.5\%$ of original quality), green to level 1 ($1/8 = 12.5\%$ of original quality).

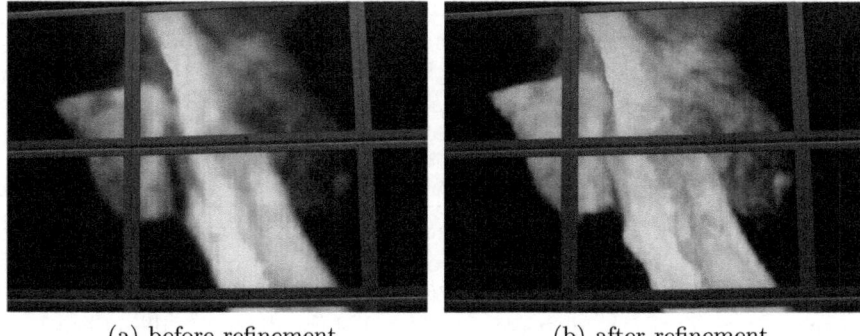

(a) before refinement   (b) after refinement

Fig. 6. Close-up before and after the refinement. The picture shown in the lower image reveals a lot more structural details after the refinement.

level 1, i.e., they display $1/8 = 12.5\%$ of the original structure. The close-up in Fig. 6 illustrates the difference between these two levels for a human mandible data set. In the upper picture each LCD displays at a wavelet level of 2, which corresponds to the detail level of the fallback texture. After refinement, the upper two LCDs switch to wavelet level 1, thereby increasing the level of detail by a factor of 8 and revealing more anatomical structures.

8   Analysis

The multi-resolution data structure is computed in a two-stage preprocessing step. In the first stage, a tool called *VolCon* computes the octree structure described in section 3.1, so that an input data set, consisting of a set of files storing slice information, is stored as a set of files storing octree bricks. In the second stage, another tool called *Compress* calculates the wavelet representation described in section 3.2 based on the results of stage one. Octree depth and maximum level of wavelet compression are passed as user-defined parameters. Generally, deeper octrees generate smaller brick files which lead to a crucially more accurate approximation of the subvolume of a tile. However, increased clipping accuracy comes cost of more file accesses. Table 1 illustrates the pre-processing time for various data sets with an octree depth of two and two levels of wavelet compression on a Core2Duo laptop machine with 2GB RAM.

We measured the time it takes each node to clip and render a scene (after interaction) using different octree depths for multiple data sets. Furthermore,

Table 1. Data set characteristics and preprocessing times for octree depth 2 (64 bricks) and two levels of wavelet compression

Data Set	Dimensions $(x \times y \times z)$	Size(MB)	VolCon	Compress
Skull	$256 \times 256 \times 113$	28.25	0m 2.5s	0m 2.7s
Mandible	$1024 \times 1024 \times 374$	1496	2m 17.2s	4m 2.5s
Toga Brain	$1024 \times 1024 \times 753$	3012	5m 9.9s	9m 45.8s

we monitored the wavelet level at which each tile displays the scene. A fixed perspective was used during measurements, i.e., the orientation and zoom level remained unchanged. The results are depicted in Fig. 7. Fig. 7(a) shows that the average time it takes to clip and render a scene decreases with increasing octree depth and thereby increasing number of bricks, except one outlier for the brain data set. The overhead of loading unnecessary parts of the data set decreases because clipped subvolumes better match the data set portion, that a tile has to display. A possible explanation for the outlier is that there is a sweep point where the overhead caused by additional I/O operations overweighs the benefits of a better subvolume approximation. Fig. 7(b) shows that at the same time, with increasing octree depth, the average detail level of the display wall increases, i.e., the average wavelet level over all fifty tiles gets smaller, because the available texture memory is used more efficiently to store structural details of the volume. The detail level of the skull data set remains constant with increasing octree depth because the volume is small enough to fit entirely into the graphics card's texture memory. Note, that the real-valued wavelet levels in Fig. 7(b) result from averaging the discrete values for each tile. Though these compression levels

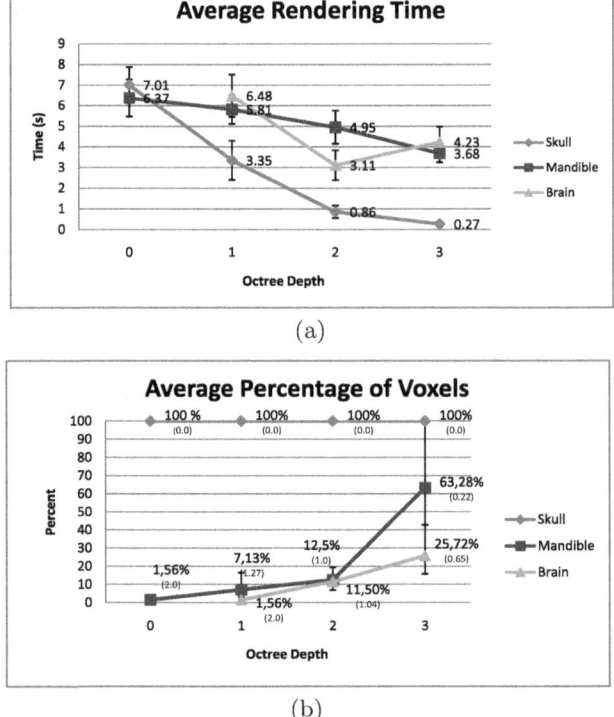

(a)

(b)

Fig. 7. (a) Average time it takes to perform frustum clipping and volume assembling. (b) Average percentage of original voxels being displayed (including average wavelet level)

cannot be achieved in practice, they give a good theoretical value describing the overall level of detail comprised in all fifty LCD panels. Further note, that the partly asymmetric variances depicted in Fig. 7(b) are due to the fact that the percentage of voxels scales non-linearly with the wavelet level, i.e., the level of detail comprised at level i is $1/8$th of level $i-1$. In general, both the average rendering time and the level of detail are positively affected by a deeper octree. Our studies show that an octree depth of four in most cases is sufficient to guarantee almost interactive behavior when working with data sets. In earlier experiments we investigated the data structure's capabilities when accessing volume data for a non-distributed application [35]. Fig. 8 compares a system using the octree-wavelet data structure to a system that uses neither spatial subdivision nor a multi-resolution representation. The unoptimized system loads the entire data by directly accessing a set of files storing slice information, i.e., slices are loaded sequentially into main memory. Fig. 8(a) compares the time it takes to load the entire mandible data set slice-wise into RAM to the time it takes to load at different wavelet levels at a fixed octree depth of three. Though the time difference observed for the system using the octree-wavelet structure is marginal between wavelet levels, loading is less than 7% of the average time measured to load the entire cross-sectional data.

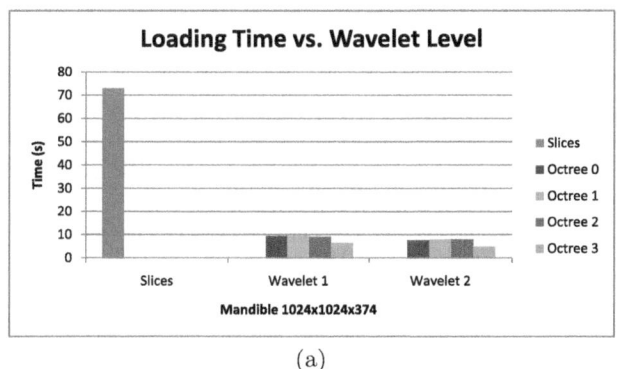

(a)

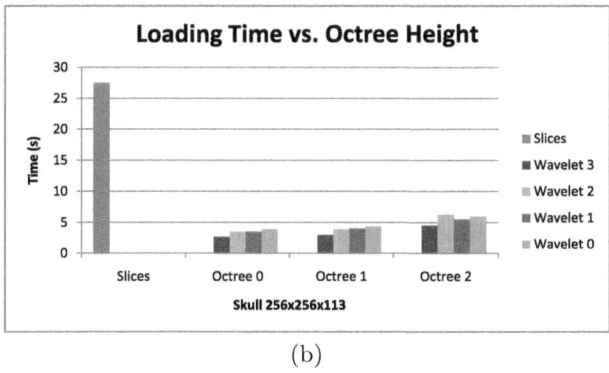

(b)

Fig. 8. (a) Loading time vs. wavelet level. (b) Loading time vs. octree height.

Fig. 8(b) illustrates the influence of octree depth on the loading time for the skull data set. It can be observed that loading takes longer with increasing octree depth, which is due to the increased number of I/O operations that have to be performed and that are generally considered to be slow. This pattern also holds for various wavelet levels.

The results of Fig. 8(b) and Fig. 7(a) seem contradictory. Whereas a higher octree depth leads to a better approximation of subvolumes during frustum clipping and reduces the amount of data that has to be loaded, the increased number of file operations works against this effect. However, the benefits of having a smaller clipping volume overweigh the negative effect of additional I/O operations.

9   Discussion

According to Molnar's [33] classification of distributed rendering algorithms the system presented in this paper implements a static sort-first algorithm. A general advantage of the sort-first strategy is the fact that communication overhead and network traffic are kept low. This is an important characteristic for the visualization of large-sized data sets because it prevents the network from being a performance bottleneck.

The data structure employed in this paper including the multi-resolution approach resembles a scenegraph-based system [1]. Scenegraphs also perform frustum culling in order to reduce scene complexity and they implement LOD techniques that often estimate an object's level of detail based on its distance to the viewing plane. However, scenegraphs are generally oriented towards geometric data and not so much suited for managing volumetric data sets. To our knowledge, no scenegraph-based system running on a distributed display cluster exploits resources for direct volume rendering with the efficiency of the technique we presented in this paper.

Note, that 3D texture mapping results in uniform sampling along the viewing ray. If one wants to sample adaptively, for example based on the distance to the eye point, this can be achieved by raycasting the volume (see section 5.1).

The algorithm we presented scales with the processing power and size of the display system. The higher the number of tiles the more compute nodes are required. If the number of compute nodes increases the subvolumes get smaller, because the relative area covered by a monitor decreases. As a consequence, the quality of visualizations improves, since the same amount of resources is used to render smaller subvolumes. Likewise, if the amount of video memory increases, the buffer sizes can be adapted in order to store more detail information. Instead of allocating 64MB for texture objects, larger memory blocks would improve the average wavelet level of tiles and thus also increase the quality of renderings.

So far, when talking about "increased quality" we refer to a higher resolution. However, visual quality also encompasses contrast, color, and shading. Thus far, these topics have been mostly untouched in our work. In the future it might be interesting to investigate how to incorporate them into our system. For instance, the human visual system is strongest in the center field of view. Objects in the periphery are perceived with less detail. In order to account for this, one could apply a focus+context technique to create areas of high contrast with complex shading in the center of the tiled display and fuzzy regions in the periphery, similar to what Baudisch et al. [4] did with the resolution of the focus+context screen.

Our display wall is a monitor-based display cluster that combines the images of multiple LCD panels to form one large high-resolution display area. In contrast, projector-based tiled displays combine the images of a set of computer projectors [26,22] and can easily exceed the dimensions of monitor-based systems. A major advantage of projector systems is their ability to form truly seamless displays [27,28] while monitor-based systems inherently suffer from monitor bezels causing discontinuities in visualizations. At the moment our implementation does not cope with sharp transitions between adjacent tiles due to different resolution levels. We found that the benefit of perceiving finer details of the data set outweighs these slight optical confusions. A user study we conducted [12] showed that sharp transitions between different levels of resolution on a tiled wall do not cause as much confusion as mismatches in brightness and color between screens. The problem of discontinuities caused by monitor bezels requires deeper investigation in the context of human-computer interaction. Software [25] as well as hardware dependent solutions [12] have already been proposed.

10   Conclusion

In this paper we presented a method to effectively visualize volumetric data sets on tiled displays. Our implementation is based on a spatial subdivision scheme using octrees and incorporates a multi-resolution wavelet representation of the data. We were able to show that our approach increases the quality of visualizations by individually exploiting the resources of each rendering node. The system is interactive and allows users to explore data sets nearly in a real-time fashion. Our implementation was tested on a fifty tile display that is driven by twenty-five rendering nodes. In the future, we plan to investigate modifications of our data structure and implement memory caching and prefetching strategies to minimize I/O latencies. Additionally, we want to exploit further features of current state-of-the-art GPUs.

Acknowledgements

This work was supported by the German Research Foundation (Deutsche Forschungsgemeinschaft, DFG) as part of the International Graduate School (International Research Training Group, IRTG 1131) in Kaiserslautern, Germany. The authors would like to thank Stephen F. Jenks and Sung-Jin Kim (University of California, Irvine), Falko Kuester and Kai-Uwe Doerr (University of California, San Diego) and the National Science Foundation for their support.

References

1. OpenSG, http://www.opensg.org/
2. Amin, M.B., Grama, A., Singh, V.: Fast volume rendering using an efficient, scalable parallel formulation of the shear-warp algorithm. In: PRS 1995: Proceedings of the IEEE Symposium on Parallel Rendering, pp. 7–14. ACM, New York (1995)
3. Bajaj, C., Ihm, I., Park, S., Song, D.: Compression-Based Ray Casting of Very Large Volume Data in Distributed Environments. In: HPC 2000: Proceedings of the The Fourth International Conference on High-Performance Computing in the Asia-Pacific Region, Washington, DC, USA, vol. 2, p. 720. IEEE Computer Society, Washington DC (2000)
4. Baudisch, P., Good, N., Stewart, P.: Focus plus context screens: combining display technology with visualization techniques. In: UIST 2001: Proceedings of the 14th Annual ACM Symposium on User Interface Software and Technology, pp. 31–40 (2001)
5. Bierbaum, A., Just, C., Hartling, P., Meinert, K., Baker, A., Cruz-Neira, C.: VR Juggler: A Virtual Platform for Virtual Reality Application Development. In: VR 2001: Proceedings of the Virtual Reality 2001 Conference (VR 2001), p. 89 (2001)
6. Cabral, B., Cam, N., Foran, J.: Accelerated Volume Rendering and Tomographic Reconstruction using Texture Mapping Hardware. In: VVS 1994: Proceedings of the 1994 Symposium on Volume Visualization, pp. 91–98. ACM, New York (1994)
7. Calderbank, A.R., Daubechies, I., Sweldens, W., Yeo, B.L.: Wavelet transforms that map integers to integers. Appl. Comput. Harmon. Anal. 5(3), 332–369 (1998)
8. CAVELib Application Programmer Interface (api), http://www.mechdyne.com/integratedSolutions/software/products/CAVELib/CAVELib.htm
9. Chen, H., Clark, D.W., Liu, Z., Wallace, G., Li, K., Chen, Y.: Software Environments for Cluster-Based Display Systems. In: CCGRID 2001: Proceedings of the 1st International Symposium on Cluster Computing and the Grid, p. 202. IEEE Computer Society, Washington DC (2001)
10. Deller, M., Thelen, S., Steffen, D., Olech, P., Ebert, A., Malburg, J., Meyer, J.: A Highly Scalable Rendering Framework for Arbitrary Display and Display-in-Display Configurations. In: Proceedings of the 2009 International Conference on Computer Graphics and Virtual Reality, CGVR 2009 (2009)
11. Doerr, K.U., Kuester, F.: http://vis.ucsd.edu/~cglx/
12. Ebert, A., Thelen, S., Olech, P.S., Meyer, J., Hagen, H.: Tiled++: An Enhanced Tiled Hi-Res Display Wall. IEEE Transactions on Visualization and Computer Graphics 16(1), 120–132 (2010)
13. Elvins, T.T.: Volume Rendering on a Distributed Memory Parallel Computer. In: VIS 1992: Proceedings of the 3rd Conference on Visualization 1992, pp. 93–98. IEEE Computer Society Press, Los Alamitos (1992)
14. Garcia, A., Shen, H.W.: An Interleaved Parallel Volume Renderer with PC-clusters. In: EGPGV 2002: Proceedings of the Fourth Eurographics Workshop on Parallel Graphics and Visualization, pp. 51–59. Eurographics Association, Aire-la-Ville (2002)
15. The Geowall2, http://www.evl.uic.edu/cavern/optiputer/geowall2.html
16. Heirich, A., Moll, L.: Scalable Distributed Visualization using off-the-shelf Components. In: PVGS 1999: Proceedings of the 1999 IEEE Symposium on Parallel Visualization and Graphics, pp. 55–59. IEEE Computer Society, Washington DC (1999)

17. Humphreys, G., Houston, M., Ng, R., Frank, R., Ahern, S., Kirchner, P.D., Klosowski, J.T.: Chromium: A Stream-Processing Framework for Interactive Rendering on Clusters. ACM Trans. Graph. 21(3), 693–702 (2002)
18. KIST Imaging Media Research: IMRC Wiki: The NAVER Framework, `http://www.imrc.kist.re.kr/wiki/NAVER_Framework`
19. Kruger, J., Westermann, R.: Acceleration Techniques for GPU-based Volume Rendering. In: VIS 2003: Proceedings of the 14th IEEE Visualization (VIS 2003), p. 38. IEEE Computer Society, Washington DC (2003)
20. LaMar, E., Hamann, B., Joy, K.I.: Multiresolution Techniques for Interactive Texture-Based Volume Visualization. In: VIS 1999: Proceedings of the Conference on Visualization 1999, pp. 355–361. IEEE Computer Society Press, Los Alamitos (1999)
21. Levoy, M.: Efficient Ray Tracing of Volume Data. ACM Trans. Graph. 9(3), 245–261 (1990)
22. Li, C., Lin, H., Shi, J.: A Survey of Multi-Projector Tiled Display Wall Construction. In: ICIG 2004: Proceedings of the Third International Conference on Image and Graphics, pp. 452–455. IEEE Computer Society, Washington DC (2004)
23. Lombeyda, S., Moll, L., Shand, M., Breen, D., Heirich, A.: Scalable Interactive Volume Rendering using off-the-shelf Components. In: PVG 2001: Proceedings of the IEEE 2001 Symposium on Parallel and large-data Visualization and Graphics, pp. 115–121. IEEE Press, Piscataway (2001)
24. Lorensen, W.E., Cline, H.E.: Marching cubes: A high resolution 3D surface construction algorithm. SIGGRAPH Comput. Graph. 21(4), 163–169 (1987)
25. Mackinlay, J.D., Heer, J.: Wideband displays: mitigating multiple monitor seams. In: CHI 2004: CHI 2004 Extended Abstracts on Human Factors in Computing Systems, pp. 1521–1524. ACM, New York (2004)
26. Majumder, A., Brown, M.S.: Practical Multi-projector Display Design. A. K. Peters, Ltd., Natick (2007)
27. Majumder, A., He, Z., Towles, H., Welch, G.: Achieving color uniformity across multi-projector displays. In: VIS 2000: Proceedings of the Conference on Visualization 2000, pp. 117–124. IEEE Computer Society Press, Los Alamitos (2000)
28. Majumder, A., Stevens, R.: Perceptual photometric seamlessness in projection-based tiled displays. ACM Trans. Graph. 24(1), 118–139 (2005)
29. Max, N.: Optical Models for Direct Volume Rendering. IEEE Transactions on Visualization and Computer Graphics 1(2), 99–108 (1995)
30. Meyer, J., Borg, R., Hamann, B., Joy, K., Olsen, A.: Network-Based Rendering Techniques for Large-Scale Volume Data Sets. In: Farin, G., Hamann, B., Hagen, H. (eds.) Hierarchical and Geometrical Methods in Scientific Visualization, pp. 283–296. Springer, Heidelberg (2002)
31. Meyer, J.: Interactive Visualization of Medical and Biological Data Sets. Ph.D. thesis, University of Kaiserslautern (1999)
32. Meyer, J., Gelder, S., Heiming, C., Hagen, H.: Interactive Rendering - A Time-Based Approach. In: SIAM Conference on Geometric Design (1997)
33. Molnar, S., Cox, M., Ellsworth, D., Fuchs, H.: A Sorting Classification of Parallel Rendering. Tech. rep., Chapel Hill, NC, USA (1994)
34. National Library of Medicine: The Visible Human Project, `http://www.nlm.nih.gov/research/visible/visible_human.html`
35. Nguyen, H.T.: Large-scale Volume Rendering using Multi-resolution Wavelets, Subdivision, and Multi-dimensional Transfer Functions. Ph.D. thesis, University of California, Irvine (2008)

36. Ni, T., Schmidt, G.S., Staadt, O.G., Ball, R., May, R.: A Survey of Large High-Resolution Display Technologies, Techniques, and Applications. In: VR 2006: Proceedings of the IEEE Conference on Virtual Reality, p. 31. IEEE Computer Society, Washington DC (2006)

37. Palmer, M.E., Totty, B., Taylor, S.: Ray Casting on Shared-Memory Architectures: Memory-Hierarchy Considerations in Volume Rendering. IEEE Concurrency 6(1), 20–35 (1998)

38. Plate, J., Tirtasana, M., Carmona, R., Fröhlich, B.: Octreemizer: a hierarchical approach for interactive roaming through very large volumes. In: VISSYM 2002: Proceedings of the Symposium on Data Visualisation 2002, p. 53. Eurographics Association, Aire-la-Ville (2002)

39. Raffin, B., Soares, L.: PC Clusters for Virtual Reality. In: VR 2006: Proceedings of the IEEE Conference on Virtual Reality, pp. 215–222. IEEE Computer Society, Washington DC (2006)

40. Reiners, D.: OpenSG: A Scene Graph System for Flexible and Efficient Realtime Rendering for Virtual and Augmented Reality Applications. Ph.D. thesis, Technische Universität Darmstadt (2002)

41. Rezk-Salama, C., Engel, K., Bauer, M., Greiner, G., Ertl, T.: Interactive volume on standard PC graphics hardware using multi-textures and multi-stage rasterization. In: HWWS 2000: Proceedings of the ACM SIGGRAPH/EUROGRAPHICS Workshop on Graphics Hardware, pp. 109–118. ACM, New York (2000)

42. Roettger, S., Guthe, S., Weiskopf, D., Ertl, T., Strasser, W.: Smart hardware-accelerated Volume Rendering. In: VISSYM 2003: Proceedings of the Symposium on Data Visualisation 2003, pp. 231–238. Eurographics Association, Aire-la-Ville (2003)

43. Rusinkiewicz, S., Levoy, M.: Qsplat: a multiresolution point rendering system for large meshes. In: SIGGRAPH 2000: Proceedings of the 27th Annual Conference on Computer Graphics and Interactive Techniques, pp. 343–352. ACM Press/Addison-Wesley Publishing Co. (2000)

44. Schaeffer, B., Goudeseune, C.: Syzygy: Native PC Cluster VR. In: VR 2003: Proceedings of the IEEE Virtual Reality 2003, p. 15 (2003)

45. Schwarz, N.: Distributed Volume Rendering of Very Large Data on High-Resolution Scalable Displays. Master's thesis, University of Illinois at Chicago (2007)

46. Schwarz, N., Venkataraman, S., Renambot, L., Krishnaprasad, N., Vishwanath, V., Leigh, J., Johnson, A., Kent, G., Nayak, A.: Vol-a-Tile - A Tool for Interactive Exploration of Large Volumetric Data on Scalable Tiled Displays. In: VIS 2004: Proceedings of the Conference on Visualization 2004, p. 598. 19. IEEE Computer Society, Washington DC (2004)

47. Soares, L.P., Zuffo, M.K.: JINX: an X3D browser for VR immersive simulation based on clusters of commodity computers. In: Web3D 2004: Proceedings of the Ninth International Conference on 3D Web Technology, pp. 79–86 (2004)

48. Weiler, M., Westermann, R., Hansen, C., Zimmermann, K., Ertl, T.: Level-of-Detail Volume Rendering via 3D Textures. In: VVS 2000: Proceedings of the 2000 IEEE Symposium on Volume Visualization, pp. 7–13. ACM, New York (2000)

49. Westover, L.: Interactive Volume Rendering. In: VVS 1989: Proceedings of the 1989 Chapel Hill Workshop on Volume Visualization, pp. 9–16. ACM, New York (1989)

50. Westover, L.: Footprint Evaluation for Volume Rendering. In: SIGGRAPH 1990: Proceedings of the 17th Annual Conference on Computer Graphics and Interactive Techniques, pp. 367–376. ACM, New York (1990)

51. Wilson, O., VanGelder, A., Wilhelms, J.: Direct Volume Rendering via 3D Textures. Tech. rep., Santa Cruz, CA, USA (1994)

Teaching Visual Design as a Holistic Enterprise

Gerrit C. van der Veer and Corné Verbruggen

Open University the Netherlands, Valkenburgerweg 177, 6419 AT Heerlen,
The Netherlands
{gvv,cvr}@ou.nl

Abstract. Our approach towards teaching visual design is based on our viewpoint of visualization as a way to elicit understanding and experience. Our teaching practice shows a permanent stress on an analytic attitude and an explicit application of design space to fit the design to the users' culture and context and still stimulate creative solutions.

Keywords: Visualization, Visual Design, Teaching Visual Design, Experience, Culture, Context.

1 Introduction

Visualization aims at the experience of a human audience. In current design education we tend to focus on designing screen images. We run the risk to forget that the audience of our design is still human and lives in a human context, as does the client of our design.

1.1 Our Focus: Visualization as Factor in Meaning and Experience

Our focus is on the human stakeholders of visualization. And here we meet an important separation: The client of design aims at representing a certain meaning, and at inducing a certain experience for the audience. The client's intentions are to be understood from the client's culture. The audience of the visualization, on the other hand, will create the meaning and the experience received [1]. The audience, first of all, is often diverse in cultural background.

1.2 Culture and Context as Factors in Meaning and Experience

Meaning and experience are, from our point of view, never to be considered objective attributes of a visual representation. Context varies in many dimensions: at home or in the car; alone or with (known or unknown) onlookers; in a hurry or with plenty of time; looking for something specific or just browsing, etc. A person using a visual representation will interpret this representation based on current specific needs, and will understand the representation according to the multiple cultures he or she considers relevant for the moment (occupational culture; geographical culture; religious or political culture; social or family culture [2]). Consequently, the meaning attributed to the representation and the experience lived with the representation can not be objectively determined and certainly not fully "designed".

A. Ebert et al. (Eds.): HCIV (INTERACT) 2009, LNCS 6431, pp. 163–172, 2011.

1.3 "Visual" is Just a Trigger at the Surface in a Context

For a human audience, "visual" is just an aspect of an artifact that is experienced in an actual context. E.g., a screen image is experienced as part of a device that has relevant characteristics like portability, opportunities for dialogue, visibility in daylight or in a building. A website may be experienced as shop window for a business that has a physical location somewhere, and the business as a whole is experienced, in addition, through manifold visual surfaces of physical artifacts like mobile phones, business cards and stationeries or leaflets, shop signs, perceived in the context of the home, a train compartment, business meetings and shopping streets.

2 Visual Design in Education – Art and Tradition

The design of visual representations seems as old as humanity. The oldest traces of what now is considered the "modern human", at least in Europe, are about as old as the oldest remains of human drawings. The earliest documented history of civilization shows the creators of visual representation to be professionals that are educated through apprenticeship. In some cases there is a distinction between the design proper and the implementation, especially in the case of large 3D representations like statues or ceremonial "buildings" (the Egyptian Pyramids). The actual design task, in all cases, seems to be based on a combination of having an explicit goal of the "client" (the ruler, the priest, the commissioner) for the representation (flattering the king or the gods, advertising the power of a tribe and impressing other tribes), understanding the audience (how to impress them, how to make them believe), and considering the context of the finished product (how the cave or the palace will be illuminated, from where the temple façade is supposed to be first perceived by the approaching believers [3, 4]).

It seems the core of this design practice did not change for many centuries, though visual artists in some recent periods claim they do not consider the audience, or they leave any interpretation completely to them. In our current society, we observe a variety of conceptions of visual design. Education in art schools itself shows a broad diversity – we will not consider this in the current paper.

2.1 Visualization for Usability

Our goal in teaching visualization as an aspect of the design is the development of usable artifacts. The current practice in this realm certainly shows differences in educational viewpoint.

Industrial design considers the artifact as a whole (considering the functionality, the physical dimensions and characteristics, and the aesthetics) focusing on its use in context, where the visual aspects are considered to support the functionality as well as to increase the product's appreciation in the intended context. How this last aspect will work is in fact hardly approached analytically, and design decisions are often based on the intuition of the designer and the subsequent perceived acceptance by the audience.

Design in the context of architecture is a different approach. Aesthetics as well as *intended* experience seem to be a main focus. Functionality could either be part of the requirements, or, in recent visions, a relatively open space of opportunities to be filled in by the future users of the artifact. The actual *lived* experience and functionality are increasingly left to the prospective users, though Alexander's design patterns [5] in fact are intended to provide the opportunities for this.

Visual design for information products (ICT and multimedia artifacts) is another case. Our current analysis is based on developing and teaching courses in this domain. The students of this type of design curricula are typically focused on the functionality (how it works and how the users work with it) and the message (the content). They frequently expect to apply some intuitive aesthetics and "creativity" for the representational aspects of their product. In many current curricula visual design is interpreted as a course in the use of drawing tools. However, increasingly, there is awareness of the importance of the individual user's experience when developing general design guidelines [6].

3   A Vision on Teaching Visual Design for Information Artifacts

Our own context is university education of design of information artifacts for users. This context is in fact rather broad, or even diverse: our teaching has been part of a variety of disciplines and curricula. In all cases we pursue the same goal: we should educate our visual designers to start considering the audience's experience from a holistic viewpoint, taking into account the culture and context of the members of the audience as well as the culture and context of the client's business. Consequently, teaching visual design cannot restrict itself to 2D electronic rendering.

The visual design of information products or of the information aspects of any artifact could be anything like:

- Developing an advertising campaigns;
- Developing a corporate image for e-commerce;
- Developing a web portal for finding courses and registering for these;
- Develop understandable dialogues for using an unmanned gas station.

In cases like this, the visuals certainly are more than just the layout of what is on the screen. Mostly there will be different types of screens involved, to be read in various contexts (indications of schedule changes at bus stops as well as SMS messages to registered bus travelers; gas quantity and price at the screen as well as printed on the receipt). Moreover, the design involves printed paper, or containers for data carriers, and in some cases promotional giveaways or logos on gadgets and tools.

In the same way (we mention this here for completeness, though we will not elaborate on it in this paper) dialogue design for information artifacts is more than designing the dialogue at the level of menu or command structure, forms and the meaning of mouse clicks. Physicality of the dialogue (how to adjust mobile device user actions to human hands, how to consider physical space, how to consider the cultural meaning of gestures and posture while using the artifact) should be part of the analytic approach to dialogue design.

4   Teaching Visual Design

Our design approach developed over the years, influenced by the design cultures in the various disciplines that hosted our teaching (Cognitive Psychology, Cognitive Ergonomics, Computer Science, Information Sciences, Architecture), by the occupational context of our students (traditional academic environments with students of ages 20-25, vs. adult distance education institutes), and by the geographical cultures that formed the context of our students (Romania, Italy, Belgium and the Netherlands, Spain).

Our general design method has been condensed into the "DUTCH" approach (Design for Users and Tasks from Concepts to Handles [7]). Visual design is just one part of this.

4.1   Holistic Visual Design Teaching

For the visual design teaching we developed a holistic approach. Designing visuals as part of information systems design should from the start proceed with an analytic attitude, where the designer has to be aware of different "forces" that contribute to the effect of the visuals:

- The client of the design intends to provide a certain message (with meaning and related experience) for his audience. The clients intuition has to be understood in relation to (a) his context (his business or "shop" with business goals and a business process) and his culture (the values of his business and the related rules, procedures, and standards); (b) the intended experiences for his customers or audience, and the related aesthetics; and (c) the "language" the client intends to use to communicate his message (with its symbols and meanings). In many cases the client is only partially aware of all this. The designer will have to enter the context of the client and try to collect indications, interpret these, and analyze their meaning for the design [8]. Techniques used here may be derived from Ethnography or Anthropology, like the use of cultural probes and the application of hermeneutics [9], [10].
- The audience of the visuals, the customers of the client of design brings their own context and culture. Increasingly, this group is heterogeneous itself, since information systems are distributed around the world, websites are available and used in a multitude of contexts, and people are distantly collaborating through information systems. Designers often are not able to know where and in what situation their products will be used, and what the background of their users will be. Designers can only try to allow for variety and to avoid representations that might cause unwanted experiences.
- Visual representations will, first of all, be perceived through humans, with the perception mechanisms, the human information processing mechanisms, human memory and decision making that is the object of Cognitive Psychology. Visual designers need to be aware of state of the art knowledge and models, in order to design for "human size" representations.

The design of visuals requires a holistic process: the main concern is not the layout of a 2D screen or print, but the total visual image of the client's business or mission as conveyed with the information system. The single visuals are elements in this, as are the dialogues between the different users and the information system, and as is the context in which the system is provided and the possible interaction with, or awareness of, other users and stakeholders of the system.

In trying to develop an analytic overview of all this, the designer in fact is mapping out a design space (what should be provided, what should be avoided, what should be considered as forces influencing understanding and experience) that reveals the freedom left for creative design solutions. From here the designer can make choices, that should be supported by reasons referring to the design space, in order to allow the client to understand and accept the design, or (possibly only in a future context) collaborate with the designer to re-specify the intentions and requirements.

4.2 Design in Context

Designers work from their own understanding and context. Their understanding is a developing awareness of the various forces mentioned above. They should be aware of this fact as well, and avoid suggesting early on to the client or the customers of the client that the design is close to being finished. Early attempts and envisioning can best be presented in what is clearly recognized as sketches, whether electronic or physical. Interactions and processes, as well, should be provided in formats like story boards. These provisional design specifications should, though, be presented to be actually used, i.e., manipulated and tried out, in context, to allow the client and his customers to imagine what the real thing would look like, feel like, behave like, and would effect their current way of doing relevant activities.

Both the client and his audience will have to be partner in developing, jointly with the designer, an understanding of the feasibility of the direction of the envisioned solution.

4.3 Teaching Design – The Process

Our courses shaped themselves based on our design vision and the students' active participation. We tried not to start with actual design activities before basic understanding was available and we tried not to bother students with seemingly endless theory and description of techniques before allowing hands on activities. Our courses currently tend to be composed of several stages:

- Introduction to Visual Design, where we illustrate the concept of visual identity, and embark on a first analysis of a client's intentions followed by an attempt to design, for a real client, visuals to support this.
- Discussion of static representations, introducing the concepts of experience and of branding. Here we also illustrate a brief history of graphic design and design styles in recent western culture, and challenge our students to develop, for a real client, designs for artifacts like a business card and stationary.
- Development of dynamic representations. We start by showing problems in actual designs like websites that send the user astray and video

recorders that refuse to be programmed, which allows us to introduce the needs and techniques for user testing. We provide our students with a model for the dynamics of experience design [1]. We discuss the concept of graphical languages and of scenarios for human-system interaction, and ask our students to develop sketch type solutions for a real client problem.

- Design for human perception and action. Now we go in depth about human information processing, and show applications of state of the art techniques like eye tracking showing how people in certain cultures read, browse, scan, and act based on visuals. We combine this with a discussion of visual design evaluation techniques and practical exercises with these.

- Developing a visual design for a real client request. In this final phase the students are asked to work in small teams (2 or 3 if we are able to arrange that) for a client from outside the university, solving a real visualization problem. This exercise starts with an analysis phase, and ends with the production of a design documented with the whole process and including the design space analyses and rationales, finalized with a presentation to the client. If we are lucky enough, we may have several design teams competing for the same client.

Taking advantage of the fact that we have such a broad variety of student populations, we always make sure we show our students examples from colleagues from other student cultures (architects vs. computer scientists; young university students vs. adult distance education students), where we stress the different ways to analyze the clients' context and the different rationales that came with the design decisions.

In the next section we will show elements of some of these final design products to illustrate how our students struggle and what we learn from this.

5   Learning from Students

The most realistic part of our courses may be found in the last phases when student teams develop competing designs for real outside clients. Our students designed for large organizations, shops, and single craftsmen's' workplaces. The actual clients profoundly influenced the analysis, the design, and the way assessment turned out to be possible in a real context, and the interpretation of it.

We show that "sketching" includes envisioning physical artifacts in a real world context. Sketching, in this case, applies tools from Adobe's Flash development tool to (physical) jig saw and paint brush. Sometimes, business cards or brochures were found to be 3-dimensional and to act as a partner in interaction.

Assessment includes having the intended audience physically manipulate the artifact (turn the brochure to read the back side, open the folder to take out the pictures). We will show that this holistic way of developing visual design, in return, has a profound effect on conceiving the meaning of visuals in context, and, hence on the "classical" screen design.

5.1   Designing for "Remote" Clients and Users

In some cases our students worked for real international organizations (including CHI conferences, IFIP TC 13). A difficulty here is that the client is often in fact not a single person but a heterogeneous group, speaking different first languages that are all different from the designers' language, and the client can be reached only through long distance communication, even if in real time.

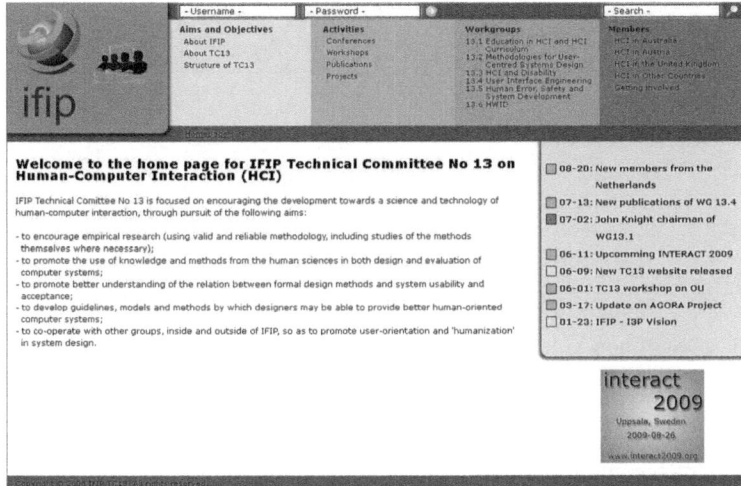

Fig. 1. Website front page design for IFIP TC13

One example considered IFIP TC13, the technical committee on human-computer interaction, which needed a new website and related paper hand out. Our design teams in this case consisted entirely of Computer Science students. The student teams developed several competing solutions. At the end, all students as well as the teacher agreed on the "winning" design where the web-based hypertext structure (See Figure 1) was, additionally, used for dynamically navigating the paper brochure, see Figure 2 and 3.

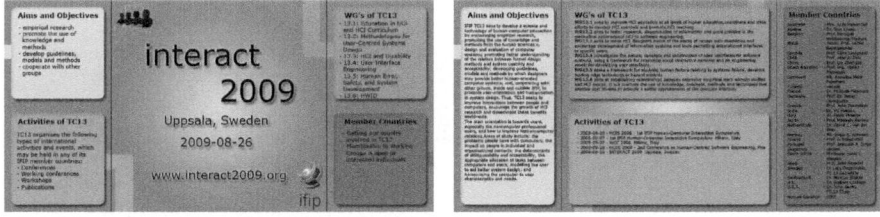

Fig. 2a and b. Single page brochure front and back side design for IFIP TC 13

The students viewed paper as just another type of information system that could be navigated in any structure to be designed. The client, though, judging as a group by email

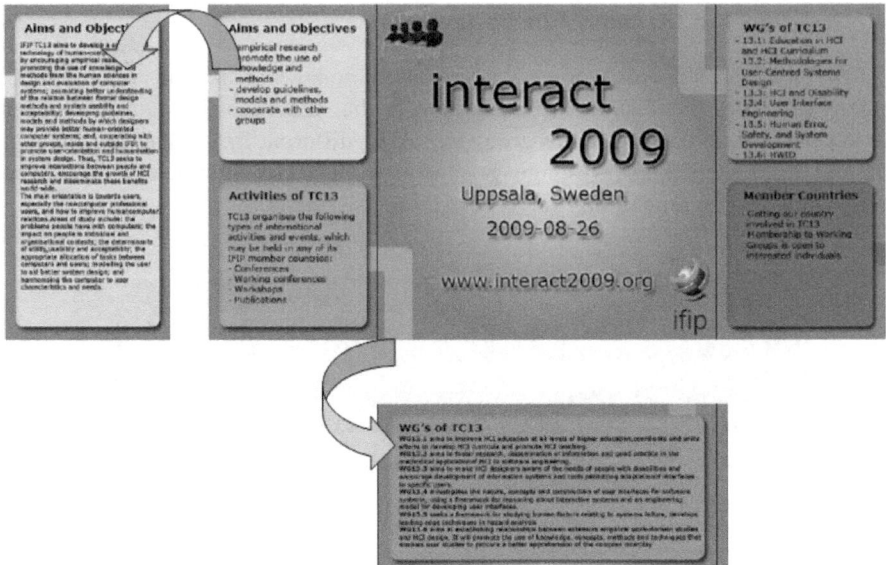

Fig. 3. Indication of how colors support the hypertext navigation for the IFIP TC 13 brochure design.

vote, chose another design where the brochure featured the traditional linear reading navigation that characterizes most products of the now centuries old printing and reading habits. TC13's culture of using paper did not match the students' design space.

5.2 Designing for an Arts and Crafts Culture

One of our clients was a jeweler couple that managed its own store, in a small alley in an old historic Sardinian town. One of the design team started with developing a "mood board" that shows an impression of the client and their customers, as well as the context and the type of products with the aesthetics.

Based on the client's production style, sketches developed (Fig. 4) that were finally transferred into a logo (Fig. 5), sketch for a new shop sign (Fig. 6), for a 3D business card finger ring not unlike the actual products of the client (Fig. 7) and for a folding brochure(Fig. 8 and 9).

Fig. 4 and 5. Sketches based on client's products, and logo based on that

Fig. 6. Sketch for a shop sign

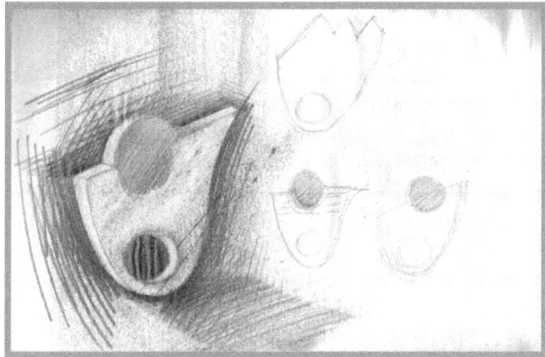

Fig. 7. Sketches for a 3D business card with the shape of a ring

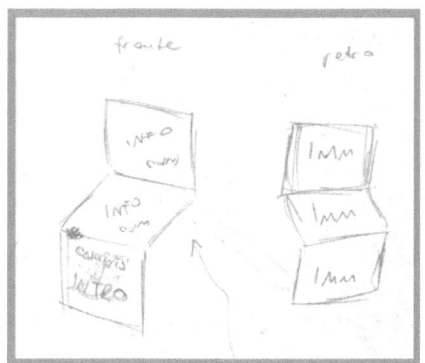
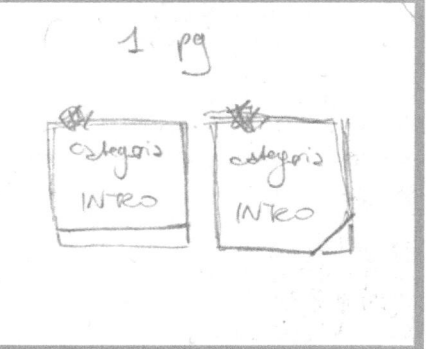

Fig. 8 and 9. Sketches for a folding brochure and the navigation with it

6 Conclusions

Teaching Visual Design for users is a holistic enterprise. It requires a permanent attention to analytics as well as a requirement for explicit design rationale. In doing so we have shown our students are able to be creative and to focus on the audience. However, cultural differences are the most difficult issue to handle. The cultural and contextual aspects of the client's intended user experience, as well as the resulting audience's actual experience, can only be managed successfully if the client is available to actually partner with the designer.

Acknowledgments. We thank all our students from many different courses, as well as the numerous clients that spend their time to help us understand the problems of holistic design and improve our teaching.

References

1. Vyas, D., van der Veer, G.C.: Experience as Meaning: Some Underlying Concepts and Implications for Design. In: Proceedings of 13th European Conference on Cognitive Ergonomics (ECCE 2006), pp. 81–91. ACM Press, NY (2006)
2. Marcus, A., Gould, E.W.: Cultural dimensions and global Web user-interface design Interactions 7(4), 32-46 (2000)
3. Parisinou, E.: Lighting practices in early Greece (from the end of the Mycenaean world to the 7th century BC. Oxford Journal of Archaeology 17(3), 327–343 (2002)
4. Damen, M.: History and Civilization, Section 5: Culture and Space, powerpoint presentation (2010), http://www.usu.edu/markdamen/1320Hist&Civ/PP/slides/05space.pdf (downloaded July 19, 2010)
5. Alexander, C.: A Pattern Language: Towns, Buildings, Construction. Oxford University Press, USA (1977)
6. Henninger, S., Haynes, K., Reith, K.M.: A Framework For Developing Experience-Based Usability Guidelines. In: Proceedings of the Symposium on Designing Interactive Systems, Ann Arbor, MI, pp. 43-53 (August 1995)
7. Van der Veer, G.C., Van Welie, M.: Designing for Users and Tasks from Concepts to Handles. In: Diaper, D., Stanton, N. (eds.) The Handbook of Task Analysis for Human-Computer Interaction, pp. 155–173. Lawrence Erlbaum, Mahwah (2003)
8. Vyas, D.M., Heylen, D.K.J., Nijholt, A., van der Veer, G.C.: Collaborative Practices that Support Creativity in Design. In: Proceedings of the Eleventh European Conference on Computer-Supported Cooperative Work, Proceedings of the Second European Conference on Computer-Supported Cooperative Work - ECSCW, pp. 151–170. Springer, Berlin (2009)
9. Benvenuti, L., Hennipman, E.P.J., Oppelaar, E.J.R.G., Van der Veer, G.C., Cruijsberg, B., Bakker, G.: Experiencing education with 3D virtual environments. In: Kinshuk, S.D.G., Spector, J.M., Isaias, P., Ifenthaler, D. (eds.) Cognition and Exploratory Learning in Digital Age (Proceedings of CELDA 2008), pp. 295–300. IADIS Press, Freiburg (2008)
10. Puerta Melguizo, M.C., Chisalita, C., van der Veer, G.C.: Assessing users mental models in designing complex systems. In: Proceedings of IEEE International Conference on Systems, Man and Cybernetics 2002, IEEE Digital Library (2002)

Erratum to: Human Aspects of Visualization

Achim Ebert[1], Alan Dix[2], Nahum D. Gershon[3], and Margit Pohl[4]

[1] University of Kaiserslautern, Computer Graphics and HCI,
Gottlieb-Daimler-Straße, 67663 Kaiserslautern, Germany
ebert@cs.uni-kl.de
[2] Lancaster University, Computing Department, Lancaster, LA1 4WA, UK
alan@hcibook.com
[3] The MITRE Corporation, 7515 Colshire Drive, McLean, VA 22102-7539, USA
gershon@mitre.org
[4] Institute of Design and Assessment of Technology,
Vienna University of Technology, Favoritenstraße 9-11/E 187, 1040 Vienna, Austria
margit@igw.tuwien.ac.at

Erratum to:
A. Ebert et al. (Eds.)
Human Aspects of Visualization
DOI: 10.1007/978-3-642-19641-6

The book was inadvertently published with an incorrect name of the copyright holder. The name of the copyright holder for this book is: © IFIP International Federation for Information Processing. The book has been updated with the changes.

The updated original online version for this book can be found at
DOI: 10.1007/978-3-642-19641-6

A. Ebert et al. (Eds.): HCIV (INTERACT) 2009, LNCS 6431, p. E1, 2011.

Author Index